Planned Obsolescence

Planned Obsolescence

Publishing, Technology, and
the Future of the Academy

Kathleen Fitzpatrick

NEW YORK UNIVERSITY PRESS

New York and London

NEW YORK UNIVERSITY PRESS
New York and London
www.nyupress.org

References to Internet websites (URLs) were accurate at the time of writing. Neither the author nor New York University Press is responsible for URLs that may have expired or changed since the manuscript was prepared.

Library of Congress Cataloging-in-Publication Data

Fitzpatrick, Kathleen, 1967–
Planned obsolescence : publishing, technology, and the
future of the academy / Kathleen Fitzpatrick.
p. cm.
Includes bibliographical references and index.
ISBN 978–0–8147–2787–4 (acid-free paper)
ISBN 978–0–8147–2788–1 (pbk. : acid-free paper)
ISBN 978–0–8147–2896–3 (ebook)
1. Scholarly publishing—United States. 2. Scholarly electronic publishing—United States. 3. Communication in learning and scholarship—Technological innovations—United States. I. Title.
Z286.S37F58   2011
070.50973—dc23   2011024719

New York University Press books are printed on acid-free paper, and their binding materials are chosen for strength and durability. We strive to use environmentally responsible suppliers and materials to the greatest extent possible in publishing our books.

Manufactured in the United States of America

Contents

Acknowledgments

The spirit of collaboration for which I advocate in this book—collaboration that extends beyond coauthorship to include a host of reading, reviewing, and project-development practices—is a key aspect of the ethos of the digital humanities, and as such, the list of people to whom I owe a debt of gratitude for the ways that this project developed is extensive.

Without the initial support of the Institute for the Future of the Book, its founder Bob Stein, and the creative and critical folks who have worked there in varying capacities, including Ben Vershbow, Dan Visel, Jesse Wilbur, and Eddie Tejeda, neither this project nor MediaCommons would ever have gotten off the ground.

Similarly, the support and encouragement I received throughout the writing, review, and revision process from New York University Press have made the seemingly impossible happen. Eric Zinner and Monica McCormick repeatedly surprised me not just with their openness to my wacky ideas but their creative thinking about how to press those ideas further than I'd have ever imagined. I'd also like to extend a particular thanks to Lisa Spiro, one of the two fantastic reviewers whom the press selected for the manuscript; not only was her review thorough, unflinching, and extraordinarily helpful, but she also agreed to participate in our open review experiment, allowing her report to be made public and commentable alongside the manuscript. This generosity is precisely the kind that I hope we can cultivate throughout the profession.

A range of colleagues made crucial contributions to this project, via Twitter discussions, conference conversations, lecture invitations, and general prodding, including Maria Bonn, Maria Bustillos, George Carr, Dan Cohen, Cathy Davidson, Neil Fraistat, Matthew Gold, Alexander Halavais, Jason Jones, Alex Juhasz, Shana Kimball, Matt Kirschenbaum, Kari Kraus, Tara McPherson, Julie Meloni, Nick Mirzoeff, Jason Mittell, Bethany Nowviskie, Gloria Origgi, Phil Pochoda, Katherine Rowe, Abby Smith Rumsey, Siva Vaidhyanathan, Michele White, George Williams, Mark Wollaeger, Paul Young, and Vika Zafrin.

I am also indebted to all of those readers whose comments in the online review process helped me clarify my ideas; I particularly want to single out

Cheryl Ball, Natalia Cecire, Barbara Fister, Michael Roy, and Julie Levin Russo for their thoughtful readings. Even more particularly, I thank Amanda French, David Parry, and Dorothea Salo, whose careful attention to the manuscript as a whole, and whose generous contributions to an atmosphere of discussion and engagement, helped make the online review process a terrific success.

Further thanks for making the online review possible go to Christian Wach, who continues to work on the CommentPress system originally developed by Eddie Tejeda for the Institute for the Future of the Book, and who was inordinately patient with a range of annoying questions and problems that I presented him with; I also owe JQuery master Jeremy Boggs a round of thanks for the nifty rollover footnote script he whipped up for me.

This project was started at the end of one sabbatical, wrapped up at the start of another, and largely written during the summers in between. I am grateful to Pomona College for the sabbatical and research support that I have received, and to my students and colleagues there for challenging my thinking about the future of digital publishing. I'm especially thankful to Kevin Dettmar, Jennifer Friedlander, Dara Regaignon, and Meg Worley for their support and encouragement in this process. I am also grateful to the NYU Department of Media, Culture, and Communication for its hospitality during the final stages of bringing the manuscript together.

Finally, to my partner in everything, Rick Blackwood: thanks for all of it, and here's to much, much more.

Portions of this book have appeared in somewhat different form in other venues, and thanks are due for the permission to reprint them here:

Part of the introduction is drawn from my essay in the May 2008 issue of *PMLA* and is reprinted by permission of the Modern Language Association of America; that material has also been published in different form in the winter/spring 2011 *ADE Bulletin* and is reprinted by permission of the Association of Departments of English.

Part of chapter 1 is drawn from my essay in the winter 2009 issue of *Cinema Journal*, and an early version of that chapter was published in the fall 2010 issue of *Social Epistemology*.

An early version of chapter 3 appeared on MediaCommons and in the fall 2007 issue of the *Journal of Electronic Publishing*.

Early drafts of many of this book's arguments appeared on a range of blogs, including *Planned Obsolescence*, *MediaCommons*, *The Valve*, and *if:book*; thanks to their editors for the platform they provided.

Introduction: Obsolescence

The old stuff gets broken faster than the new stuff is put in its place.
—Clay Shirky, "Newspapers and Thinking the Unthinkable"

In many cases, traditions last not because they are excellent, but because influential people are averse to change and because of the sheer burdens of transition to a better state.
—Cass Sunstein, *Infotopia*

The text you are now reading, whether on a screen in draft form or in its final, printed version, began its gestation some years ago in a series of explorations into the notion of obsolescence, which culminated in my being asked to address the term as part of the workshop "Keywords for a Digital Profession," organized by the Committee on the Status of Graduate Students at the December 2007 Modern Language Association (MLA) convention in Chicago. However jaded and dispiriting the grad students' choice of "obsolescence" as a keyword describing their own futures might appear, the decision to assign me this keyword was entirely appropriate. My work has circled the notion of obsolescence for quite a while, focusing on the concept as a catch-all for multiple cultural conditions, each of which demands different kinds of analysis and response. As I said at the MLA workshop, we too often fall into a conventional association of obsolescence with the death of this or that cultural form, a linkage that needs to be broken, or at least complicated, if the academy is going to take full stock of its role in contemporary culture and its means of producing and disseminating knowledge. For instance, the obsolescence that I focused on in my first book, *The Anxiety of Obsolescence: The American Novel in the Age of Television*, is not, or at least not primarily, material in nature; after all, neither the novel in particular, nor the book more broadly, nor print in general is "dead." My argument in *The Anxiety of Obsolescence* is, rather, that claims about the obsolescence of cultural forms often say more about those doing the claiming than they do about the object of the claim. In fact, agonized claims of the death of technologies like print and genres like the novel sometimes function to re-create an elite cadre of cultural producers and consumers, ostensibly operating on the margins of contemporary culture and profiting from their claims of marginality by creating a sense that their values, once part of a utopian mainstream and now apparently waning, must be protected. One might here think of the oft-cited reports published by the National Endowment for the Arts, *Reading at Risk* (2004) and *To Read or Not to Read* (2007). Each of these reports, like numerous other such expressions of anxiety about the ostensible decline of reading (a decline that comes to seem inevitable, of course, given the narrowness with which "reading" is defined: book-length printed and bound fiction and poetry consumed solely for pleasure), works rhetorically to create a kind of cultural wildlife preserve within which the apparently obsolete can flourish.[1] My argument in *The Anxiety of Obsolescence* thus suggests that obsolescence may be, in this case at least, less a material state than a political project aimed at intervening in contemporary public life, perhaps with the intent of shoring up a waning cultural hierarchy.

I'm beginning this new project by discussing my last project in no small part because of what happened once the manuscript was finished. Naively, I'd assumed that publishing a book that makes the argument that the book isn't dead wouldn't be hard, that publishers might have some stake in ensuring that such an argument got into circulation. What I hadn't counted on, though, as I revised the manuscript prior to submitting it for review, was the effect that the state of the economy would have on my ability to get that argument into print. In December 2003, almost exactly seventy-two hours after I'd found out that my college's cabinet had taken its final vote to grant me tenure, I received an email message from the editor of the scholarly press that had had the manuscript under review for the previous ten months. The news was not good: the press was declining to publish the book. The note, as encouraging as a rejection can ever be, stressed that in so far as fault could be attributed, it lay not with the manuscript but with the climate; the press had received two enthusiastically positive reader's reports, and the editor was supportive of the project. The marketing department, however, overruled him on the editorial board, declaring that the book posed "too much financial risk . . . to pursue in the current economy."

This particular cause for rejection prompted two immediate responses, one of which was most clearly articulated by my mother, who said, "They were planning on making money off of your book?" The fact is, they were— not much, perhaps, but that the press involved needed the book to make money, at least enough to return its costs, and that it doubted it would, highlights one of the most significant problems facing academic publishing today: an insupportable economic model.

To backtrack for a second: that there is a problem in the first place is something about which I hope, by this point, anyone reading this doesn't really need to be convinced; "crisis in scholarly publishing" has become one of the most-heard phrases in certain kinds of academic discussions, and organizations including the American Council of Learned Societies (ACLS) and the Association of Research Libraries (ARL), publishers such as Lindsay Waters and Bill Germano, scholars including Cathy Davidson and John Willinsky, and, perhaps most famously, past MLA president Stephen Greenblatt have been warning us for years that something's got to give. So of course the evidence for this crisis, and for the financial issues that rest at its heart, extends far beyond my own individual, anecdotal case.

Though the notion of a crisis in scholarly publishing came into common circulation well over a decade ago (see, e.g., Thatcher 1995), the situation suddenly got much, much worse after the first dot-com bubble burst in 2000. During this dramatic downturn in the stock market, when numerous university endowments went into free fall—a moment that, in retrospect, seems like mere foreshadowing—university presses and university libraries were among the academic units whose budgets took the hardest hits. And the cuts in funding for libraries represented a further budget cut for presses, as numerous libraries, already straining under the exponentially rising cost of journals, especially in the sciences, managed the cutbacks by reducing the number of monographs they purchased. The result for library users was perhaps only a slightly longer wait to obtain any book they needed, as libraries increasingly turned to consortial arrangements for collection-sharing, but the result for presses was devastating. Imagine: for a university press of the caliber of, say, Harvard's, the expectation for decades had been that they could count on every library in the University of California system buying a copy of each title they published. Since 2000, however, the rule was increasingly that *one* library in the system would buy that title.[2] And the same has happened with every such system around the country, such that, as Jennifer Crewe (2004, 27) noted, sales of monographs to libraries were less than one-third of what they had been two decades before—and they've continued to drop since then. So library cutbacks have resulted in vastly reduced sales for university presses, at precisely the moment when severe reductions in the percentage of university press budgets subsidized by their institutions have made those presses dependent on income from sales for their survival. (The average university press, as we'll see, receives well under 10 percent of its annual budget from its institution. We can only imagine what will happen to that figure in the current economic climate.) The results, of course, are that many presses have reduced the number of titles that they publish, and that marketing concerns have come at times, and of necessity, to outweigh scholarly merit in making publication decisions.

Despite the fact that *The Anxiety of Obsolescence* was finally published—by a smaller press with more modest sales expectations[3]—my experience of the crisis in academic publishing led me to begin rethinking my argument about the continued viability of the book as a form. Perhaps there is a particular type of book, the scholarly monograph—or, even more specifically (given that marketing departments prefer known quantities), the *first* scholarly monograph—that is indeed threatened with obsolescence. Even so, this is not to say that the monograph is "dead." Even first books are still published, after all, if not quite in the numbers they might need to be in order to satisfy all our hiring and tenure requirements, and they still sell, if not exactly in the numbers required to support the presses that put them out. The scholarly press book is, however, in a curious state, one that might usefully trouble our associations of obsolescence with the "death" of this or that cultural form, for while it is no longer a *viable* mode of communication, it is, in many fields, still *required* in order to get tenure. If anything, the scholarly monograph isn't dead; it is *undead*.

The suggestion that one particular type of book might be thought of as undead indicates that we need to rethink, in a broad sense, the relationship between old media and new, and ask what that relationship bodes for the academy. If this traditional mode of academic publishing is not dead, but undead—again, not viable, but still required—how should we approach our work and the publishing systems that bring it into being? There's a real question to be asked about how far we want to carry this metaphor; the suggestion that contemporary academic publishing is governed by a kind of zombie logic, for instance, might be read as indicating that these old forms refuse to stay put in their graves, but instead walk the earth, rotting and putrescent, wholly devoid of consciousness, eating the brains of the living and susceptible to nothing but decapitation—and this might seem a bit of an overresponse. On the other hand, it's worth considering the extensive scholarship in media studies on the figure of the zombie, which is often understood to act as a stand-in for the narcotized subject of capitalism, particularly at those moments when capitalism's contradictions become most apparent.[4] And, of course, there's been a serious recent uptick in broad cultural interest in zombies, perhaps exemplified by the spring 2009 release of *Pride and Prejudice and Zombies*.[5] If there is a relationship between the zombie and the subject of late capitalism, the cultural anxiety that figure marks is currently, with reason, off the charts—and not least within the academy, as we not only find our ways of communicating increasingly threatened with a sort of death-in-life, but also find our livelihoods themselves decreasingly lively, as the liberal arts are overtaken by the teaching of supposedly more pragmatic fields, as tenure-track faculty lines are rapidly being replaced with more contingent forms of labor, and as too many newly-minted Ph.D.s find themselves without the job opportunities they need to survive. The relationship between the zombie status of the scholarly book and the perilous state of the profession isn't causal, but nor is it unrelated, and until we develop the individual and institutional will to transform our ways of communicating, we're unlikely to be able to transform our broader ways of working.[6]

Just to be clear: I am not suggesting that the future survival of the academy requires us to put academic publishing safely in its grave. I'm not being wholly facetious either, though, as I do want to indicate that certain aspects of the academic publishing process are neither quite as alive as we'd like them to be, nor quite as dead as might be most convenient. If the monograph were genuinely dead, we'd be forced to find other forms in which to publish. And if the book were simply outmoded by newer, shinier publishing technologies, we could probably get along fine with the undead of academic publishing, as studies of forms like radio and the vinyl LP indicate that obsolete media have always had curious afterlives.[7] There are important differences between those cases and that of academic publishing, however: we don't yet have a good replacement for the scholarly monograph, nor do we seem particularly inclined to allow the book to become a "niche" technology within humanities discourse. It's thus important for us to consider the work that the book is and isn't doing for us; the ways that it remains vibrant and vital; and the ways that it has become undead, haunting the living from beyond the grave.

A few distinctions are necessary. The obsolescence faced by the first academic book is not primarily material, any more than is the putative obsolescence of the novel; a radical shift to all-digital delivery would by itself do nothing to revive the form. However much I will insist in what follows that we in the humanities must move beyond our singular focus on ink-on-paper to understand and take advantage of pixels-on-screens, the form of print still functions perfectly well, and numerous studies have indicated that a simple move to electronic distribution within the current system of academic publishing will not be enough to bail out the system, as printing, storing, and distributing the material form of the book represent only a fraction of its current production costs (see Crewe 2004). In fact, as many have pointed out, digital forms may be *more* prone to a material obsolescence than is print. Consider, for instance, the obsolescence one encounters in attempting to read classic hypertext fiction such as Michael Joyce's *Afternoon* (1987/90) on a Mac these days: Apple fully retired its support for "Classic" mode with the advent, on the hardware side, of Intel-based processors that can't boot into OS 9, and on the software side, the release of OS 10.5, which eliminated Classic support for PowerPC machines as well. Couple this forward march of technology with the fact that Eastgate, the publisher of many of the most important first-generation hypertexts, has after more than eight years still failed to release those texts in OS X-native editions. Technologies move on, and technological formats degrade, posing a set of dangers to digital textual futures that the Electronic Literature Organization has been working to bring into public view, both through its "acid-free bits" campaign and through its more recent work with the Library of Congress to archive digital literary texts (see, e.g., Liu et al. 2005; Montfort and Wardrip-Fruin 2004). Without such active work to preserve electronic texts, and without the ongoing interest of and commitment by publishers, many digital texts face an obsolescence that is not at all theoretical, but very material.

As I discuss in chapter 4, however, the apparent ephemerality of digital text in fact masks unexpected persistences. Let me point, by way of example, to my more than nine-year-old blog, which I named *Planned Obsolescence* as a tongue-in-cheek jab at the fact that I'd just finished what seemed to be a long-term, durable project, the book, and was left with the detritus of many smaller ideas that demanded a kind of immediacy and yet seemed destined to fade into nothingness. The blog is the perfect vehicle for such ephemera, as each post scrolls down the front page and off into the archives—and yet, the apparent ephemerality of the blog post bears within it a surprising durability, thanks both to the technologies of searching, filtering, and archiving that have developed across the web, as well as to the network of blog conversations that keep the archives in play. Blogs do die, often when their authors stop posting, sometimes when they're deleted. But even when apparently dead, a blog persists, in archives and caches, and accretes life around it, whether in the form of human visitors, drawn in by Google searches or links from other blogs, or spam bots, attracted like vermin to the apparently abandoned structure. A form of obsolescence may be engineered into a blog's architecture, but this ephemerality is misleading; the ways that we interact with blogs within networked environments keep them alive long after they've apparently died.

I want to hold up alongside the blog's persistent ephemerality the state of the scholarly monograph, which I'd argue faces an obsolescence that is primarily institutional, arising from the environment in which it is produced. If, after all, there's something obsolete about the book, it's not its content; despite my general agreement with calls to decenter the book as the "gold standard" for tenure and place greater value on the publication of articles, there's a kind of large-scale synthetic work done in the form of the book that's still important to the development of scholarly thought.[8] Nor is the problem the book's form; the pages still turn just fine. What has ceased to function in the first academic book is the system surrounding its production and dissemination, the process through which the book comes into being, is distributed, and interacts with its readers. I mentioned earlier that the message I'd received from that press, declining my book on financial grounds, produced two immediate responses. The first was my mother's bewildered disbelief; the second came from my colleague Matt Kirschenbaum, who left a comment on *Planned Obsolescence* saying that he did not understand why I couldn't simply take the manuscript and the two positive readers' reports and put the whole thing online—voilà: peer-reviewed publication—where it would likely garner a readership both wider and larger than the same manuscript in print would. "In fact I completely understand why that's not realistic," he went on to say, "and I'm not seriously advocating it. Nor am I suggesting that we all become our own online publishers, at least not unless that's part of a continuum of different options. But the point is, the system's broken and it's time we got busy fixing it. What ought to count is peer review and scholarly merit, not the physical form in which the text is ultimately delivered" (Kirschenbaum 2003).

This exchange with Matt, and a number of other conversations that I had in the ensuing months, convinced me to stop thinking about scholarly publishing as a system that would simply bring my work into being, and instead approach it as the object of that work, thinking seriously about both the institutional models and the material forms through which scholarship might best circulate. I began, in early 2004, to discuss in a fairly vague way what it would take to found an all-electronic community-run scholarly press, but it took a while for anything more concrete to emerge. What got things started was a December 2005 report by the online journal *Inside Higher Ed* on the work that had been done to that point by an MLA task force on the evaluation of scholarship for tenure and promotion, and on the multiple recommendations thus far made by the panel. At the request of the editors of *The Valve*, a widely read literary studies–focused blog, I wrote a lengthy consideration of the recommendations made by this panel, and extended one of those recommendations to reflect one possible future, in the hopes of opening up a larger conversation about where academic publishing ought to go, and how we might best take it there.

Many of the recommendations put forward by the MLA task force (expanded in the task force's final report; see Modern Language Association of America, December 2006) were long in coming, and many stand to change tenure processes for the better; these include calls for departments

- to clarify the communication of tenure standards to new hires via memorandums of understanding;
- to give serious consideration to articles published by tenure candidates— thus, as I noted, decentering the book as the gold standard of scholarly production—and to communicate that expanded range of acceptable venues for publication to their administrations;
- to set an absolute maximum of six letters from outside evaluators that can be required to substantiate a tenure candidate's scholarly credentials, to draw those evaluators from comparable institutions rather than more prestigious ones, and to refrain from asking evaluators to make inappropriate judgments about the tenure-worthiness of candidates based on the limited portrait that a dossier presents;

and, perhaps most importantly, at least for my purposes,

- to acknowledge that scholarship of many different varieties is taking place online, and to evaluate that scholarship without media-related bias.

These were extremely important recommendations, but there was a significant degree of "easier said than done" in the responses they received (particularly the last one), and for no small reason: they require a substantive rethinking not simply of the processes through which the academy tenures its faculty, but of the ways those faculty do their work, how they communicate that work, and how that work is read both inside and outside the academy. Those changes cannot simply be technological; they must be both social and institutional. This recognition led me to begin two projects, both aimed at creating the kinds of change I think necessary for the survival of scholarly publishing in the humanities into the twenty-first century.

The first of these is MediaCommons, a field-specific attempt to develop a new kind of scholarly publishing network, which my collaborators and I have been working on with the support of the Institute for the Future of the Book, a National Endowment for the Humanities (NEH) Digital Start-Up Grant, and the NYU Digital Library Technology Services group. MediaCommons is working to become a setting in which the multiplicity of conversations in and about media studies taking place online can be brought together, through projects like *In Syndication*, which aggregates a number of the leading blogs in the field. We're also publishing a range of original projects, the longest-running of which is *In Media Res*, which asks five scholars a week to comment briefly on some up-to-the-minute media text as a means of opening discussion about the issues it presents for media scholars, students, practitioners, and activists. We hope to foster that discussion as part of a much broader scholarly ecosystem, understanding that the ideas we circulate range in heft from the blog post through the article to the monograph. Those heftier forms are published through MediaCommons Press, a project in which we produce longer texts for open discussion, some of which move through the digital phase on their way to a primary life in print. (For example, we launched an experiment in open peer review in March 2010 on behalf of *Shakespeare Quarterly*, for a special issue on Shakespeare and New Media.) Other projects are meant to have a primary digital existence, including Nick Mirzoeff's *The New Everyday*, an experimental "middle-state" publication. But the chief importance of MediaCommons, as far as I'm concerned, is the network it aims to build among scholars in the field, getting those scholars in communication with one another, discussing and possibly collaborating on their projects. To that end, we've built a peer network backbone for the system—Facebook for scholars, if you like. Through this profile system, members can gather the writing they're doing across the web, as well as citations for offline work, creating a digital portfolio that provides a snapshot of their scholarly identities.

Working on MediaCommons has taught me several things that I mostly knew already, but hadn't fully internalized: first, any software development project will take far longer than you could possibly predict at the outset; and second, and most important, no matter how slowly such software development projects move, the rate of change within the academy is positively glacial in comparison.

My need to advocate for such change is what led to this project, for although numerous publications in the last few years have argued for the need for new systems and practices in scholarly publishing—to name just two, John Willinsky's *The Access Principle* (2006) and Christine Borgman's *Scholarship in the Digital Age* (2007)—these arguments too often fail to account for the fundamentally conservative nature of academic institutions and (the rhetoric of a David Horowitz notwithstanding) the similar conservatism of the academics that comprise them. In the main, we're extraordinarily resistant to change in our ways of working; it is not without reason that a senior colleague once joked to me that the motto of our institution (one that I think might usefully be extended to the academy as a whole) could well be "We Have Never Done It That Way Before." As Donald Hall has noted, scholars often resist applying the critical skills that we bring to our subject matter to an examination of "the textuality of our own profession, its scripts, values, biases, and behavioral norms" (Hall 2002, xiv); such self-criticism is a risky endeavor, and those of us who have been privileged enough to succeed within the extant system are often reluctant to bite the hand that feeds us. Changing our technologies, our ways of doing research, and our modes of production and distribution of the results of that research are all crucial to the continued vitality of the academy—and yet none of those changes can come about unless there is first a profound change in the ways that scholars think about their work. Until scholars really believe that publishing on the web is as valuable as publishing in print—and more importantly, until they believe that their institutions believe it, too—few will be willing to risk their careers on a new way of working, with the result that that new way of working will remain marginal and undervalued.

In what follows, then, I focus not just on the technological changes that many believe are necessary to allow academic publishing to flourish into the future, but on the social, intellectual, and institutional changes that are necessary to pave the way for such flourishing. In order for new modes of communication to become broadly accepted within the academy, scholars and their institutions must take a new look at the mission of the university, the goals of scholarly publishing, and the processes through which scholars conduct their work. We must collectively consider what new technologies have to offer us, not just in terms of the cost of publishing or access to publications, but in the ways we research, write, and review.

In chapter 1 I argue that we need to begin with the structures of peer review, not least because of the persistent problem they present for digital scholarship, and the degree to which our values (not to mention our value) as scholars are determined by them. Peer review is at the heart of everything we do—writing, applying for grants, seeking jobs, obtaining promotions. It is, arguably, what makes the academy the academy. However, the current system of peer review is in fact part of what's broken, of what threatens a vibrant mode of scholarly communication with obsolescence. As I explore in the next chapter, a rather extraordinary literature is available, mostly in the sciences and social sciences, on the problems with conventional peer review, including its biases and flaws. It also requires an astonishing amount of labor, for which academics can't currently receive any "credit." And thus when Kirschenbaum says that "what ought to count is peer review and scholarly merit, not the physical form in which the text is ultimately delivered," I agree, but at the same time feel quite strongly that the system of peer review as we know it today is flawed, a backchannel conversation taking place between editor and reviewer that too often excludes the author from its benefits, and that too often impedes rather than assists in the circulation of ideas. For that reason, I want to force us to take a closer look at what we mean when we say peer review, and what it is we expect the process to accomplish, in order to make sure that we're not installing a broken part in a new machine.

A dramatically changed peer-review system such as the one that I propose, however, would require us to think about new structures of authorship. In chapter 2, I argue that a turn from pre-publication review to post-publication review will almost certainly necessitate a parallel turn from thinking about academic publishing as a system focused on the production and dissemination of individual *products* to imagining it as a system focused more broadly on facilitating the *processes* of scholarly work, as the time and effort required to maintain a community-oriented, gift-economy-driven system of peer-to-peer review will oblige scholars, much like the developers of large-scale open-source software projects, to place some portion of their emphasis not on their own individual achievements, but rather on finding their self-interest served by the advancement of the community as a whole. This is a utopian ideal, of course, and it largely goes against our training as scholars, particularly within the humanities; what we accomplish, we accomplish alone. (Or, as a commenter on Twitter put it after hearing a talk of mine, "Being helpful is not really part of academic culture.") As I reconsider authorship within digital networked publishing structures, I argue, using the example of blogs, that what we will need to let go of is not what we have come to understand as the individual voice, but rather the illusion that such a voice is ever fully alone. Roland Barthes, of course, claimed back in 1967 that no text is a single "line of words," but that each is instead a "multi-dimensional space in which are married and contested several writings, none of which is original: the text is a fabric of quotations" (Barthes 1967/86, 52–53). We have long acknowledged the death of the author—in theory, at least—but have been loath to think about what such a proclamation might mean for our own status as authors, and have certainly been unwilling to part with the lines on the CV that result from publishing.

Digital networks, as structures that facilitate interaction, communication, and interconnection, will require us to think differently about what it is we're doing as we write. As the example of the blog might suggest, communities best engage with one another around writing that is open rather than closed, in process rather than concluded. If we were to shift our focus in the work we're doing as authors from the moment of completion, from the self-contained product, to privilege instead the process of writing, discussion, and revision, we'd likely begin to "publish" work—in the sense of making it public in readable form—earlier in its development (at the conference paper stage, for instance) and to remain engaged with those texts much longer after they've been released to readers. Although this idea makes many scholars nervous—about getting "scooped," about getting too much feedback too soon, about letting the messiness of our processes be seen, about the prospect of never being fully "done" with a project—it's worth considering why we're doing the work in the first place: to the degree that scholarship is about participating in an exchange of ideas with one's peers, new networked publishing structures can facilitate that interaction, but will best do so if the discussion is ongoing, always in process.

This foregrounding of conversation, however, will likely also require authors, who are in dialogue with their readers—who are, of course, themselves authors—to relinquish a certain degree of control over their texts, letting go of the illusion that their work springs wholly from their individual intelligence and acknowledging the ways that scholarship, even in fields in which sole authorship is the norm, has always been collaborative. (We resist this, of course; as Lisa Ede and Andrea Lunsford [2001] have pointed out, no matter how much we claim to value the collective or collaborative, the proof of our profoundly individualistic sense of accomplishment rests in the literally unthinkable nature of the multi-author dissertation.) Sometimes the result of these new conversational publishing practices might be productive coauthoring relationships, but it need not always be so; we may instead need to develop new methods of citation that acknowledge the participation of our peers in the development of our work. Along the way, though, we'll also need to let go of some of our fixation on the notion of originality in scholarly production, recognizing that, in an environment in which more and more discourse is available, some of the most important work that we can do as scholars may more closely resemble contemporary editorial or curatorial practices, bringing together, highlighting, and remixing significant ideas in existing texts rather than remaining solely focused on the production of more ostensibly original texts. We must find ways for the new modes of authorship that digital networks will no doubt facilitate—process-focused, collaborative, remix-oriented—to "count" within our systems of valuation and priority.

In the later chapters, I explore a number of other such changes that will be required throughout the entire academic community if such new publishing practices are to take root. Publishers, for instance, will need to think differently about their business models (which may need to focus more on services and less on objects), about their editorial practices (which may require a greater role in developing and shepherding projects), about the structures of texts, about their ownership of copyright, and about their role in facilitating conversation; they'll also need to think in concert with libraries about archival and preservation practices, ensuring that the texts produced today remain available and accessible tomorrow. Universities, in the broadest sense, will need to rethink the relationship between the library, the university press, the information technology center, and the academic units within the institution, reimagining the funding model under which publishing operates and the institutional purposes that such publishing serves—but also, and crucially, reimagining the relationship between the academic institution and the surrounding culture. As new systems of networked knowledge production become increasingly prevalent and influential online, the university and the scholars who comprise it need to find ways to adapt those systems to our needs, or we will run the risk of becoming increasingly irrelevant to the ways that contemporary culture produces and communicates authority.

In the end, what I am arguing is that we in the humanities, and in the academy more broadly, face what is less a material obsolescence than an institutional one; we are entrenched in systems that no longer serve our needs. But because we are, by and large, our institutions—or rather, because they are us—the greatest challenge we face is not that obsolescence, but our response to it. Like the novelists I studied in my first book, who may feel their cultural centrality threatened by the rise of newer media forms, we can shore up the boundaries between ourselves and the open spaces of intellectual exchange on the Internet; we can extol the virtues of the ways things have always been done; we can bemoan our marginalization in a culture that continues marching forward into the digital future—and in so doing, we can further undermine our influence on the main threads of intellectual discussion in contemporary public life. The crisis we face, after all, does not stop with the book, but rather extends to the valuation of the humanities within the university, and of institutions of higher education within the culture at large. We tend to dismiss the public disdain for our work and our institutions as a manifestation of the ingrained anti-intellectualism in U.S. culture, and perhaps understandably so, but until we take responsibility for our culture's sense of our irrelevance, we cannot hope to convince it otherwise. Unless we can find ways to speak with that culture, to demonstrate the vibrancy and the value of the liberal arts, we run the risk of being silenced altogether.

And we will be silenced, unless we can create new ways of speaking both with that culture and among ourselves. We can build institutional supports for the current, undead system of scholarly publishing, and we can watch as the profession itself continues to decline. Or we can work to change the ways we communicate and the systems through which we attribute value to such communication, opening ourselves to the possibility that new modes of publishing might enable, not just more texts, but better texts, not just an evasion of obsolescence, but a new life for scholarship. The point, finally, is not whether any particular technology can provide a viable future for scholarly publishing, but whether we have the institutional will to commit to the development of the systems that will make such technologies viable and keep them that way into the future.

1

Peer Review

In a world where knowledge is being made available at a rate of millions of pages per day, it is comforting to know that some subset of that knowledge or science has been critically examined so that, were we to use it in our thinking for our work, we would be less likely to have wasted our time.

—Ray Spier, "The History of the Peer-Review Process"

[E]lectronic publishing distinguishes between the phase where documents are placed at the disposal of the public (publishing proper) and the phase where "distinctions" are being attributed. It used to be that being printed was "the" distinction; electronic publishing changes this and leads us to think of the distinction phase completely separately from the publishing phase.

However, doing so changes the means by which distinction is imparted, and imparting distinction is a sure sign of power. In other words, those who now hold that privilege are afraid of losing it ("gate keepers") and they will [use] every possible argument to protect it without, if possible, ever mentioning it.

—Jean-Claude Guédon and Raymond Siemens,
"The Credibility of Electronic Publishing:
Peer Review and Imprint"

We police ourselves into irrelevance and insignificance.

—Cathy Davidson, "'Research': How
Peer Review Counts and Doesn't"

For the past few years, I have worked with the Institute for the Future of the Book, my colleague Avi Santo, and a range of prominent scholars in media studies on MediaCommons, an all-electronic scholarly publishing network. During the planning phases of the project, we blogged, held meetings, and tested some small-scale implementations of the network's technologies—and in all of the feedback that we received, in all of the conversations we had with scholars both senior and junior, one question repeatedly resurfaced: What are you going to do about peer review?

I've suggested elsewhere (Fitzpatrick 2007a) that peer review threatens to become the bottleneck in which the entire issue of electronic scholarly publishing gets wedged, preventing many innovative systems from becoming fully established. This is a flippant response, to be sure; such concerns are quite understandable, given that peer review is in some sense the *sine qua non* of the academy. We employ it in almost every aspect of the ways that we work, from hiring decisions through tenure and promotion reviews, in both internal and external grant and fellowship competitions, and, of course, in publishing. The work we do as scholars is repeatedly subjected to a series of vetting processes that enable us to indicate that the results of our work have been scrutinized by authorities in the field, and that those results are therefore themselves authoritative.

But as authors such as Michael Jensen (2007a, 2007b) of the National Academies Press have recently argued, the nature of authority is shifting dramatically in the era of the digital network. Scholars in media studies have explored such shifts as they affect media production, distribution, and consumption, focusing on the extent to which, for instance, bloggers are decentralizing and even displacing the authority structures surrounding traditional journalism, or the ways that a range of phenomena including mashups and fan vids are shifting the previously assumed hierarchies that existed between media producers and consumers, or the growing tensions in the relationship between consumers, industries, and industry regulators highlighted by file-sharing services and battles with the Recording Industry Association of America. These changes are at the heart of much of the most exciting and influential work in media studies today, including publications such as Siva Vaidhyanathan's *The Anarchist in the Library* (2004), Henry Jenkins's *Convergence Culture* (2006), and Yochai Benkler's *The Wealth of Networks* (2006), projects that have grown out of an interest in the extent to which the means of media production and distribution are undergoing a process of radical democratization in the age of blogs, Wikipedia, and YouTube, and a desire to test the limits of that democratization.

To a surprising extent, however, scholars have resisted exploring a similar sense in which *intellectual* authority might likewise be shifting in the contemporary world.[1] Such a resistance is manifested in the often unthinking and over-blown academic response to Wikipedia—for instance, the Middlebury College history department's ban on the use of the online encyclopedia as a research source and the debate that ensued—which seems to indicate a serious misunderstanding about the value of the project.[2] Treating Wikipedia like any other encyclopedia by consulting only the entries runs the risk of missing the point entirely; as Bob Stein (2006) has suggested, a user has to learn to read Wikipedia differently, given that the real intellectual heart of the project lies on the history and discussion pages, where the controversies inherent in the production of any encyclopedia entry are enacted in public, rather than smoothed over into an untroubled conventional wisdom (see Visel 2006; Stein 2006). More centralized projects, such as Citizendium, that seek to add traditional, hierarchical modes of review to a project like Wikipedia overlook the facts that the wiki is in its very architecture a mode of ongoing peer review, and that not only the results of that review but the records of its process are available for critical scrutiny.[3] Failing to engage fully with the intellectual merits of a project like Wikipedia, or with the ways in which Wikipedia represents one facet of a far-reaching change in contemporary epistemologies, is a mistake that we academics make at our own peril. As one librarian frames the issue, "Banning a source like Wikipedia (rather than teaching how to use it wisely) simply tells students that the academic world is divorced from real-world practices" (Bill Badke, quoted in Regalado 2007). The production of knowledge is the academy's very reason for being, and if we cling to an outdated system for establishing and measuring authority while the nature of authority is shifting around us, we run the risk of becoming increasingly irrelevant to contemporary culture's dominant ways of knowing. We too often keep our work as scholars hidden away from the cultural mainstream, pointing toward a pervasive anti-intellectualism that disqualifies the public from engaging with our ideas. Today's funding climate for higher education requires, however, that we look more deeply within for the sources of our resistance to public engagement and the ways that resistance hinders rather than supports us as professionals. As Janice Radway (2004, 217) has argued, the rise of professionalization in the academy "had everything to do with specialization, with the growing emphasis on laboratory research, and with the creation of a communications infrastructure that enabled the publication, circulation, and discussion of research results not only among peers but within a larger society called upon to finance such research, to support it with students, and to understand its value," thus reminding scholars that our very professional existences (and the support that we need in order to maintain them) may depend on communicating, not just among ourselves, but with a broader public, so that they understand the value of academic ways of knowing. We must open ourselves up in order to be *part of* rather than *apart from* contemporary culture, and in order to do so, we need to expand and rethink the very idea of who our peers are today.

For this reason, what I am absolutely *not* arguing in what follows is that we need to ensure that peer-reviewed journals online are of equivalent value to peer-reviewed journals in print; in fact, I believe that such an equation is part of the problem I'm addressing. Imposing traditional methods of peer review on digital publishing might help a transition to such publishing in the short term, enabling more traditionally minded scholars to see electronic and print scholarship as equivalent in value, but it will hobble us in the long term, as we employ outdated methods in a public space that operates under radically different systems of authorization. Instead, we must find ways to work with, improve, and adapt those new systems for scholarly use—but we must also find ways to convince ourselves, our colleagues, our colleges and universities, our disciplinary organizations, and the academy at large of the value that is produced by the use of such systems.

Traditional Peer Review and Its Defenses

David Shatz notes in the introduction to his 2004 volume on peer review that his text is not only "the first book-length study of peer review that utilizes methods and resources of contemporary philosophy," but also "the first wide-ranging treatment of the subject by a scholar in the humanities," a fact that becomes all the more surprising when he points out that

> [b]esides its ethical aspect, the topic also has dimensions of epistemological significance, since it implicates such concepts as truth, bias, relativism, conservatism, consensus, and standards of good argument. Philosophers and other humanities scholars have produced a voluminous literature on these subjects. Yet they have not applied their approaches to these topics to peer review itself, that is, to the very procedures and practices that produced much of the voluminous literature in ethics, epistemology, and so many other fields. (Shatz 2004, 4)

Shatz indicates a number of reasons why this may be so, including that the more nebulous (or, rather, problematized) understanding of "truth" in the humanities precludes such scholars from being able to "show that a peer review was wrong" (p. 6), and that a critical study of peer review might require empirical work of a sort for which humanists are neither trained nor rewarded. Beyond these factors, however, I'd argue that a critical study of the epistemological practices of peer review requires a form of self-analysis that, as Donald Hall has argued in *The Academic Self* (2002), many of us resist.

Such resistance might suggest an underlying anxiety about the outcome of the analysis, a concern that the time-honored procedures and standards of the humanities might be shown to be flawed—and thus that the work that has developed through those procedures and according to those standards might be even further marginalized within the academy's mission of knowledge-production. However, as Hall argues, genuinely "owning" our careers and the ways in which we conduct them requires taking the risk of applying our critical skills to an examination of "the textuality of our own profession, its scripts, values, biases, and behavioral norms" (Hall 2002, xiv). Too often, such examinations and proposals for change are met with stern reminders that We Have Never Done It That Way Before. The apparently intractable nature of the way things have always been done is precisely the kind of signal that, in other institutions, impels scholars to critical analysis; a resistance to turning the same critical eye on our own seemingly naturalized assumptions may create (or deepen) an atmosphere of intellectual oppression and stultification, as we allow systems in which we do not genuinely have faith to dictate our engagements with the world and with one another. Opening up the basis of those engagements through a thorough reconsideration of peer review may be precisely what we need in order to allow our work to help shape ways of knowing in the contemporary world.

Resistance to considering the merits of a more open mode of publishing often runs something like that expressed—in, I assume, an intentionally hyperbolic fashion—by Shatz:

> It is hard to say who would have the biggest nightmare were open review implemented: readers who have to trek through enormous amounts of junk before finding articles they find rewarding; serious scholars who have to live with the depressing knowledge that flat earth theories now can be said to enjoy "scholarly support"; or a public that finds the medical literature flooded with voodoo and quackery. Let us not forget, either, that editors and sponsoring universities would lose power and prestige even while their workload as judges would be eliminated. (2004, 16)

The vehemence of such resistance often reveals something about the nervousness of those who express it, and, as in much psychotherapeutic discourse, only after some initial projection and displacement does the real source of that anxiety come out: the loss of "power and prestige."[4] However, in responding to those earlier displacements of anxiety, one can provide certain kinds of reassurance. The computer technologies that make open review possible also make possible the implementation of analytical tools that can help filter "rewarding" articles from any "junk" in which they may be mired, whether those tools employ the results of the open review system themselves or use other modes of sophisticated textual analysis and recommendation. Further, serious scholars depressed by the apparent anything-goes nature of open publishing can see to it, by participating in the review system, that "flat earth" theories obtain the reception that they deserve. In fact, the public is already flooded with voodoo and quackery, as revealed by even the most cursory look at the relationship between the pharmaceutical industry and the bulk of publicly available medical information; post-publication review might actually help readers know how to interpret the material that's out there.[5] But finally, if the loss of power and prestige is our primary concerns in clinging to closed review, we would be best served by admitting this to ourselves up front. If we enjoy the privileges that obtain from upholding a closed system of discourse sufficiently that we're unwilling to subject it to critical scrutiny, we may also need to accept the fact that the mainstream of public intellectual life will continue, in the main, to ignore our work. Public funds will, in that case, be put to uses that seem more immediately pressing than our support. This can no doubt be rationalized as the inevitable, unenviable fate of genius in a world of mediocrity.

The History of Peer Review

It would be worthwhile, however, to explore several of the assumptions we make about the benefits of peer review in order to avoid clinging to our present ways of working out of the mistaken sense that as they have ever been thus, so they should remain. In fact, peer review as we currently know it has a different history than we might assume. Very little investigation of the historical development of peer review has been done, and the few explorations that do attempt to present some sense of the system's history largely cite the same handful of brief texts.[6] Moreover, nearly all of the texts exploring the history of peer review focus on the natural and social sciences, and almost none mention peer review in scholarly book publishing.[7] Although it is beyond the scope of this chapter to fill in all of those gaps, it is worth noting a few wrinkles in the history of peer review as it is conventionally understood. Most often, authors date the advent of what we now refer to as editorial peer review—the assessment of manuscripts by more than one qualified reader, usually not including the editor of a journal or press—to the Royal Society of London's 1752 creation of a "Committee on Papers" to oversee the review and selection of texts for publication in its nearly century-old journal, *Philosophical Transactions*.[8] A number of authors complicate this history by pointing to the existence of at least one earlier instance of formalized peer review in a scientific journal: the Royal Society of Edinburgh seems to have had such a system in place as early as 1731 (Kronick 1990).[9]

However, Mario Biagioli (2002) argues that a deeper excavation of the genealogy of peer review suggests that its origins may lie in seventeenth-century *book* publishing, and that peer review of journal articles formed a significantly later stage in the process's development. Biagioli ties the establishment of editorial peer review to the royal license that was required for the legal sale of printed texts; this mode of state censorship, employed to prevent sedition or heresy, was delegated to the royal academies through the imprimatur granted them at the time of their founding. The Royal Society of London, for instance, took on that imprimatur by passing a resolution in December 1663, one year after its founding, which stated, "No book be printed by order of the council, which hath not been perused and considered by two of the council, who shall report, that such book contains nothing but what is suitable to the design and work of the society" (quoted in Biagioli 2002, 21). The purpose of such review, as Biagioli (2002, 23) emphasizes, remained more related to censorship than to quality control: "As in traditional book licensing, the review was about making sure that a text did not make unacceptable claims rather than to certify that it made good claims." Because the members of the royal academies were, if not literally part of the government, certainly dependent upon the state for their livelihoods, the concept of "peer review" in this instance indicates an early ambiguity between review by one's peers and review by a peer of the realm; as Biagioli suggests, "[B]ecause of the 'pre-disciplining' of academicians, the simple requirement that manuscripts had to be reviewed by the whole academy or by a committee made it almost impossible that anything controversial would go to press" (p. 15). Gradually, however, scholarly societies facilitated a transition in scientific peer review from state censorship to self-policing, allowing them a degree of autonomy but simultaneously creating, in the Foucauldian sense, a disciplinary technology, one that produces the conditions of possibility for the academic disciplines that it authorizes.

Biagioli's argument leads us to understand peer review not simply as a system that produces disciplinarity in an intellectual sense, but as a mode of disciplining knowledge itself, a mode that is "simultaneously repressive, productive, and constitutive" of academic ways of knowing (2002, 11). He pertinently distinguishes Michel Foucault's disciplinary reference points in medicine and the prison from the discipline of peer review, however, as only in the academy do we find "that the roles of the disciplined and the discipliner are often reversed during one's career" (p. 12), indicating the ways that peer review functions as a self-perpetuating disciplinary system, inculcating the objects of discipline into becoming its subjects. Though peer review may have shed "its negative symbolic connections to early modern absolutism," as Biagioli concludes, and instead become "the new symbol of the relationship between science and liberal societies," and though its work today "is now about technical accuracy, not legal approbation" (pp. 32, 34), its roots in early modern book censorship are revealed by its continued appeal to the imprimatur it grants.

Peer review thus long pre-dates the invention of the scholarly journal, originating with the formation of the royal academies themselves.[10] Membership in these societies required scientists to demonstrate their bona fides in the form of publication, experimentation, or invention in order to be eligible for election—arguably subjecting their work to a form of peer review (see Kronick 2004, 96). Further, early scientists circulated letters among their peers or read papers in society meetings, reporting the results of their investigations with the explicit intention of eliciting response.[11] The application of peer-review processes to scientific journal publishing thus becomes a further extension of society business—reviewing and discussing the reports of work done by the society's members. Moreover, Drummond Rennie argues that early journal peer-review processes were less focused on quality control than we would now assume:

> [S]ystems of peer review, internal and external to journals, were put in place by editors during the eighteenth century in order to assist editors in the selection of manuscripts for publication. It was appreciated from the start that the peer review process could not authenticate or endorse because the editors and reviewers could not be at the scene of any crime. . . . [T]he journals from the beginning threw the ultimate responsibility for the integrity of the article squarely upon the author. (Rennie 2003, 2).

Early peer review in scientific journal publishing was meant to augment editorial expertise rather than to exercise more conventionally understood modes of quality control. Moreover, as Jean-Claude Guédon and Raymond Siemens (2002, 18) indicate, while peer review developed in order to augment the expertise of the editor, the process "nevertheless rested on procedures that put the editor-in-chief in absolute control, albeit in an acceptable way," namely, through editorial control over the selection of reviewers. Thus, while we attribute the arbitration of value in scholarly publishing to the review process to which work has been subjected, that process was not early on imagined to guarantee the quality of publications, nor did it wholly diffuse the authority of the editor.

On the one hand, peer review has its deep origins in state censorship, as developed through the establishment and membership practices of state-supported academies; on the other, peer review was intended to augment the authority of a journal's editor rather than assure the quality of a journal's products. Given those two disruptions in our contemporary notions about the purposes of peer review, it may be less surprising to find that the mode of formalized review that we now value in the academy seems not to have become a universal part of the scientific method, and thus of the scholarly publishing process, until as late as the middle of the twentieth century; *Science* and the *Journal of the American Medical Association*, for instance, did not vet manuscripts through outside reviewers until the 1940s (Burnham 1990; Spier 2002).[12] The history of peer review thus appears to have been both longer and shorter than we may realize. And yet, because of the role that it has played in authorizing academic research—because we ourselves, as Biagioli suggests, are both the subject and the object of its disciplining gestures—it has become so intractably established that we have a hard time imagining not just a future without it, but any way that it could conceivably change.

The Future of Peer Review

The issue of peer review's future has nonetheless been taken up in various forms by a number of recent publishing experiments. One such experiment is arXiv, an open-access "e-print" (or pre-print) repository, founded at Los Alamos and now housed at Cornell University, through which scientists have increasingly obtained and disseminated working papers in physics, mathematics, computer science, and quantitative biology (see fig. 1.1). Such papers are often submitted to arXiv before they are submitted to journals—sometimes because the authors want feedback, and sometimes simply to get an idea into circulation as quickly as possible. However, a growing number of influential papers have *only* been published on the arXiv server, and some observers have suggested that arXiv has in effect replaced journal publication as the primary mode of scholarly communication within certain specialties

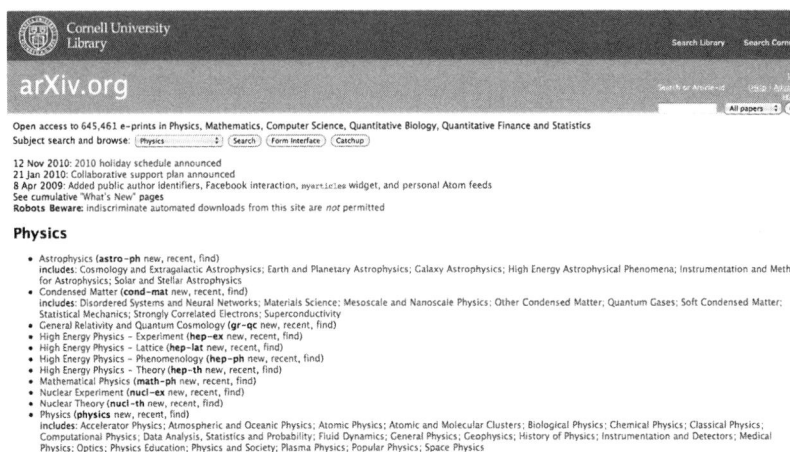

Fig. 1.1. The arXiv e-print server (arXiv.org)

in physics. As Paul Ginsparg indicates, arXiv has had great success as a scholarly resource despite employing only a modicum of review:

> From the outset, a variety of heuristic screening mechanisms have been in place to ensure insofar as possible that submissions are at least *of refereeable quality*. That means they satisfy the minimal criterion that they would not be peremptorily rejected by any competent journal editor as nutty, offensive, or otherwise manifestly inappropriate, and would instead at least in principle be suitable for review (i.e., without the risk of alienating or wasting the time of a referee, that essential unaccounted resource). These mechanisms are an important—if not essential—component of why readers find the site so useful: though the most recently submitted articles have not yet necessarily undergone formal review, the vast majority of the articles can, would, or do eventually satisfy editorial requirements somewhere. (Ginsparg 2002, 12 [emphasis in original])

In 2004, however, arXiv added a layer of author verification to its system by implementing an endorsement process that requires new authors to be vouched for by established authors before submitting their first paper to any subject area on the site. The site is at great pains to indicate that the endorsement process "is not peer review," but it is a process for the review of peers and as such bears a direct relationship to the site administrators' desire to maintain the consistently high quality of submissions to the site, a means of verifying that "arXiv contributors belong [to] the scientific community" (Cornell University Library).[13] The site administrators do note, however, that "[e]ndorsement is a necessary but not sufficient condition to have papers accepted in arXiv; arXiv reserves the right to reject or reclassify any submission," suggesting that the open server is nonetheless subject to a degree of editorial control, if not in the form of traditional peer review.

Another peer review experiment in scientific publishing that received significant attention was undertaken in 2006 by *Nature* and was accompanied by a debate, published on the journal's website, about the future of peer review (see fig. 1.2). The experiment was fairly simple: the editors of *Nature* created an online open review system that ran parallel to its traditional anonymous review process. "From 5 June 2006," the editors wrote, "authors may opt to have their submitted manuscripts posted publicly for comment. Any scientist may then post comments, provided they identify

Fig. 1.2. *Nature*'s peer-review debate (nature.com)

themselves. Once the usual confidential peer-review process is complete, the public 'open peer review' process will be closed. Editors will then read all comments on the manuscript and invite authors to respond. At the end of the process, as part of the trial, editors will assess the value of the public comments" (Campbell 2006). The experiment was closed in early December of that year, after which the editors analyzed the data resulting from it and, later in the month, declared the experiment to have failed, announcing that "for now at least, we will not implement open peer review." The statistics cited by the editors indicate serious issues in the open system they implemented: only 5 percent of authors who submitted work during the trial agreed to have their papers opened to public comment; of those papers, only 54 percent (or 38 out of 71) received substantive comments. And, as Linda Miller, the executive editor of *Nature*, told a reporter for *Science News*, the comments that the articles received weren't as thorough as the official reviews: "They're generally not the kind of comments that editors can make a decision on" (Brownlee 2006, 393).

Certain aspects of the experiment, however, raise the question of whether the test was flawed from the beginning, destined for a predictable failure because of its constraints. First, no real impetus was created for authors to open their papers to public review; in fact, the open portion of the peer-review process was wholly optional and had no bearing whatsoever on the editors' decision to publish any given paper. This points to the second problem, as no incentive was created for commenters to participate in the process: Why go to all the effort of reading and commenting on a paper if your comments serve no identifiable purpose?

As several entries in the web debate held alongside *Nature*'s peer-review trial made clear, though, the editors had not chosen a groundbreaking model; the editors of several other scientific journals that already use open review systems to varying extents posted brief comments about their processes. *Electronic Transactions on Artificial Intelligence (ETAI)*, for instance, has a two-stage process, with a three-month open review stage followed by a speedy up-or-down refereeing stage (with some time for revisions, if desired, in between). This process, the editors acknowledge, has produced some complications in the notion of "publication," as the texts in the open review stage are already freely available online; in some sense, the journal itself has become a vehicle for republishing selected articles.

ETAI's dual-stage process highlights a bifurcation in the purpose of peer review: first, fostering discussion and feedback among scholars with the aim of strengthening the work that they produce; and second, providing a mechanism through which that work may be filtered for quality, such that only the best is selected for final "publication." By foregrounding the open stage of peer review—by considering an article "published" during the three months of its open review, but then only "refereed" once anonymous scientists have held their up-or-down vote, which comes only after the article has been read, discussed, and revised—such a dual-stage process promises to return the center of gravity in peer review to communication among peers.

ETAI's process thus highlights the relatively conservative move that *Nature* made with its open peer-review trial. First, the journal was at great pains to reassure authors and readers that traditional, anonymous peer review would still take place alongside open discussion. There was, moreover, a relative lack of communication between the two forms of review: open review took place at the same time as anonymous review, rather than as a preliminary phase, preventing authors from putting the public comments they received to use in revision. And though the open review was on some level expected to serve as a parallel to the closed review process—thus Miller's disappointment that the comments weren't as thorough as traditional peer reviews—they weren't really allowed to serve a parallel function: while the editors "read" all such public comments, it was decided from the beginning that only the anonymous reviews would be considered in determining whether any given article was published.

Anonymity

Perhaps *Nature*'s cautious approach to open review was an attempt to avoid throwing out the baby of quality control with the bathwater of anonymity. The editors of *Atmospheric Chemistry and Physics*, however, presented evidence (based on their two-stage review process) that open review significantly increases the quality of articles a journal publishes:

> Our statistics confirm that collaborative peer review facilitates and enhances quality assurance. The journal has a relatively low overall rejection rate of less than 20%, but only three years after its launch the ISI journal impact factor ranked *Atmospheric Chemistry and Physics* twelfth out of 169 journals in 'Meteorology and Atmospheric Sciences' and 'Environmental Sciences'.
>
> These numbers support the idea that public peer review and interactive discussion deter authors from submitting low-quality manuscripts, and thus relieve editors and reviewers from spending too much time on deficient submissions. (Koop and Pöschl 2006)[14]

Such evidence begins to suggest that traditional closed, anonymous peer-review processes and quality control aren't quite as related as we often assume. The primary results of a closed peer-review process may, in fact, be negative. As Fiona Godlee (2000, 65) has argued, anonymous review "has the effect of giving reviewers power without responsibility," since reviewers are freed by the veil of anonymity to behave, in some instances, in a variety of unprofessional ways, ranging from the relatively innocuous unleashing of snark on an undeserving target to several utterly unacceptable forms of academic dishonesty. Such behaviors are not the norm, but they occur frequently enough that they should give us pause.[15] On the other side of the review process, of course, are the authors, ostensibly equal participants in a conversation about their work. The anonymous peer-review process, however, effectively closes the author out of the main chronology of the conversation, which instead becomes a backchannel discussion between the reviewer and the editor. As such, the author is hindered in her ability to learn from the review process *even if she is given a copy of the reviewer's comments*, as there is no forum in which she can respond to those comments in kind. By the time the comments arrive, generally speaking, the decision about the manuscript's fate has been made, the conversation is over, and the author is too often left with no one listening.[16]

Reviewer anonymity, however, has been a part of the process long enough that many academics express alarm at the thought of that protection being removed, insisting that their anonymity as reviewers is necessary in order for them to have the freedom to say that a manuscript should not be published. Such a position would certainly be justifiable if the primary purpose of peer review is quality control, and if it can be demonstrated that the process is both scrupulous and effective. However, as Douglas Peters and Stephen Ceci famously uncovered in their 1982 article "Peer Review Practices of Psychological Journals," reviewer reliability is not at all a given. In their experiment, Peters and Ceci selected one article from each of twelve journals in the field, published between eighteen and thirty-two months previously, and resubmitted the article *to the same journal*, with some minor modifications: they changed the authors' names (but, significantly, not their sexes); they created new institutional affiliations for their authors (notably replacing "high-status" institutions with low- or no-status ones); and they slightly altered the phrasing, but not the meaning, of the articles' opening paragraphs. Only three of these twelve articles were discovered by either the editors or the reviewers to have been previously published, and of the nine that went undiscovered, eight were rejected, most on the grounds of "serious methodological flaws"

(Peters and Ceci 1982/2004, 202).[17] Their conclusion is that one of two things has occurred: either the initial reviewers who approved the articles as originally published were incompetent—which seems unlikely—or "systematic bias was operating to produce the discrepant reviews" (ibid.).[18]

One of the correctives suggested in response to evidence of such "systematic bias," as well as some of the more egregious abuses of peer review, is a further layer of anonymity: blind review, in which the identity of the author is cloaked, as well as that of the reviewer. Blind review is imagined by many (including Shatz) to be a mode of avoiding certain forms of reviewer bias—for instance, preventing the continuation of an "old boys' network" that excludes the work of women, or ensuring that personal grudges play no role in the review process. And, it must be acknowledged, such blind review did have, at its introduction, the effect of opening the venues for academic discourse to women. However, the effectiveness of blind review in genuinely masking authorial identity has been subject to some critical scrutiny by authors who suggest, for instance, that blinding is futile: "Alas, anyone capable of evaluating research in a given specialty generally knows that specialty sufficiently to identify the probable author of the manuscript under review" (Guédon and Siemens 2002, 18).[19] In many cases, in fact, the author has previously presented and discussed the material in public, whether via informal networks or in more formal conference settings. Moreover, blind review can only correct for ad hominem bias and cannot compensate for the reviewer who operates within a cloud of intellectual bias, dismissing any arguments or conclusions that disagree with his or her own.[20]

It's also necessary to point out that neither reviewer nor author identity are hidden from the editor, who may have his or her own biases. As Godlee notes, "Evidence suggests that editors may be susceptible to the pull of prestige"; she cites the results presented by Harriet Zuckerman and Robert K. Merton (1971), which suggest that "if a paper had higher-ranking authors, editors were more likely to come to a decision without sending it out for peer review" (Godlee 2000, 73). Moreover, the editor's selection of reviewers for a manuscript may be influenced by the author's identity, and the editor's evaluation of the reviewers' reports may similarly be affected by the differing levels of prestige of reviewer and author.

Finally, one cannot help but wonder about the logic of correcting for the abuses of anonymity on one side of a conversation by establishing anonymity on the other, creating further barriers between peers rather than encouraging open, effective, productive discussion of intellectual issues. As Drummond Rennie (1994, 1143) argued, "We have an ample history to tell us that justice is ill served by secrecy. And so it is with peer review. Two or three hundred years ago, scientific papers and letters were often anonymous. We now regard that as quaint and primitive. I hope that in 20 years, that's exactly how we will look on our present system of peer review."

Credentialing

If closed peer-review processes aren't serving scholars in their need for feedback and discussion, and if they can't be wholly relied upon for their quality-control functions—if they appear, at least to some, "quaint and primitive"—why do we cling so ferociously to them? Arguably, the primary purpose that anonymous peer review actually serves today, at least in the humanities,[21] is that of institutional warranting, of conveying to college and university administrations that the work their employees are doing is appropriate and well-regarded in its field, and thus that these employees deserve ongoing appointments, tenure, promotions, raises, and so forth. As Rennie (2003, 10) has noted, "[E]ditorial peer review is seen by investigators and research institutions as a convenient quality control mechanism, for which they usually do not have to pay." This mechanism, on the level of the academic book, has been described by Lindsay Waters (2004) as a means for departments to "outsource" the evaluation of junior scholars to university presses; the existence of a book by a reputable press comes to serve as a convenient binary signifier of the quality of that scholar's work.[22]

We need to ask ourselves whether using the results of peer review as a shortcut in faculty performance evaluations isn't misguided in and of itself; much of the most important work published by scholars today is already issued in forms that aren't subject to conventionally understood modes of peer review, such as edited volumes. Moreover, understanding the successful navigation of peer review as a sufficient sign of quality work is a category error of sorts. As Ginsparg (2002, 9) has argued, the mere existence of an author's peer-reviewed publication is insufficient evidence, for hiring and promotion purposes, of the scholar's level of accomplishment; "otherwise there would be no need to supplement the publication record with detailed letters of recommendation and other measures of importance and influence. On the other hand, the detailed letters and citation analyses would be sufficient for the above purposes, even if applied to a literature that had not undergone that systematic first editorial pass through a peer review system." In other words, our institutional misunderstanding of peer review as a necessary prior indicator of "quality," rather than as one means among many of assessing quality, dooms us to misunderstand the ways that scholars establish and maintain their reputations within the field.

Another obvious question to ask is whether peer review as it is currently practiced is really able to support credentialing in the ways we assume. It's at least imaginable, if as yet untested, that the intellectual purposes that we expect of peer review—most importantly, quality control—could be undermined by this functionalist use of the process's results, as some extremely well-meaning reviewers, all too aware of the stakes of their evaluations, could unconsciously tend toward a sort of scholarly grade-inflation. And many scholars work with a sense, however vague, that certain publications use peer review as a means of supporting predetermined ideas held by a field's in-group, resulting in a mode of gatekeeping that is not simply about quality but instead about policing the limits of a discursive field. Moreover, the pressure to get a certain quantity of work through the peer-review process in a limited amount of time has unquestionable effects on junior scholars' work, as they are advised to focus not on the *important* but on the *publishable*, avoiding risk-taking in the interest of passing the next review.[23] All this suggests that the credentialing cart may have been put before the peer-review horse.

The Internet, as Guédon and Siemens indicate in one of this chapter's epigraphs, has in any event disrupted our ability to draw an association between the fact that a scholarly text has been published and the quality of work it may therefore contain. The result, conventionally, has been the dismissal by many faculty and administrators of all electronically published texts as inferior to those that appear in print, or, where those authority figures are sufficiently forward-looking as to argue for the potential value of electronic publishing, the insistence that the new forms adhere to older models of authorization—and thus the reinforcement of "the way things have always been done" at the expense of experimental modes that might produce new possibilities. Such conservatism shouldn't come as much surprise, of course; those faculty and administrators who are in the position of assessing the careers of other, usually younger, faculty are of necessity those who have benefited from the current credentialing system. As Guédon and Siemens suggest, those who hold such privilege will find ways to keep it, preferably without drawing attention to their having done so, precisely by making a virtue—and a besieged one, at that—out of the status quo.

Although I have spent a great deal of time in this chapter on the various abuses and shortcomings of the peer-review process as currently constituted, peer review has played an important role in opening fields to more voices, and the core notion behind it—that one's work as a scholar should be reviewed and assessed by one's peers—is a good one. The problem is in the implementation of that notion as an exercise in gatekeeping, and its subsequent transformation into a means of creating authority in and of itself. Those two shifts not only have the potential to interfere with peers' ability to communicate directly and fully with one another, but they also create enormous amounts of extra, unproductive work for everyone involved. Scholars pour countless hours into peer review each year, time which is not only usually uncompensated but which also results in a product for which reviewers can receive no "credit," as peer reviews, unlike post-publication reviews, cannot be counted among the reviewer's published work. For all of these reasons, I suggest that the time has come for us to consider whether we might all be better served by separating the question of credentialing from the publishing process, by allowing everything through the gate, and by designing a post-publication peer-review process that focuses on how a scholarly text should be received rather than whether it should be out there in the first place. What if peer review learned from social software systems such as Slashdot and Digg and became peer-to-peer review?

The Reputation Economy

The notion of "peer-to-peer review" that I have been circulating in talks and articles for the last couple of years draws upon the convergence of the kinds of discussion many scholars would like peer review to produce and the decentralized peer-to-peer networks that have sprung up across the Internet. In fact, just as Biagioli (2002) suggested a shift, across the early modern development of the scientific academy, in the definition of the term "peer"—from a member of the royal court to a scholarly colleague—so Chris Anderson (2006b) has argued that the term is once again being redefined in online communities: "In the Internet age, 'peer' is coming to mean everyman more than professional of equal rank. Consider the rise of peer-to-peer networks and the user-created content of 'peer production,' such as the millions of blogs that now complement mainstream media." Anderson uses this transformation in the notion of a peer to suggest that the academy might fruitfully find ways to open its review processes to "the wisdom of the crowds," allowing new models of authority in online information distribution to augment more traditional review systems. For instance, Anderson's reading of Wikipedia contradicts many of the conventional academic assumptions about the project, calling it "not so much anti-elitist as . . . 'anti-credentialist,'" a distinction that indicates that site editors' "contributions are considered on their merit, regardless of who they are or how they became knowledgeable. If what they write stands up to inspection, it remains; otherwise it goes" (Anderson 2006b).[24] Such systems of communal knowledge-production are thus far from the free-for-all that many have assumed—and, in fact, are at least in theory bringing into being a new mode of authority production; those editors whose work consistently "stands up" to community inspection may be accorded a kind of clout within the community that then affects assumptions about their future work.

I say "in theory" because one of the most important criticisms leveled at Wikipedia has been about its acceptance of anonymous contributions, which hinders the ability of readers to assess particular Wikipedians' work based upon their reputations. Reputation in this sense should be understood as separate from credentials; the point is not whether a particular Wikipedia editor has a degree in the appropriate subject area, but rather whether his or her work on the site has repeatedly stood up to community scrutiny.[25] There is, of course, no small irony in the fact that the academic outcry against the anonymous nature of much of Wikipedia's production occurs at the very same time that we cherish our own anonymity as peer reviewers, and we might take the implications of this contradiction to heart.

In a recent experiment with community-based peer review, Noah Wardrip-Fruin published the manuscript of his book-in-progress, *Expressive Processing*, in a CommentPress-based format on his coauthored blog *Grand Text Auto* (*GTxA*), seeking review from the blog's community of readers, at the same time that MIT Press sent the manuscript to traditional anonymous peer reviewers (see fig. 1.3). Although a number of articles—including, most notably, one in the *Chronicle of Higher Education*—represented this experiment as a "head-to-head" competition between open and closed peer-review systems (see Young 2008), Wardrip-Fruin was clear that such a contest was not his goal. The important aspect of the experiment was in getting feedback from a community he trusted:

> In most cases, when I get back the traditional, blind peer review comments on my papers and book proposals and conference submissions, I don't know who to believe. Most issues are only raised by one reviewer. I find myself wondering, "Is this a general issue that I need to fix, or just something that rubbed one particular person the wrong way?"...
>
> But with this blog-based review it's been a quite different experience. This is most clear to me around the discussion of "process intensity" in section 1.2. If I recall correctly, this began with Nick's comment on paragraph 14. Nick would be a perfect candidate for traditional peer review of my manuscript—well-versed in the subject, articulate, and active in many of the same

communities I hope will enjoy the book. But faced with just his comment, in anonymous form, I might have made only a small change. The same is true of Barry's comment on the same paragraph, left later the same day. However, once they started the conversation rolling, others agreed with their points and expanded beyond a focus on *The Sims*—and people also engaged me as I started thinking aloud about how to fix things—and the results made it clear that the larger discussion of process intensity was problematic, not just my treatment of one example. In other words, the blog-based review form not only brings in more voices (which may identify more potential issues), and not only provides some "review of the reviews" (with reviewers weighing in on the issues raised by others), but is also, crucially, *a conversation* (my proposals for a quick fix to the discussion of one example helped unearth the breadth and seriousness of the larger issues with the section).

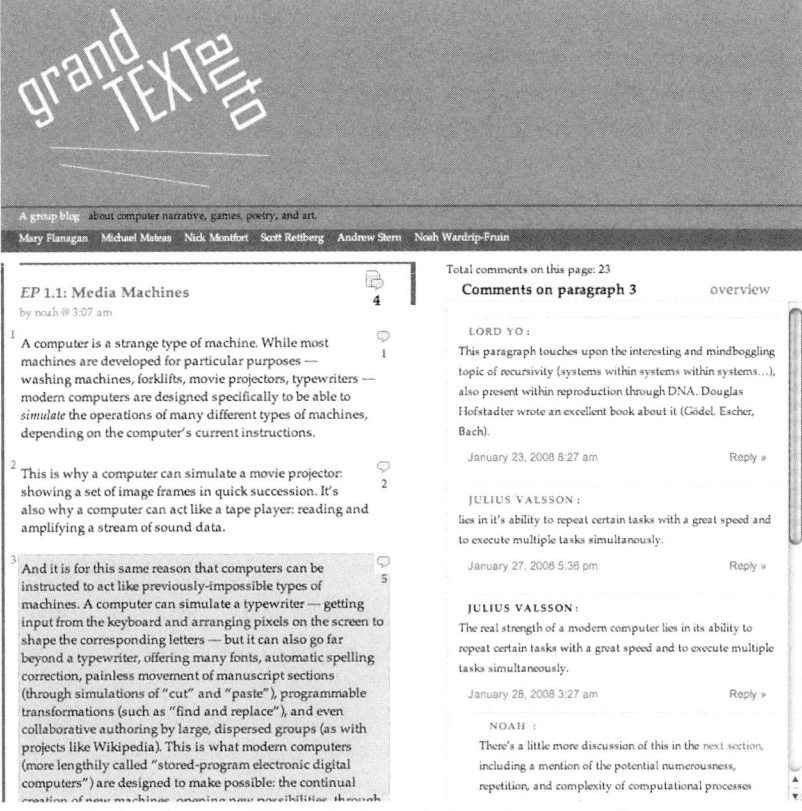

Fig. 1.3. Blog-based review of *Expressive Processing* (grandtextauto.org)

In the end, he notes, "the blog commentaries will have been through a social process that, in some ways, will probably make me trust them more" (Wardrip-Fruin 2008). Knowing the reviewers' reputations, and seeing those reputations as part a dynamic process of intellectual interaction, produced the authority of the comments, and thus affected the authority of the book that Wardrip-Fruin finally published (Wardrip-Fruin 2009b).

Given this, we might begin to posit an intimate relationship between reputation and authority in the intellectual sphere. This relationship has long existed within the academy, manifested in our various mechanisms of assessment and review, but digital networks give us new modes of determining reputation, as well as new requirements for such reputation-determining metrics. Not all networked publishing structures are concerned with reputation, of course: Wikipedia, for instance, only makes tangential use of a reputation-based system in assessing the authority of its entries. Other systems, most notably online retailers such as eBay, draw heavily on customer feedback in evaluating the reliability of service provided by individual merchants within the network. And the news and discussion forum Slashdot, most famously, uses a system of rating contributions to assess the reputations of individual contributors.

The Slashdot system evolved out of a more traditional system of comment moderation, in which twenty-five people weeded out the nonsense and highlighted the valuable; when the work became too much for those moderators, they selected four hundred more moderators based on the reputations they'd developed as users of the site. However, this hierarchical moderation system, in which some users had power that others didn't, quickly led to abuses, and the site's owners began developing what they refer to as a system of "mass moderation." In this system, nearly every active contributor to the site has the potential to receive, for a period of time, a degree of power to rate the site's contributions, through being given a number of "points of influence"; each time the contributor rates a comment on the site, he expends one influence point. These influence points expire rapidly if unused, and contributors cannot rank comments in threads in which they actively participate, thus preventing influence from becoming a currency within the system, and preventing moderators from controlling the discourse. The power to moderate, moreover, is only granted by the system based upon the contributor's "karma" within the site—that is, based upon the ways that the contributor's own comments have been moderated—which is understood to be a community-based assessment of whether or not the contributor's comments have been a helpful, positive addition to the community (see "How Did the Moderation System Develop?").

One weakness of a reputation system such as Slashdot's, in which the value of a user's contributions to the community can become subject to manipulation and attack, is that it potentially replaces substantive discourse and engagement with a networked popularity contest. And there are other, deeper problems with the site, as my use of "he" in describing the moderation system is intended to highlight; Slashdot is felt by many to be a highly male-dominated, if not downright misogynist, environment: see, for example, what happens in the comment thread when a poster asks for advice on handling being the lone woman working for an IT firm ("Breaking Gender Cliques at Work?" 2006). As we think about peer-to-peer review, it will be important to consider the ways that network effects bring out both the best and the worst in the communities they connect, and the kinds of vigilance that we must bring to bear in guarding against the potential reproduction of the dominant, often exclusionary ideological structures of the Internet within the engagements between scholars and readers online. In large part, this will require scholars of good will to confront such behavior head-on, to ensure that what Bill Readings (1996) has described as our ethical obligation to listen to one another is met.

This vigilance might take a couple of different forms, one of which may well have computational elements, developing what Advogato, an online forum for free and open-source software developers, refers to as "trust metrics." As one user argues:

> If you believe that "in any sufficiently large crowd, the majority are idiots," then this can be applied to Slashdot moderators too. All moderators have equal powers and the system is supposed to work as a kind of democracy. But if the majority does not think very much about what they are doing (because of lack of time, lack of interest, lack of intelligence or many other reasons), then it becomes easy to abuse the system. . . . I hope that something similar to the trust metrics implemented on Advogato could help. (Quinet 2000)

Advogato's "trust metrics" are intensively computational, evaluating each "node," or user, within the network via its interconnections with the network's many other nodes, certifying each node through three levels of trust (apprentice, journeyer, and master). One of the benefits of this system, as its developer writes, is its "resistance to catastrophic failure in the face of a sufficiently massive attack" (Levien). Reputation, in this implementation, cannot be hacked; on the other hand, it is entirely objectively calculated, leaving little to no room for subjective judgment.

While such "trust metrics" might seem inappropriate as a model for reconsidering peer review, they may help point us in the direction of a more sophisticated, partially computational, partially review-based system for determining authority in networked scholarly publishing, the kind of model Michael Jensen (2007a) imagines under the rubric of "Authority 3.0." Such a system, whatever its particulars, must operate in accordance with three key principles. First, it must be as non-manipulable as possible, preventing the importation of in-group favoritism, logrolling, and other interpersonal abuses from traditional peer review into the new system. Second, the system must achieve a critical mass of participation, and thus will need to operate within an ethos of "quid pro quo"; in contrast with Slashdot's system, in which users earn the right to become reviewers by publishing within the system, scholars must earn the right to publish within these new electronic publishing networks by actively serving as reviewers. And finally, and most significantly, the key activity of such a peer-to-peer review system must be not the review of texts, but the review of the reviewers. It is the reviewers, after all, whom a reader within such a network needs to trust; as Jonathan Schwartz, the COO of Sun Microsystems, has argued in numerous interviews, "[T]rust is the currency of the participation age."[26]

It's no accident that trust is here defined through an economic metaphor; while the "currency" that reputation affords within the academy is far less spendable than its counterpart in the corporate world, there's nonetheless an economic reality at its root, and thus at the root of the peer-review mechanisms through which reputation is currently granted. Print-based publishing operates within an economics of scarcity, with its systems determined largely by the fact that a limited number of pages, journals, and books can be produced; the competition among scholars for those limited resources requires pre-publication review, to make sure that the material being published is of sufficient quality as to be worthy of the resources it consumes. Electronic publishing faces no such material scarcity; there is no upper limit on the number of pages a manuscript can contain or the number of manuscripts that can be published, or at least none determined by available resources, as the Internet operates within an economics of abundance. We might think, for a moment, of Cory Doctorow's "Whuffie," in *Down and Out in the Magic Kingdom* (2003), a currency of sorts that measures the esteem one is held in, a system designed specifically for a world in which material shortages have become obsolete.[27] As Doctorow explained in an interview, Whuffie becomes important in the digital sphere precisely because such a sphere "isn't a tragedy of the commons; this is a commons where the sheep s*** grass—where the more you graze, the more commons you get" (Tweney 2003). Such is the abundance of the Internet, and given this abundance, imposing artificial scarcity through a gatekeeping model of peer review makes little sense.

However, in a self-multiplying scholarly commons, some kind of assessment of the material that has been published becomes even more important, but not because of scarce resources; instead, what remain scarce are time and attention.[28] For this reason, peer review needs to be put not in the service of gatekeeping, or determining what should be published for any scholar to see, but of filtering, or determining what of the vast amount of material that has been published is of interest or value to a particular scholar. As Clay Shirky (2008, 98) has argued, "Filter-then-publish, whatever its advantages, rested on a scarcity of media that is a thing of the past. The expansion of social media means that the only working system is publish-then-filter." In using a computational filtering system, of course, the most important thing to understand is its algorithm—what criteria, in what balance, it's using in making decisions to include or exclude various pieces of data.[29] Similarly, in using a human filtering system, the most important thing to have information about is not the data that is being filtered but the human filter itself: who is making the decisions, and why. Thus, in a peer-to-peer review system, the critical activity is not the review of the texts being published, but the review of the reviewers.

Community-Based Filtering

A relatively simple example of such a system is Philica, which bills itself as "the journal of everything." Philica is an open publishing network, co-founded by British psychologists Ian Walker and Nigel Holt, that invites scholars from any field to post papers, which are then made freely available for reading and review by any interested user (see fig. 1.4). Philica describes itself as operating "like eBay for academics. When somebody reviews your article, the impact of that review depends on the reviewer's own reviews. This means that the opinion of somebody whose work is highly regarded carries more weight than the opinion of somebody whose work is rated poorly" ("An Introduction to Using Philica").[30] Account registration is open, though members are asked to declare their institutional affiliations if they have them, and encouraged to obtain "confirmation" of their status within the academy by sending the site administrators a letter on institutional letterhead, or a letter detailing appropriate credentials as an independent researcher. The site's FAQ indicates that membership is in theory restricted to "fully-quali-

 **Philica,**
Where ideas are free

 my Philica

ISSN 1751-3030
Log in
Register

208 Articles and Observations available | Content last updated 7 December, 14:40   Philica entries accessed 653 893 times

Philica front page	**Instant academic publishing with transparent peer-review**	
Search		
About Philica	## Most recent Articles	### Read a specific entry
Take the tour	(Select a discipline from on the right to see a more selective list)	Article num. [____] (Go)
	DFEM-Computation of a Zero-point-energy Converter with realistic	Observation num. [____] (Go)
Publish your work	Parameters for a practical Setup [**Physics**]	
Work needing review	Turtur, C. (7th Dec 2010).	### Quick search
Most popular entries	Participatory Action Research to Reduce Youth Violence [**Psychology**]	
Highest-rated entries	Pickens, J. (3rd Dec 2010).	(No need for wildcards: entering GRAV finds gravity, gravitational, etc.)
Recent reviews	Energetic properties of ether [**Physics**]	Search: [All of Philica ⬍]
	Margulis, M. (19th Nov 2010).	(Search) Advanced search

The sun was a red giant 4.6 billion years ago - the planets were born from the solar wind of the red giant sun. [**Astronomy & cosmology**]
Bar-Zohar, D. (6th Nov 2010).

The sun can absorb large amount of energy from weak magnetic fields due to its low resistivity [**Astronomy & cosmology**]
Bar-Zohar, D. (16th Oct 2010).

Example of a simple Algorithm for the Construction of Zero-point-energy Converters [**Physics**]
Turtur, C. (9th Oct 2010).

The fundamental Principle of the Conversion of Zero-point-energy of the Vacuum [**Physics**]
Turtur, C. (28th Sep 2010).

MULTILAYER PROTEIN GROWTH IN CENTRAL VENOUS CATHETERS [**Medicine**]
Sotolongo-Costa, O. & Fernandez-Barbero, A. (23rd Sep 2010).

Most recent Observations
(Select a discipline from on the right to see a more selective list)

A suggestion about the BP oil spill [**Environmental studies**]
chen, c. (4th Jun 2010).

Proposal for a test of a motionless zero-point-energy converter [**Physics**]
Turtur, C. (4th Jun 2010).

Laser interferometers failed? Don't worry, it's even better. [**Astronomy & cosmology**]
Tatrocki, P. (4th Apr 2010).

How to cite Philica
FAQs
Support Philica
Contact us

NEWS: The SOAP Project, in collaboration with CERN, are conducting a survey on open-access publishing. Please take a moment to give them your views

New to Philica? Click here!

Publish your work today

Read a random Observation

RSS FEED 2.0
🔲 anthro.philica.com Anthropology
🔲 astro.philica.com Astronomy & cosmology
🔲 bio.philica.com Biological sciences
🔲 chemo.philica.com Chemistry & chemical engineering
🔲 compu.philica.com Computer science
🔲 econo.philica.com Economics & development
🔲 edu.philica.com Education
🔲 engi.philica.com Engineering
🔲 enviro.philica.com Environmental studies
🔲 geo.philica.com Geography & geology
🔲 histo.philica.com History
🔲 humani.philica.com Humanities
🔲 inter.philica.com International studies
🔲 juris.philica.com Law
🔲 linguo.philica.com Language & linguistics
🔲 mani.philica.com Management & Business studies
🔲 matho.philica.com Mathematics
🔲 medi.philica.com Medicine
🔲 musi.philica.com Music
🔲 neuro.philica.com Neuroscience
🔲 philoso.philica.com Philosophy

Fig. 1.4. Philica (philica.com)

fied academics," though without confirmation, one could simply claim such a status, and thus the system makes an unconfirmed membership "much less useful than a confirmed membership, since (a) unconfirmed members' reviews carry less weight than confirmed members' reviews and (b) readers are less likely to trust research from unconfirmed authors. In other words, there's not really much point joining if you do not go on to prove your status" ("Philica FAQs"). Reviewing articles published on Philica is open to registered, logged-in members, whether "confirmed" or not, though confirmed members' reviews are noted with a check mark. Articles are evaluated by reviewers both quantitatively (rating "originality," "importance," and "overall quality" on a 1-to-7 scale) and qualitatively, via comments. Article authors each have a page that details their work on the site, including the number of articles and notes that they have published, the mean peer-review ratings their work has received, and the number of reviews and comments that the author has contributed to other work. The site notes that the author's ratings "will change whenever a new review of this author's work appears, as well as whenever somebody reviews the work of anybody who has reviewed" the work of the author in question.[31]

While Philica's system presents some compelling possibilities for the future of scholarly publishing, it nonetheless has a number of apparent shortcomings: though the articles uploaded to the site are reviewed, and reviews are weighted based on the assessed quality of the work of the reviewers, the *quality of the reviews themselves* isn't assessed, and thus these reviews don't count among the "work" used in determining the value of a reviewer's comments. In part this is due to the fact that while the comments made by a particular reviewer are associated with one another, they are not associated with their authors by name, but are rather submitted anonymously. Each review entry page contains the following notice: "Unless you sign your review, which you are welcome to do if you wish, it will be anonymous to the author and to other Philica readers. Nevertheless, the administrators can see who you are if necessary so please be sure your review is not abusive." Thus, Philica only opens the comments produced by peer review to public scrutiny; though reviewers are accountable to the site's administrators, they are not directly accountable to the article's authors, or to the network's community as a whole. And while the reviewers' own peer-review ratings affect the way the system weights the ratings they assign to others, the working of this algorithm remains partially hidden behind the veil of anonymity.

Further, as a "journal of everything," Philica runs the risk of precisely the kind of overflow that makes Internet skeptics worry; if "everything" is published there, how will researchers find what they need—and will they, as Shatz (2004, 16) suggested, be required to "trek through enormous amounts of junk before finding articles" that are at all "rewarding"? Such concerns are well-founded, in this case, as work published on Philica is organized by discipline, but as of April 2010, only twenty-seven such disciplinary categories exist on the site, with no further subdivisions, tags, or other metadata allowing the reader to find relevant material. The site thus suffers from a too-general mode of organization; the "humanities" as a whole, for instance, represents a single field on Philica (though history, philosophy, music, and linguistics have been given separate categories). The result, however, has not been overflow but, if anything, underflow; only 185 articles or notes were published on Philica between March 2006 and April 2010, a mere four of which were in the humanities. Such a minuscule rate of participation, like that experienced in the *Nature* open-review trial, could be taken to indicate a general resistance among academics to new publishing models—and yet, it's hard to imagine that a traditional, closed-review, print-based "journal of everything" would fare much better. The purpose of scholarly publishing, after all, is not merely making the results of research public, but also making those results public *to the appropriate community*. Because Philica has no particular disciplinary focus, it seems to have been unable to build a community.

The development and maintenance of such a community is key to the scholarly publishing network of the future, and in particular to its implementation of peer-to-peer review, because while the post-publication filtering mechanisms that such a system will require may in part be computational, they cannot be wholly automated; the individual intelligences and interests of the members of this social network are the bedrock of community-based filtering. One might, for instance, look at Chris Anderson's explanation for the success of MySpace as a promoter of the more obscure music that lies well down the "long tail" from the mainstream, where other such networks like MP3.com had failed: "The answer at this point appears to be that it is a very effective combination of community and content. The strong social ties between the tens of millions of fans there help guide them to obscure music that they wouldn't otherwise find, while the content gives them a reason to keep visiting" (Anderson 2006a, 149). The absence of the kind of community that MySpace fosters—a user base committed to the site as a means of self-expression, whose relationships with one another are built precisely around that self-expression—prevented MP3.com from becoming a flourishing site for the exploration of new and obscure music, precisely because the absence of social ties among users left them no way of assessing the recommendations others were making. And the more niche-based the mode of cultural communication becomes—the further down the "tail" that communication moves—the more important such community-based knowledge becomes.

Given the case of Philica, in fact, one might begin to speculate that, in electronic scholarly publishing, the community is necessary not just to the post-publication review and filtering process but to the production of content itself. Scholarly communication, generally speaking, is *all* tail, aimed at a comparatively small niche group of similarly focused readers; for that reason, Internet technologies seem particularly well-positioned to enable those readers to find and communicate with one another, as well as to set community-based standards for the evaluation of their work. Only once it is clear to scholars that the standards of this community are *their* standards—that this is a community to which they belong—will many of them venture to contribute their work to it. In order for such a community to be established, however, its individual members must know one another, at least by reputation, and thus the process of review—the setting of standards by the community—must itself be open to continual review.

It seems self-evident that the more open such systems are, the more debate they foster, and that the more communal value is placed on participating in them, the better the material they produce will be. However, all of these aspects of the community must be carefully nurtured in order for it to avoid turning into what Cass Sunstein describes, in *Infotopia*, as a deliberative cocoon, in which small groups of like-minded persons reinforce one another's biases and produce unspoken social pressures toward conformity with what appears to be majority opinion, resulting in a mode of "group-think" that propagates errors rather than correcting them. Sunstein points out that new, Internet-based knowledge-aggregation systems such as wikis, open-source software, and blogs "offer distinct models for how groups, large or small, might gather information and interact on the Internet. They provide important supplements to, or substitutes for, ordinary deliberation" (Sunstein 2006, 148), enabling correctives for the errors that small groups of decision-makers can produce. Using such new technologies for purposes of deliberation, however, requires that all members of the network be equally empowered—and in fact, equally compelled—to contribute their ideas and voice their dissent, lest the network fall prey to a new mode of self-reinforcing groupthink.

The significance of dissent in Sunstein's assessment of networked discussion might usefully remind us of Bill Readings's model of the University of Thought, the mode of rethinking the contemporary academic institution that in his assessment is the only one with a chance of escaping the corporatizing effects of the University of Excellence. As he points out, despite the equal emptiness of the two signifiers, "Thought does not function as an answer but as a *question*. Excellence works because no one has to ask what it means. Thought demands that we ask what it means, because its status as mere name—radically detached from truth—enforces that question" (Readings 1996, 159–60). Moreover, Thought provides a means of ethical engagement with our community, which, crucially, functions not by creating and enforcing consensus, but by encouraging and dwelling within dissensus. I would argue that while the current model of closed, pre-publication review enacts the most oppressive aspects of the consensus model of community—a forced agreement about standards, an assumption that we're all speaking the same language, an ability to hide behind the notion of excellence—open peer review provides space for Readings's dissensus. Such an open system of discussion and dissent has the potential to allow many more ideas into circulation, no doubt many of which we won't agree with, and some of which we'll find downright appalling. But only in allowing those ideas to be aired and argued against can we really obtain the openness in scholarly thought we claim to value.

Readings's understanding of the ethical obligation we bear toward one another, which primarily manifests as an obligation to listen, must be extended not just to the scene of teaching or to the faculty meeting, but also to the scene of publishing; we need to think about our work as reviewers as part of an ongoing process of "thinking together," one necessary for our full participation in the scholarly community. In this sense, the key to avoiding the groupthink Sunstein fears is not heightened intellectual individualism—separating oneself from the network—but, paradoxically, placing the advancement of the community's knowledge ahead of one's own personal advancement. Sunstein (2006, 205) presents evidence that the propagation of errors is "far less likely when each individual knows that she has nothing to gain from a correct *individual* decision and everything to gain from a correct *group* decision." Such a turn toward a communally distributed mode of knowledge production, however, will not come easily in a culture in which credentialing processes focus precisely on individual achievement. I turn my attention more fully to the issue of collaboration and community in chapter 2; for now, I simply suggest that the success of a community-based review system will hinge on the evaluation of one's contributions to reviewing being considered as important as, if not more important than, one's individual projects. Genuine peer-to-peer review will require prioritizing members' work on behalf of the community within the community's reward structures.

MediaCommons and Peer-to-Peer Review

This need to focus on the communal aspects of peer-to-peer review—in particular, the review of the reviewers—led me and my colleagues, in the early stages of our planning, to start thinking about MediaCommons as less a digital scholarly *press* than a digital scholarly *network*. Although the social aspects of MediaCommons are not its primary product, we've increasingly come to believe that they're a precondition for the success of the publishing aspects of the network. Too many digital publishing experiments, like Philica, have lagged due to an assumption that might be summed up as "if you build it, they will come." In fact, such publishing experiments often would benefit from examining the relative success of MySpace in comparison with MP3.com, thus placing a greater focus on getting users to come in the first place, on drawing them in by demonstrating the ways that the network's connections will benefit their work. For this reason, the first part of Media-Commons that we built was the community, in order to create a network of trust between authors and reviewers. Rather than "eBay for academics," for our purposes a more appropriate analogy between MediaCommons and other "Web 2.0" systems might well have been "Facebook for scholars," as we focused on building a network structure that allows people, and not just texts, to interconnect. And the most salient point of that comparison is this: as some scholars have argued, the success of Facebook, compared with earlier social-networking systems such as Friendster and Orkut, derived in no small part from the decision its developers made to keep the network relatively closed in its early days by limiting its use to students at a small number of colleges and universities and by focusing on the pre-existing connections among the members of those institutions.[32] The emphasis, in other words, was not on allowing users to create new social networks, but rather on helping them extend their offline social networks into digital environments. MediaCommons similarly began by facilitating the relationships among scholars who were already connected—who already attended the same conferences, published in the same journals, and read one another's work.

At this writing, the MediaCommons systems are still very much in development, so what follows remains somewhat speculative; the future functioning of the network may well wind up being a bit different than what I here project.[33] We are fairly certain, however, that the peer-to-peer system we build will remain the backbone of MediaCommons, and accordingly, we have already developed and implemented the first stages of this system, which includes:

- a networked user profiling system that enables scholars to define their interests in taggable, complexly searchable ways;
- a portfolio system that allows users to build and maintain a comprehensive record of their writing within the site and in other networked spaces, both formal and informal, allowing scholars both to maintain publicly accessible versions of their work and to receive some sort of academic "credit" for the kinds of work—which will soon include peer reviews, but already includes participation in online forums—that too often remain invisible.

We are still in the process of developing the system that will transform this network into a new kind of peer-review system, however; to this end, we are working on:

- a sophisticated recommendations system that uses the information in a member's profile, along with robust textual analysis of documents in the network, to present the user with frequently updated suggestions for texts to read, discussions in which to participate, and collaborators with whom to work;
- a "reputation" system that will allow users of the network to review the reviewers and to assess the "value" of a particular scholar's work within the network.

Many systems like these have been developed in isolation from one another, both in open-source and proprietary variants, but they have not yet been brought together to create such a dynamic community structure, nor have they been put to the uses that scholars might make of them. A social-networking system such as Facebook, for instance, allows its users to create profiles and join groups, but its publishing tools are limited in effectiveness.[34] Drupal, an open-source content-management system, allows users to create limited profiles and tracks user participation in a site, but that information remains relatively static rather than being used dynamically to help generate connections among users. BuddyPress, a WordPress plugin, uses this same profile and user-tracking information in conjunction with the ability to form and publish with groups, but like Drupal, the system requires extensive customization to work in a complex publishing environment. Recommendation systems of varying stripes are in use at a number of commercial sites (usually extending the "customers who bought x also bought y" type to text recommendations), but they usually rely upon keywords rather than full textual analysis, and little use of such systems has been made in the organization and dissemination of scholarly research. "Reputation" systems, such as that in use in a large-scale discussion forum like Slashdot, have proven effective at filtering out unhelpful or nuisance commentary, but their potential use in a system of scholarly review has yet to be explored.

MediaCommons intends to bring such systems together, providing scholars with a range of tools through which to connect with one another; to produce and publish networked, multimodal texts; to review those texts; and then, most crucially, to review the work of the reviewers, enabling the community to determine its own standards and adjudicate their implementation.

In a peer-to-peer reviewing system, "reputation" will be determined not simply through an assessment of the scholar's own production, but through an assessment of her reviewing practices. Reviews might, for instance, be rated on numerical scales that measure both their incisiveness and their helpfulness, resulting in a reviewer reputation score. Reviews written by scholars with better reputations would then be accorded more weight in determining the status of texts published through the network.

The emphasis in MediaCommons's peer-to-peer reviewing system is thus not simply on being smart, but on being helpful—and I don't want to underestimate the enormity of that shift; as my Twitter commenter pointed out in the introduction, little in graduate school or on the tenure track inculcates helpfulness, and in fact much militates against it. However, for network-based publishing to succeed, the communal emphasis of network culture will have to take the lead over academic culture's individualism. Again, this is not meant to paint a rosy picture of a community governed by consensus, in which we all just happily get along, but rather to suggest that our ethical commitment to one another requires an active participation in discussion and debate, particularly as listeners; "helpful" criticism avoids logrolling, but it also avoids snark, instead working to press both author and reader toward a deeper understanding of the questions involved. This open discussion will have to become the primary point of network members' commitment, placing the advancement of the community as a whole alongside the advancement of their own work; only in that way can both the individual scholar and the field as a whole succeed. In order to promote such a commitment, MediaCommons will need to find a way to implement a pay-to-play system of sorts, requiring community members to become active participants in the network's review processes in order to take advantage of its publishing capabilities. This might be done by constructing a point system, in which a scholar must earn credits by reviewing, which can then be spent on publishing, but it might also be done by linking the scholar's reputation as a reviewer to her own published texts, encouraging authors to improve their "karma," in Slashdot-speak, and thus the rankings of their work as a whole, by publishing more, and more helpful, reviews of texts by others.

Before moving on, I need to acknowledge another serious difficulty in the system I am proposing: it will require a phenomenal amount of labor on the part of all scholars as readers and discussants of one another's work, as well as additional labor on the part of the author in responding to reader comments. That having been said, it might also be worth pointing out that such labor is already being done, arguably in a less equitably distributed fashion; editors repeatedly call upon the subset of scholars who take their roles as reviewers seriously, who do the work well, and who do it on time. If reviewing were a prerequisite for publishing, we'd likely see more scholars become better reviewers, which would in turn allow for a greater diversity of opinion and a greater distribution of the labor involved. Review is certainly a function within which we'd do well to draw upon the "wisdom of the crowds," particularly as there are far more potential readers for any given text than two or three select reviewers, and as such "crowdsourced" review will enable us to see how critical opinion of a text develops over time.

Credentialing, Revisited

The idea of texts and authors being "ranked" and "rated" within the system raises several important concerns, most notably about the quantification of assessment across the academy. Faculty in the humanities in particular are justifiably anxious about the degree to which accrediting bodies and the U.S. Department of Education are demanding empirical, often numerical, accounting of things like "student learning outcomes," even in fields in which the learning itself isn't empirically driven, but rather focused on interpretation and argument. Certainly we don't want our own work to be subject to the same kinds of "bean-counting" principles, in which statistics overtake more nuanced understandings of significance; as Lindsay Waters (2004, 9) suggests, the danger in assuming that all knowledge can be quantified is that "[e]mpiricism makes people slaves to what they can see and count," and the values of the humanities are largely non-countable. Moreover, our colleagues in the sciences might provide a bit of a cautionary tale: even in fields whose methods and evidence are largely empirically produced, concerns about the reliance on citation indexes and impact factors as metrics of faculty achievement are growing.[35] We certainly don't want to suggest to tenure and promotion review committees that the data produced through online peer-to-peer review more accurately evaluate faculty performance simply because they contain numbers.

On the other hand, we're already relying upon a system that's even more reductive than the kinds of metrics that the web can provide; the results of the current system of peer review are a simple binary: either the article or monograph was published in a peer-reviewed venue or it was not. There is precious little nuance in such a mode of evaluation, little room for considering whether a text published in a non-traditional format has been important in its field, little means of assessing the value of a scholar's contributions to a field outside of standardized modes of publishing. Network-based peer-to-peer review can provide us with certain kinds of information that can help complicate this practice, including quantitative elements such as the number of inbound links, comments, and citations, as well as statistical analyses of community-based review practices, but also a wide range of qualitative, evaluative, interpretative commentary from the other authors and readers interacting with the texts we produce. No single measure can offer demonstrative proof of scholarly significance, but a range of such information, including both the numerical and the narrative, the empirical and the ephemeral, can help illuminate the wide variety of ways in which texts interact with the community of scholars.

The question remains whether the various credentialing bodies that currently rely on peer review's gatekeeping function will be satisfied with the kinds of information that such a system can provide. This is the point at which I must fall back on polemic, and simply insist that they must—that we must say to hiring committees, tenure and promotion review bodies, and, most importantly, ourselves, that the fact that ostensibly anonymous reviewers didn't determine whether an article or monograph was worthy of publication shouldn't matter. A system of peer-to-peer review won't give us an easy binary criterion for determining "value"—but then, if we're honest, it never has. It will, however, give us invaluable information about how a scholar is situated within her field, how her work has been received and used by her peers, and what kind of effect she is having on her field's future. Moreover, we need to remind ourselves, as Cathy Davidson (2009) has pointed out, that the materials used in a tenure review are meant in some sense to be metonymic, standing in for the "promise" of all the future work that a scholar will do. We currently reduce such "promise" to the existence of a certain quantity of texts; we need instead to shift our focus to active scholarly engagement of the sort peer-to-peer review might help us produce. Requiring an up-or-down measurement of impact, promise, or engagement, or even relying on computationally produced metrics, can never provide an adequate substitute for the real work that such credentialing bodies must do: reading and assessing the scholarship and engaging with expert analysis on the relationship between the scholarship and the field. It is in part our desire for shortcuts, for a clear and quantifiable set of benchmarks by which we can judge "quality" without having to do the labor ourselves, that has gotten the academy into its current predicament, in which the very systems of production on which it relies are crumbling. Until institutional assumptions about how scholarly work should be assessed are changed—but moreover, until we come to understand peer review as part of an ongoing conversation among scholars rather than a convenient means of determining "value" without all that inconvenient reading and discussion—the processes of evaluation for tenure and promotion are doomed to become a monster that eats its young, trapped in an early-twentieth-century model of scholarly production that simply no longer works.

2

Authorship

> If I have seen further, it is only by standing on the shoulders of giants.
>
> —Sir Isaac Newton

> While all of this is familiar in philosophy, as in literary criticism, I am not certain that the consequences derived from the disappearance or death of the author have been fully explored or that the importance of this event has been appreciated.
>
> —Michel Foucault, "What Is an Author?"

> The digital author connotes a greater alterity between the text and the author, due in part to the digital nature of the writing. I claim that digital writing is both a technological inscription of the author and a term to designate a new historical constellation of authorship, one that is emergent, but seemingly more and more predominant.
>
> —Mark Poster, *What's the Matter with the Internet?*

The transformation in our thinking about peer review that I call for in the previous chapter bears serious implications for our understandings of the nature of authorship and, in particular, for our relationships to ourselves as authors. In fact, the suggestion that a peer-to-peer review system will require the members of such a scholarly network to place their primary emphasis on the advancement of the community as a whole, rather than their own individual advancement, will no doubt produce a significant degree of concern among many academic readers, especially those in the humanities: however communally minded our publishing practices might become, within our current practices writing is still something that we must undertake—and be evaluated on—alone.

These concerns are made all the more pressing by the fact that each of us lives with a host of anxieties about writing and about ourselves as writers, anxieties that can interfere with our work and yet make it difficult to change the ways that we approach that work.[1] Though this chapter's title and much of its research indicate that it is focused on a much more abstract, conceptual sense of "authorship," it is underwritten by those anxieties—and not just abstract anxieties, felt "out there," by some amorphous group of "academics," but my own anxieties as well. As I began drafting this chapter, I found myself having extraordinary difficulty organizing my thoughts, attempting to figure out what the chapter was about and how to approach it. My partner tried to talk with me about the chapter, hoping to help me think my way through the problem, but I grew increasingly irritable and withdrawn, and as he and I later cleared the air, I heard myself telling him that I have a very hard time talking about my writing projects while they're in progress. Some part of that difficulty comes from a sense that someone else's opinions might interfere with my thought processes, confusing my sense of the issues that I'm exploring before I've been able to establish my position fully. It took a moment for me to process what I'd said and to realize that the anxiety I felt about the boundary between "my" ideas and someone else's was exactly what I was attempting to write about. And, in fact, the blog entries I'd written in the previous week were similarly about my writerly anxieties, including one titled "The Bolter Principle," in which I reflected rather textbook concerns about originality ("I eagerly anticipate at some as yet undetermined point in the future having a complex thought of which I do not later discover Jay David Bolter has already said a portion, both more intelligently and a decade earlier"), and one titled "Future Writing, Take Two," in which I worried about my focus and productivity levels over the previous five years. For someone whose entire first book is about writerly anxieties and their displacements, it took me an awfully long time to recognize that I'm subject to precisely the same concerns and evasions about which I've been writing, and that those anxieties have similarly profound effects on my work.

Academic anxieties about writing often circle around such questions about originality, creativity, productivity, ownership, and so on. Each of these issues has deep roots, being embedded not just in the complexities of academic life (such as the often painful changes in focus required to move from teaching through committee meetings and into writing), and not just in the enormous weight placed upon the quantified outcomes of our writing within academic systems of reward, but in the very nature of authorship as we have constructed it in Western culture. This is why so many academic self-help books focused on issues around writing have been published: from *Academic Writing for Graduate Students* (Swales and Feak 2004) to *Writing Your Dissertation in Fif-*

teen Minutes a Day (Bolker 1998), from Bill Germano's *From Dissertation to Book* (2005) to his *Getting It Published* (2001), and from Beth Luey's *Handbook for Academic Authors* (2002) to Robert Boice's *Professors as Writers* (1990) to Paul Silvia's on-the-nose *How to Write a Lot* (2007), just to name a few. The existence of such an enormous selection of guides to the academic writing process suggests that many of us are in substantive need of advice and assistance in our writing lives that we're not getting elsewhere, whether in grad school or beyond. It also suggests that we believe that someone out there knows how to be a successful author, and that if they could just put their process into clear enough words, we could put them into practice. We thus seem to imagine something transitive embedded in the writing process itself that creates a relationship between writer and reader capable of solving the most intractable problems: I have an idea, I write it, you read it, and now you have that idea, too; even better, I can do something, I put that something into words, you read the words, and now you can do that something, too. But by containing this transmission in books, we also seem to imagine the writing process to be radically individualized, something that each author must figure out alone.

In what follows, I argue that we all need—myself not least among us—to rethink our authorship practices and our relationships to ourselves and our colleagues as authors, not only because the new digital technologies becoming dominant within the academy are rapidly facilitating new ways of working and of imagining ourselves as we work, but also because such reconsidered writing practices might help many of us find more pleasure, and less anxiety, in the act of writing. This is not to suggest that digital publishing networks will miraculously solve all of the difficulties that we face as writers; rather, network technologies might help us feel less alone and less lost in the writing process. But such change will require facing our anxieties head-on, and thus we need to take the time to question our assumptions about authorship and how they impose themselves on our writing lives.

There is a mild irony in the suggestion that we need to spend some time rethinking the nature of authorship, as it certainly seems that, at least in literary fields, we've done nothing but that for the last four decades or so; authorship, its institutions, and its practices give every impression of having been under continual scrutiny since poststructuralism's moment of conception. Nonetheless, the kinds of changes in publishing practices that I'm discussing here reveal the degree to which our interrogation of the notion of authorship has been, in a most literal sense, theoretical. However critically aware we may be of the historical linkages among the rise of capitalism, the dominance of individualism, and the conventionally understood figure of the author, our own authorship practices have remained subsumed within those institutional and ideological frameworks.[2] Examining those structures closely, with the intent of making any kind of practical change, will no doubt be uncomfortable for many of us—myself included; enough of my ego is bound up in whatever I am writing that, as my partner unfortunately discovered, I have a hard time discussing my work-in-progress, much less imagining a different way of approaching it. And perhaps we should be made nervous by such change; as James O'Donnell (1996, 48) asserts, "The categories by which we *do* our intellectual business in the academic world are so deeply ingrained in us that to turn our power to relativize those categories, historicize them, and leave them as it were *sous rature*, intact but relativized, is, and *rightfully* is, unsettling and disturbing." Academic authorship as we understand it today has evolved in conjunction with our publishing and employment practices, and changing one aspect of the way we work of necessity implies change across its entirety—an unnerving thought, indeed.

As I argued earlier, however, all of these practices may benefit from certain kinds of change: some of our publishing practices are economically unsustainable, some of our employment practices are out of step with our actual intellectual values, and some of our writing practices are more productive of anxiety than they are of good work. Again, digital scholarly publishing itself cannot solve these problems; none of them has an easy technological fix. However, adopting new technologies will require us to face these problems; as Lawrence Lessig's work has explored, the networks of electronic communication carry embedded values within the codes that structure their operation, and many of the Internet's codes, and thus its values, are substantively different from those within which scholars—at least those in the humanities—profess to operate.[3] We must examine our values, and the ways that our new technologies may affect them, in order to make the most productive use of those new forms.

Having said that, I now need to perform the ritual of forswearing technological determinism; I'm not arguing, in McLuhanesque fashion, that the technologies with which we work determine the social, intellectual, or institutional structures within which we use them. Computers do not *make* us think differently. At the same time, however, I would not argue that they have no effect on the world in which they operate, or that their development is ultimately determined by cultural constraints; clearly computers, like all of our other technologies, have had certain effects on our lives, some intended and some not. Rather than asserting either an obviously flawed technological determinism or an equally flawed anti-determinism, I suggest that technologies and cultures are mutually determining and thus must evolve in concert.

As—*of course*—Jay David Bolter (1996, 254) has argued, "Technological constraints and social construction always interact in such a way that it is impossible to separate the two." Social and institutional structures develop new technologies to serve their purposes, but the design of those technologies can have effects that are often unforeseen.

The example of the word processor might be relevant here. In the not too distant past, many professors had secretaries, or perhaps typists, or at the very least *wives*, who handled a key aspect of the production of their work. Over the last three decades, a series of technological and social changes have made such a phenomenon all but unheard of; with very few exceptions, everybody operates his (or her!) own word processor, manages his own email, writes his own memos, and so forth. Such changes have taken hold in any number of professions, but the impact for scholars on the writing process has been significant. Typing has ceased to be a technological process that follows the intellectual act of writing, which thus allowed it to be outsourced, and has instead become the core of the writing process itself. This change has in turn had often dramatic effects on the ways we write.[4] This chapter, for instance, was composed in the kind of fits and starts that would have been all but impossible if I'd been tied to a typewriter; first, I put together a very spotty outline, and then fleshed that outline out, moving and changing sections as the logic of the chapter began to unfold. I then gradually transformed that outline into ugly, hacky prose, and then into a more polished, more readable draft. And all of this took place within the same document, within the same window on my laptop screen. Things got moved around, deleted, inserted, revised; I jumped between sections as various thoughts occurred to me; I began sentences having no idea where they would end; I trashed entire concepts in midstream. None of this would have been possible—or, where possible, certainly would have been much less pleasant—back in the days when I wrote my term papers in longhand on legal pads before laboriously typing up the final draft. The word processor has allowed my writing to become much more about *process*—more recursive, non-linear, open-ended, and spontaneous—than my previous technologies permitted.

Even more to the point, the technologies that support Internet-based writing and communication developed in a milieu—among scientific researchers—in which a higher value was placed on the sharing of information than on the individual authorship or ownership of particular texts. From Vint Cerf's development of the "transmission control protocol" at the heart of TCP/IP, to Tim Berners-Lee's creation of the World Wide Web, to Marc Andreessen's invention of the graphical web browser, the Internet's technologies have been designed to promote the open exchange of data in a content-agnostic fashion. As Lessig explains in *The Future of Ideas* (2001, 35–40), the "end-to-end" design of the networks that make up the Internet produce its neutrality; the network treats any packet of data just like any other, leaving it to the applications located at the network's ends to determine how such data should be interpreted. Similarly, in the design of the HTTP and HTML protocols that make the web possible, Berners-Lee privileged an ideal of open communication based upon the interconnectability of all documents on the network, regardless of their location, and he gave those protocols away for free, enabling others to build upon them. And every major web browser since the beginning has allowed users to view any page's source code, encouraging the sharing of new technologies and designs (Lessig 2006, 146). Since those early days of its development, of course, the web has changed enormously, including an increase in technologies for the regulation and restriction of certain kinds of communication, but the values of open, shared protocols and codes that encouraged the web's development still linger in its culture. And just as many seemingly well-established industries—the music industry most famously, but only because they were hit first—are being forced to reinvent the ways that they do business in the wake of the model established by a small group of theoretical physicists, so many of us in the academy would benefit from taking a long, hard look at the ways that we work, and from trying to imagine how current and future technological developments might continue to affect the ways that we write.

In fact, some of these effects may be even more significant than those enabled by the word processor, precisely because of the networked structures of the newer technologies and the kinds of interconnections and interactions that they make possible. Writing and publishing in networked environments might require a fundamental change not just in the tools with which we work, or in the ways that we interact with our tools, but in our sense of ourselves as we do that work, and in the institutional understandings of the relationships between scholars and their now apparently independent silos of production. As Carla Hesse wrote in 1996, in an examination of the historical development of the culture surrounding the book:

> The striking parallels between the late eighteenth and late twentieth centuries' cultural debates suggest to me that what we are witnessing in the remaking of the "modern literary system" at the end of the twentieth century is not so much a technological revolution (which has already occurred) but the public reinvention of intellectual community in its wake. (Hesse 1996, 29)

The technologies of a new literary system, in other words, are here; they've taken root and are quickly becoming dominant, both in the culture at large and in the academy in particular. What we need to consider, in this sense, is less whether we ought to change our tools than what shifts and reinventions in our intellectual lives the changes already underway will require of us.

I suggest, however, that such shifts are not, in actuality, radical alterations of the nature of authorship, but rather an acknowledgment and intensification of things that have been going on beneath the surface all along. In that sense, what this chapter aims to do is less to disrupt all our conventional notions of authorship than to demonstrate why thinking about authorship from a different perspective—one that's always been embedded, if dormant, in many of our authorship practices—could result in a more productive, and hopefully less anxious, relationship to our work. This relationship will be more productive both because we'll have the opportunity to re-center our understanding of what we're doing when we're writing, and what others are doing when they're reading what we've written, within the framework of an ongoing conversation, a process of communication among peers that can be promoted and supported by the technologies of the Internet. Such a return to communication, to interconnection, as the focus of our writing practices will, furthermore, enable academic authors to think about the multiple audiences they address and the different forms in which they can be addressed, potentially drawing the academy back into broader communication with the surrounding social sphere.

In all of this, the key issue is interaction. The author is not operating—and has never operated—in a vacuum, but has always been a participant in an ongoing conversation.[5] Some aspects of the interactions made possible by new network technologies may seem daunting or alarming to us today, but in the long run, used with care, they'll provide significant possibilities for the kind of knowledge advancement that we all seek, which requires a broad communal framework. Earlier thinking about the intersection between authorship and computer technologies often overlooked this communal framework, in part because such examinations were focused on standalone computers running discrete hypertexts. Howard Bloch and Carla Hesse argued, for instance, in their introduction to the "Future Libraries" special issue of *Representations*:

> The potential loss of the object book, the disappearance of the author and reader as coherent imagined selves constituted through the stabilizing form of the bound book, the disordering of authorial agency in favor of an increasingly active reader (or alternatively, the empowerment of

FITZPATRICK, KATHLEEN.

PLANNED OBSOLESCENCE: PUBLISHING, TECHNOLOGY, AND
THE FUTURE OF THE ACADEMY.
                                    Paper   245 P.
NEW YORK: NEW YORK UNIVERSITY PRESS, 2011

AUTH: POMONA COLLEGE. ARGUES NEED TO TRANSFORM
SCHOLARLY PUBLISHING & ITS ROLE W/IN THE UNIV. TLS
LCCN 2011-24719
  ISBN 0814727883   **Library PO#**   /NR

		List	23.00	USD
8395 NATIONAL UNIVERSITY LIBRAR		**Disc**	5.0%	
App. Date 10/30/13 SOE	8214-08	**Net**	21.85	USD

SUBJ: 1. SCHOLARLY PUBLISING--U.S. 2. SCHOLARLY
ELECTRONIC PUBLISHING--U.S

CLASS Z286   DEWEY# 070.50973   LEVEL ADV-AC

YBP Library Services

FITZPATRICK, KATHLEEN.

PLANNED OBSOLESCENCE: PUBLISHING, TECHNOLOGY, AND
THE FUTURE OF THE ACADEMY.
                                    Paper   245 P.
NEW YORK: NEW YORK UNIVERSITY PRESS, 2011

AUTH: POMONA COLLEGE. ARGUES NEED TO TRANSFORM
SCHOLARLY PUBLISHING & ITS ROLE W/IN THE UNIV. TLS
  LCCN 2011-24719
  ISBN 0814727883   **Library PO#**   /NR

		List	23.00	USD
8395 NATIONAL UNIVERSITY LIBRAR		**Disc**	5.0%	
App. Date 10/30/13 SOE	8214-08	**Net**	21.85	USD

SUBJ: 1. SCHOLARLY PUBLISING--U.S. 2. SCHOLARLY
ELECTRONIC PUBLISHING--U.S

CLASS Z286   DEWEY# 070.50973   LEVEL ADV-AC

the "online" author in control of the uses and distribution of texts), the displacement of a hermeneutical model of reading by one premised on absorption, the transformation of copyright into contract: all point toward the subsuming fear of a loss of community. (Bloch and Hesse 1993, 8)

I suggest, however, that while these senses of loss are indeed linked, the dominant fear toward which they point in the age of "Web 2.0" may not, in fact, be the fear of loss of community, but rather of loss of individuality, revealed in the assumption that "coherent imagined selves" require separation rather than interconnection to be thought coherent, and that the "disordering of authorial agency in favor of an increasingly active reader" is a disruption of authority inasmuch as a changing relationship. If academic writing is to move productively into a digital environment, and if, as Mark Poster (2001, 91) has argued, "the shift in the scene of writing from paper and pen or typewriter to the globally networked computer is a move that elicits a rearticulation of the author from the center of the text to its margins, from the source of meaning to an offering, a point in a sequence of a continuously transformed matrix of signification," then we must stop to consider where, in the age of the Internet, authority lies.

The Rise of the Author

As Poster also indicates, however, our modern ideas about authorship are relatively recent inventions. Early books, he suggests, were products of the sociocultural structure of the guild, and thus were the product of collective labor rather than the individual intelligence: "Our print culture contains two principles," Poster points out, "neither of which applied in the first century or so of book production: that the copy one sees in one's hands is an exact duplicate of all others, especially those of the same edition, and that the 'author' of the book may be trusted to have written the words one reads" (2001, 87). The suggestion, of course, is that the values that we currently associate with print authorship, and in particular with *book* authorship—individuality, originality, completeness, ownership—were not a direct product of their technologies, nor were they the proximate cause of the development of those technologies. Instead, the technology of print and the concept of authorship that we associate with it each grew out of related but distinct historical formations affecting the breadth of Western political, social, and economic structures.

This is not the history of the book that provided the conventional wisdom for much of the late twentieth century. Beginning with Marshall McLuhan's

The Gutenberg Galaxy (1962), continuing through Elizabeth Eisenstein's *The Printing Press as an Agent of Change* (1979), and beyond, scholars conceived of modern notions of authorship as part of "print culture," literally, that culture brought into existence by the form of print. As Adrian Johns (1998, 2) argues, the "self-evidence" of many of the assumptions that we make when approaching a book—for instance, that it was in fact written by the author named on its cover and published by the organization named on its spine, that the copy we hold is complete and identical to every other copy available, and that those facts together create an imprimatur for the text through which we grant it authority—"encourages us to ascribe all these characteristics to a technological order of reality. If called upon, we may assert that printed texts are identical and reliable because that is simply what printing *is*." McLuhan and Eisenstein rely upon this argument: print created print culture, of which the modern author was a key aspect. However, as Johns goes on to argue, these assumptions about print's authority were not always self-evident, and in fact were brought into being alongside, not through, print technologies, a process requiring the active labor of those who worked on the book's behalf. By focusing on these social processes that existed alongside the new technology of print, more recent scholars exploring the history of the book have argued that a direct relationship exists between the reliability of texts and the individuality of the author—in both cases, "authority"—and the production of modern political and economic states.

Enough such work has been done that rehearsing all of it here would be both unnecessary and impossible; I will instead focus on one key text in this line of thought, Carla Hesse's "Books in Time," in which she explores the political purposes served by the transformation in the notion of authorship in revolutionary France. At the outset of the revolution, the right of monopolistic ownership over a text was a concession granted by the king, rather than a fact emerging from the text's composition. In response to this manifestation of monarchic privilege, Enlightenment thinkers such as Nicolas de Condorcet (1743–1794) argued that knowledge could best be disseminated through "authorless and opened-ended [*sic*] texts, circulating freely between all citizens: he imagined the periodical press supported through the mechanism of subscription rather than through the institution of royalties to authors or monopolies to publishers" (Hesse 1996, 24).[6] Such an "ideally transparent mode of exchange" led, however, to a chaos of sedition, libel, and piracy, and as the revolution settled down into the First Republic, Condorcet himself sponsored legislation reinstating the legal notion of authorship, but in a liberal mode: "Through the legal notion of a 'limited property right,' the

National Convention reshaped the political and legal identity of the author, transforming that cultural agent from a privileged creature of the absolutist state into a property-owning civic hero, an agent of public enlightenment" (pp. 25–26).

In unpacking this history, Hesse demonstrates the weaknesses in the assumption that the printing press produced the author as a function of print culture, and instead focuses on the emergence of what she calls the "modern literary system" from the political revolutions of the late eighteenth century, a system that reflects those revolutions by embodying, within the person of the author, "the ideals of the autonomous, self-creating and self-governing, property-owning individual," as well as such liberal values as the "universal access to knowledge, and the assurance of cautious public reflection and debate" (1996, 28). Our assumptions about authorship, then—that the author is a unitary voice, expressing original ideas in a complete and polished form, over which he retains legal property rights—derive less from the technologies and processes that produce the author's texts than from the legislative and economic systems that govern those technologies and processes. This is not to say, however, that such a modern literary system would have evolved without the assistance of print; as Poster argues:

> The legally defined rights of the author required a print technology that could reproduce large quantities of texts, a market system that could determine printed products as objects for sale, and distribution institutions that could make identical copies available in many places, a discursive regime in which individuals were understood as agents capable of inventing new things and as proprietors with interests in accumulating capital. . . . Authorship also required, as I shall argue below, a technology of the analogue: a conviction that what was printed in the book was a direct representation of an author's intention, be it in the form of idea, style, or rhetoric; in short, that the book was an analogue reproduction of an original, authentic author. (Poster 2001, 65)

In other words, the development of the modern concept of authorship required both the facilitation of print and the influence of the multiple social systems within which print was embedded.

This understanding of the origins of authorship bears significant consequences for thinking about ourselves as authors and ameliorating the anxieties that such work often produces in us; if in part our attachments to the idea of authorship arise from deeply seated beliefs about the locus of individual intelligence and about the placement of the individual within liberal society, we might recognize a certain conflict between that notion of authorship and the more communally oriented ideals of academic life. And if, as Hesse (1996, 27–28) suggests, we are today "facing the anxieties that attend the possibility of losing the means of associating a particular work or text with an individual agency, or of losing the writer's and even the reader's individuality, the possibility of a disappearance, perhaps, of the Enlightenment sense of self and of a sociability based upon a Rousseauesque model of intellectual community and of a liberal model of public life rooted in individualism and private property," we must explore the possibility that these losses arise less from technological shifts than from "sociopolitical choices" and other legal, economic, and institutional frameworks surrounding authorship. This is to say that our anxieties about writing are not produced by our tools, but by the cultural significance of the ways in which we use them. Similarly, those anxieties won't be assuaged by new tools, as the shift from a print-based mode of authorship to one based in digital networks cannot in and of itself produce a new mode of authorship; rather, changes in our understandings of the nature of the author might be required in order for us to embrace new network technologies.

The Death of the Author

Such shifts in thinking about authorship have been underway, at least theoretically, since the late 1960s, when the rise of poststructuralism in literary theory and philosophy brought into prominence arguments aimed at changing our understandings of the relationship between the author and the text. The most famous among these, of course, is Roland Barthes's 1967 essay announcing the "death" of the author, which seeks to undermine the critical and political "authority" invested in that figure, in part by insisting upon the structuring power of language over the subject, such that it becomes impossible for any author to fully "own" or control the text he or she produces, as the language with which it is produced has already itself constructed the consciousness of the writing subject:

> [L]inguistics furnishes the destruction of the Author with a precious analytical instrument, showing that the speech-act in its entirety is an "empty" process, which functions perfectly without its being necessary to "fill" it with the person of the interlocutors: linguistically, the author is nothing but the one who writes, just as *I* is nothing but the one who says *I*: lan-

guage knows a "subject," not a "person," and this subject, empty outside of the very speech-act which defines it, suffices to "hold" language, i.e., to exhaust it. (Barthes 1967/86, 51)

The author, therefore, comes into being at the moment of writing—the author is not, Barthes says, the subject of which his writing is predicate, but is rather born *subject to* the process of writing itself—and in so "holding" language, in claiming ownership over the product of writing, perversely deprives it of meaning: "To assign an Author to a text is to impose a brake on it, to furnish it with a final signified, to close writing. This conception is quite suited to criticism, which then undertakes the important task of discovering the Author (or his hypostases: society, history, the psyche, freedom) beneath the work: once the Author is found, the text is 'explained,' the critic has won" (p. 53). If the purpose of the critic is to close down the text's meaning, and that meaning is thus closed through the identification of the Author (and, one assumes, his intention, whether conscious or unconscious) or the broader societal structures that support and sustain the author (and thus determine his intention), then the figure of the author is actually detrimental to meaning, rather than productive of meaning, as our conventional wisdom assumes, and the intimate association of a text with its author serves not to give the text life but instead to choke it off. In order to give life to a text by granting it openness, to prevent the work of criticism from degenerating into an act of butterfly-pinning, and "to restore to writing its future," Barthes finally argues, "the birth of the reader must be requited by the death of the Author" (p. 55).

As contemporary critics, thoroughly inculcated in poststructuralist and postmodernist thought, we can read this and nod: yes, of course, the death of the author, a moment of radical empowerment for us, as we can finally fully overcome the intentional fallacy, ignore the author, and focus instead on producing more imaginative new readings of the texts with which we work. But—and one almost hesitates to ask—what does this death of the author bode for *ourselves as authors*? Given that our work with the texts in our field is itself productive of more new texts, are we willing, or indeed able, to find ourselves so decentered, to think of ourselves as "scriptors" rather than "authors," equally called into being subject to language rather than exercising authority over it? If the author is dead, how can we continue to think of writing as part of our work—and how can we continue to evaluate the careers of academics based upon their writing?

Michel Foucault provides a partial answer, if not a particularly reassuring one, in his 1969 rejoinder, "What Is an Author?" In contrast to Barthes's sense of the liberatory effects that the author's death might produce for the reader, Foucault seems to suggest that though the author is indeed dead (in his analysis, killed off by the act of writing itself, a notion that might go some distance toward understanding anxieties about writing), the networks of power that produce cultural "authority" remain fully in place, existing wholly independently of the figure of the individual author. True, the author may have been demoted to the status of an "author function," which is the result of "a complex operation whose purpose is to construct the rational entity we call an author . . . these aspects of an individual, which we designate as an author (or which comprise an individual as an author) are projections, in terms always more or less psychological, of our way of handling texts" (Foucault 1969/77, 127), and thus the role of the author function is no more than "to characterize the existence, circulation, and operation of certain discourses within a society" (p. 124). The author, as a function of language, becomes a convenient handle by which to pick up texts and carry them around, something significantly less than the independent liberal actors we like to imagine ourselves to be as writers. Of course, the possibility remains that we can think of ourselves as that special category of author that Foucault argues arose in Europe during the nineteenth century, whose "transdiscursive" position resulted in their "distinctive contribution": "they produced not only their own work, but the possibility and the rules of formation of other texts" (p. 131). Such transdiscursivity, the ability to transcend the mere production of discourse, perhaps, or to transform it at its root, appears reserved, however, for a precious few authors: Karl Marx, Sigmund Freud, and, one might expect, Foucault himself.

The rest of us are ostensibly working in a post-authorial era, in which the "removal of the Author" has become "not only a historical fact or an act of writing: it utterly transforms the modern text (or—which is the same thing—the text is henceforth produced and read so that the author absents himself from it at every level)" (Barthes 1967/86, 51–52). But questions remain: How has this theoretical death of the author actually changed the text's production? Has it had any material effect on our writing practices? Early proponents of new modes of electronic writing and publishing, including George Landow and Jay David Bolter, have pointed to hypertext as a digital manifestation of the poststructuralist decentering of the author, fragmentation of the text, and activation of the reader. Landow (1997, 2), for instance, points toward the convergence of literary theory and computing in hypertext, noting that practitioners in both fields "argue that we must abandon conceptual systems founded upon ideas of center, margin, hierarchy, and linearity and replace them with ones of multilinearity, nodes, links, and networks," and that "critical theory promises to theorize hypertext and hypertext proposes to embody and thereby test aspects of theory, particularly those concerning textuality, narrative, and the roles or functions of reader and writer." What Landow describes as the open, intertextual, multivocal, decentered, rhizomatic mode of hypertext thus becomes the emblem of deconstruction; moreover, as Bolter (1991, 153) notes, electronic writing "complicates our understanding of literature as either mimesis or expression, it denies the fixity of the text, and it questions the authority of the author." If literary theory had not succeeded in putting the figure of the author in its grave, it seems, hypertext would be along behind, ready to finish the job.

And yet authorship remains far from dead, even in such electronic forms; these arguments, like those of Barthes and Foucault, are compelling in theory, but in application hypertext did not result in the revolution in authoring practices, the decentering of authority, or the empowerment of the reader that had been projected. As I explore further in the next chapter, hypertext is somewhat deceptive in its claims to activate the reader; though the reader is required to make choices and click on them in order to advance a hypertext narrative, such activities have always, to differing extents, been part of the reading process. *Do I want to keep reading this book? Then I'll turn the page. Do I just want to find out how it all turns out? Then I'll flip to the end.* While arguments such as these—that the book-reading process has always been as active, if not more active, than the process of reading hypertext—are often tendentious, designed to defuse the significant claims made for electronic modes of communication and reduce them to mere novelty, they have a point: upon picking up a book to read, I have the entire text in my hands, all at once, and I can do anything with it that I choose—read the entire thing in a linear fashion, read the end before the beginning, use the index to find the only three pages I really need to read, flip back and forth between different sections. With a hypertext, not only do I not have the entire text available to me at the outset—some pathways only becoming activated by prior choices, some choices remaining hidden—but it is also often unclear what options I do have before me, what choices I can make, and what relationship those choices bear to the shape of the text as a whole. All I can do as a reader is follow the choices that the author has allowed. The process of reading a hypertext is thus, in its way, more determined than the process of reading a book, and the experience of reading can at times seem more focused on attempting to divine the author's encoded intent than on creating a reader-centered text.

The apotheosis of such a reinscription of authorial primacy might be found in Shelley Jackson's "Skin" (2003); Jackson, previously best known for

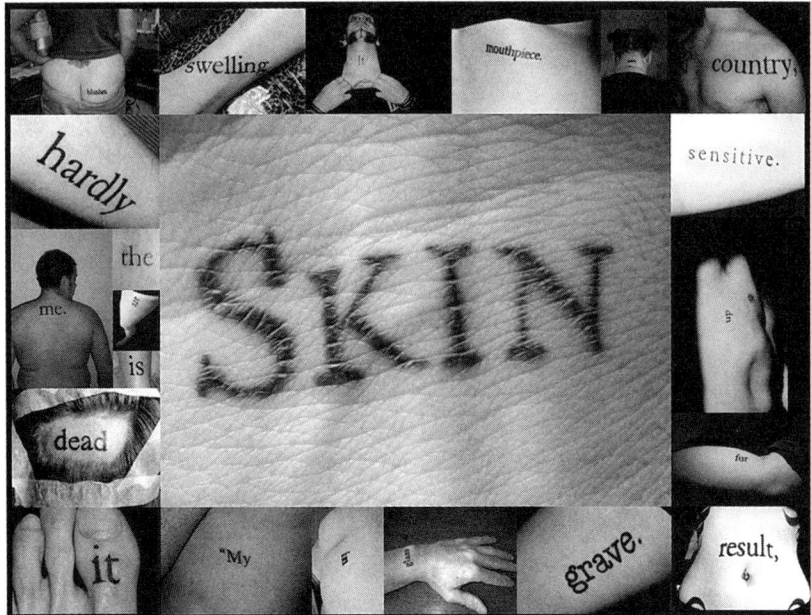

Fig. 2.1. Cover page of Shelley Jackson's *Skin* (ineradicablestain.com)

her experiments in hypertext fiction such as *Patchwork Girl*, launched this project in August 2003 with a call for participants, each of whom "must agree to have one word of the story tattooed upon his or her body" (see fig. 2.1). The story would thus be distributed not just across physical space but across the bodies of those who elect to interact with the text. Moreover, though the story is legible, at least in part, to anyone who encounters a participant in the project, the text in its entirety—all of the words, in the correct sequence— is available only to those who participate, as well as, of course, the author herself. And lest this sense of "participation" come to sound like a mode of active readership, the participants, those few who have the option of reading the full story, are potentially deactivated by the project, considered something simultaneously more and less than readers:

> From this time on, participants will be known as "words." They are not understood as carriers or agents of the texts they bear, but as its embodiments. As a result, injuries to the printed texts, such as dermabrasion, laser surgery, tattoo cover work or the loss of body parts, will not be considered to alter the work. Only the death of words effaces them from the text. As

words die the story will change; when the last word dies the story will also have died. The author will make every effort to attend the funerals of her words.

Aside from the arguable violence to be found in the author's desire to inscribe—literally—the text into the flesh of her audience, the project's description manages both to convey the potential for shifting relationships among author, reader, and text in the contemporary moment while re-centering the author within the structures of meaning-making; readers disappear, transformed into signs, and signs "owned" by the author, at that ("her words"). The author remains singular, unique, individual, while the words she uses, and the readers she inscribes them upon, are an indifferent, effaceable mass.[7]

One must wonder, then, whether authorship, or at least our thinking about it, can have changed all that much in this ostensibly postmodern, post-structuralist, decentered, digital world. While Poster (2001, 68) argues that "[d]igital writing *may* function to extract the author from the text, to remove from its obvious meaning his or her intentions, style, concepts, rhetoric, mind—in short, to disrupt the analogue circuit through which the author makes the text his or her own, through which the mechanisms of property solidify a link between creator and object" (emphasis mine), the difference may be one of degree, in which the "digital author connotes a greater alterity between the text and the author" (p. 69), suggesting rather than absolutely determining a separation between the two. Rather than existing in the "postauthor utopia" Poster derives from the end of Foucault's "What Is an Author?," in which "discourse would circulate without any need for an author" (Foucault 1969/77, 138), our actual digital authorship practices seem instead to be caught between two regimes, bound to assumptions about the ownership and originality of texts that derive from older, Enlightenment-era notions of the self, while using technologies that lend themselves to the distributed, the collective, the process-oriented, the anonymous, the remix. Although the digital has already begun to have significant effects on our work, both in the ways that we write and the ways that our writing moves throughout the academy and the broader public sphere, a full acknowledgment of the benefits of digital authorship practices for our writing, much less any further acceptance of the digital as a primary mode of our work, will require significant shifts in our thinking about ourselves in the act of writing—what we're doing, how and with whom we're doing it, and the relationship between ourselves and the texts we produce.

The first of the shifts I discuss has to do with the status of the texts that we produce when we write, including their very shape and structure. We are all attuned to the form of the book review, the essay, the article, the book, but digital publishing has thus far produced a number of new forms, none of which comfortably fit in our old structures. The blog, for instance, is arguably the first successful web-native electronic publishing platform,[8] one with a number of structural elements that cannot be replicated in print, and one that therefore encodes different expectations than do print texts. A perfunctory bit of background, for those still unfamiliar with the form: "blog" is a neologism drawn from a contraction of "web log," a term first used to designate the web journals kept by a number of active web-surfers, logging and commenting on their online finds. "Blog" has since come to refer to a wide range of ongoing web publications in an equally wide range of genres, all of which have in common frequently updated entries that appear on the published page with the newest posts up top, receding into the past as one scrolls down the page.[9] Blogging has developed from a mildly peculiar and somewhat self-regarding web-publishing practice limited to a small sector of the techno-elite into a surprisingly widespread phenomenon, thanks in part to a number of free software packages and services that make blogging no more difficult than writing itself. Blogger, the first of those tools, was released in October 2000; by July 2008, Technorati.com was tracking the activity on 112.8 million blogs.[10] Among those blogs, the type and level of discourse vary greatly: some blogs are exclusively personal journals, others focus on politics or other aspects of the public sphere, and many are a blend of the two; some blogs are single-authored while others are the work of groups; some blogs exclusively publish text while many others include other forms of media. And, of course, some blogs are "good," while others aren't. None of this variation should distract us from the key point: the rapid spread of blogs and the relative robustness of their platforms should suggest that their tools might be useful to a range of potential, specialized digital publishing modes.

Among the tools most commonly associated with blogs is the ability of readers to comment on entries, creating multivocal and wide-ranging conversations; another is the link, whether standard HTML links created within blog entries in order to comment on other web-based texts or those automatically generated and transmitted by blogging engines in order to leave an indication on a linked-to text that it has been commented upon elsewhere (known as "trackbacks" or "pingbacks"). I discuss commenting and linking later in this chapter and further explore the implications of such tools for new textual structures in chapter 3. For the moment, however, I'd like to focus on "versioning," a third feature provided by some blog engines, as well as by other web publishing platforms such as wikis, and how it might affect our thinking about the life of scholarly writing online.

All three of these features—commenting, linking, and versioning—produce texts that are no longer discrete or static, but live and develop as part of a network of other such texts, among which ideas flow. Of these features, however, versioning may in some ways be the most disconcerting for traditional authors, including academics, whose work lives have been organized around writing conceived not as an ongoing action but rather as an act of completing discrete projects. In part this emphasis on the completeness and stability of written texts developed in conjunction with the ideas subtending the modern literary system discussed earlier; one of the assumptions that the technologies, implementations, and organizations surrounding print publishing have produced is that any text that comes into our hands, whether a book or a journal, is present in its entirety and will be consistent from copy to copy. We further assume that any changes made to the text in further printings will be corrections or emendations meant to bring the printed text into line with the author's or publisher's intentions; changes more substantive than these, we assume, will be revisions of a sort labeled by the publisher as a "second" or "revised" edition. We rely on such stability as a sign of a text's authority, and where it doesn't exist, the resulting oddities often become the object of scholarly investigation.[11]

There's another factor, however, one perhaps peculiar to academic authorship, that puts additional pressure on completion as the most significant moment in the writing process. Only at the point of completion, after all, can our projects at last attain their final purpose: the entry of a new item on the CV. This emphasis on the academic version of the bottom line—evidence of scholarly "productivity" that must be demonstrated in order to obtain and maintain a professorial appointment—brings a distinctly Fordist, functionalist mode of thinking to bear on our work as writers. Bill Readings, in *The University in Ruins*, calls attention to the ways that the metaphor of "production" in scholarly life transforms the university into "a bureaucratic apparatus for the production, distribution, and consumption of knowledge" (1996, 163) whose purpose rapidly degenerates from the knowledge that is produced to the fact of production itself: "Produce what knowledge you like, only produce more of it, so that the system can speculate on knowledge differentials, can profit from the accumulation of intellectual capital" (p. 164).[12] Such functionalism, however, cannot become so endemic to our institutions without being reflected in our individual approaches to the work we do as members of them. Lindsay Waters (2004, 6) links the emphasis on scholarly productivity to the crisis in academic publishing, arguing that "there is a causal connection between the corporatist demand for increased productivity and the draining of publication of any significance other than as a number"; Waters goes on to indicate that the loss of "significance" produced by this emphasis on productivity is not just about the status conveyed by scarcity, but in fact about quality:

> The problem of ridiculous articles by humanists was caused partly by the vast increase of the numbers of publications that humanists (and all academics) are expected to perpetrate on paper or on one another as talks at conferences. It all sounds like a world gone wrong, but the problem is not limited to the humanities. We are experiencing a generalized crisis of judgment that results from unreasonable expectations about how many publications a scholar should publish. (Waters 2004, 18)

Writing has, in this view, been reduced from a process of discovery, exploration, and communication to a system for the assembly of more and more new products. If this is the case, and if the result is, as Waters claims, that many scholars feel "more and more like the figure portrayed by Charlie Chaplin in the film *Modern Times*, madly and insensibly working to produce" (p. 45), it is little wonder that many of us experience unresolved anxieties about our writing. As long as we are in the process of writing, we have not yet completed it, and without completion, we cannot get credit for what we have produced; we haven't accomplished anything. We must put a close to our texts, put them into print, and walk away, not least in order to move on to the next project.

But being "done" with a project published online runs to some extent counter to the network's open-endedness.[13] What made blogs so immediately popular, both with readers and with writers, was the very fact that they changed and developed over time, existing not as a static, complete text but rather as an ongoing series of updates, additions, and revisions. This is to be expected of a journal-like format, and might easily be compared to any form of periodical or serial publication; the blog as a whole remains relatively constant, even as new "issues" or posts are added to it. But the fact that a blog's readers return again and again in order to find those new posts might encourage us to ask whether there is something in the structure of digital authorship that privileges and encourages development and change, even beyond the obviously diachronic aspect of the blog's structure. When web pages are not regularly updated and attended to, after all, they're subject to rapid degeneration: aging styles, outdated standards, and worst, perhaps, "link rot."[14] Such ephemerality makes it arguable that the unspoken contract between the author and the reader of a piece of digital text is radically different from that between the author of a book and its reader; the reader of a digital text may not assume that the text is fixed, complete, and stable. As Clifford Lynch (2001) suggests, we do not yet fully understand what "reader expectations about updating published work" will be; will the assumption come to be that a text must be up-to-date, with all known errors corrected, reflecting new information as it comes to light, in order to maintain the "authority" that print has held? Sites such as Wikipedia seem to indicate a growing assumption that digitally published texts not only will but *should* change over time. Digital text is, above all, malleable, and the relationship between the reader and the text reflects that malleability; there is little sense in attempting to replicate the permanence of print in a medium whose chief value is change.

On the other hand, allowing a text to grow and change over time shouldn't—and needn't—efface earlier incarnations by simply overwriting them with newer versions. Versioning preserves the history of a text, allowing it to live and breathe while maintaining snapshots of the text at key moments, as well as the ability to compare those snapshots, permitting readers to approach a text not just in a finished state, but throughout its process of development. That ability to focus on process may well lead to new modes of criticism; as Luca Toschi (1996, 200) has argued, "[t]he true task" involved in the creation of the sort of "genetic criticism" he calls for, which explores the coming-into-being of a piece of literature, "is to return to the fixity of a written text a third dimension, of movement and of transformation." This third dimension, which demands a publishing format that is able to support change while maintaining the history that makes the change visible, can best be provided through the implementation of versioning in our publishing technologies, and an attention to process in our writing. As Hesse suggested well before any but the very first blogs had been established,

> What appears to be emerging from the digital revolution is the possibility of a new mode of temporality for public communication, one in which public exchange through the written word can occur without deferral, in a continuously immediate present. A world in which we are all, through

> electronic writing, continuously present to one another. There is, I would like to suggest, something unprecedented in this possibility of the escape of writing from fixity. What the digitalization of text seems to have opened up is the possibility for writing to operate in a temporal mode hitherto exclusively possible for speech, as *parole* rather than *langue*. (Hesse 1996, 32)

This "continuously immediate present" of writing could allow our writing projects, and our conversations around those projects, to develop in a more fruitful, more organic fashion.

But this will require a fairly radical shift in our understandings of what it is we're doing as we're writing, because if our texts are going to continue to grow even as they're published online, we're going to need to be present in those texts in order to shepherd that growth—perhaps not forever, but certainly for longer than we have been with traditional print publishing. This thought will make many of us nervous, in part because we already have difficulties with completing a project; if we have the opportunity to continue working on something forever, well, we just might. On the other hand, would that necessarily be such a bad thing? What if we were freed—by a necessary change in the ways that we "credit" ongoing and in-process work— to shift our attention away from publication as the moment of singularity in which a text transforms from nothing into something, and instead focus on the many important stages in our work's coming-into-being? What if we were able to think of our careers as writers in a more holistic sense, as an ongoing process of development, perhaps with some key moments of punctuation, rather than solely as a series of discrete, closed projects, the return to the scene of which—whether in order to reveal changes in one's thinking about something one once committed to print or to take old material in new directions—seems somehow vaguely scandalous? Such abilities would no doubt lead to work that was better thought-through, more "significant," in Waters's sense. In order to take advantage of those abilities, however, we will first have to learn to value process over product, and to manifest that value in our assessments of one another's work.

Even more frighteningly, perhaps, we'll have to become willing to expose some of our process in public, to allow our readers—and our colleagues— to see some of the bumps and false starts along the way. This, I confess, is the aspect of my argument that I find the most alarming, and yet as soon as I admit to my own anxiety, I have to recognize that, through my blog, I'm already doing some of this in-public work. Many of the ideas in this text, for instance, were first articulated in somewhat nebulous blog posts, clarified in discussions with commenters, expanded into conference papers and lectures, formalized into articles, and revised into chapters. That process was absolutely key to the project's formation: I didn't at all have the sense, as I wrote those early blog posts, that I was embarking on a book-length project; I only knew that I had a small, persistent question that I wanted to think about a bit. Having formulated an initial stab at one possible answer, and having been disagreed with, supported, and encouraged by my commenters to think in more complex ways about the issues I'd presented, only then was I able to recognize that there was more to be said, that there was something in the ideas to which I was compelled to commit myself. Without the blog and the inadvertent process of drafting in public to which it led me, not to mention the online publication of the draft of this manuscript, none of the ideas in this text could have come together.

This is not to say, of course, that every stage of this project was conducted in front of an audience, or that every academic blogger has experienced the same relationship between the in-public work of the blog and the more traditionally private work of scholarly writing. In January 2008, I spoke on a conference panel with fellow academic bloggers Laura Blankenship (of *Geeky Mom*) and Timothy Burke (of *Easily Distracted*), and each of us presented a very different perspective on the relationship between blogging and scholarship: my talk (which was a stage along the way toward chapter 3) focused on the technical and social possibilities that new modes of blog-based publishing might present for the drafting and revision processes; Tim's explored a typology of projects that he argued would be good candidates for blog-based drafting (as well of those that wouldn't); Laura's reported on the process and results of drafting her dissertation on a blog.[15] Despite the obvious similarities in these talks, however, each of us drew slightly different conclusions in thinking about the kinds of projects, the stages within those projects, and the circumstances in which some mode of writing-in-public might be beneficial. Tim and I, for instance, saw public drafting as a potential means of creating a robust, open-access scholarship for an already-established community of peers within a field, while Laura, writing her dissertation in relative isolation, was able to create community through her drafting process, building a support network of colleagues she wouldn't otherwise have had. And each of us had developed slightly different boundaries between our selves, our blogs, and our scholarship, with slightly different senses of what material we're willing to reveal, and in what state.[16]

My interest in the possibilities that versioning could present for shifting our focus in writing from product to process is thus not meant to suggest that every author need expose every draft of every sentence online, in real time. What constitutes a "version," and at what stage it is made public, will be, and indeed ought to be, different for each author. But approaching our writing from the perspective of process, thinking about how ideas move and develop from one form of writing to the next, and about the ways that those stages are represented, connected, preserved, and "counted" within new digital modes of publishing, will be necessary for fostering work that takes full advantage of the web's particular temporality. Everything published on the web exists, in some sense, in a perpetual draft state, open to future change; we need to recognize both the need this creates for careful preservation of the historical record of the stages in a text's life and the equal importance for authors of approaching our work openly, thinking about how our texts might continue to grow even after they've seen the light of day.

From Individual to Collaborative

Beyond this, however, it is also important to recognize that even if we never return to an article and revise it after it's been published online, the article's meaning will nonetheless shift and change depending on the ways that other writers interact with it, as links to and from other texts, past and future, will expand the text's connections within the network. This has always been true of scholarship—critical authority exists in a state of continual reassessment, as new texts are published and fields grow and transform—but print publishing hasn't made the changes produced by a text's reception and the responses to it quite so materially evident. In a digital publishing environment, the links among texts are literal, and thus each text published exists in direct interaction with those to which it is linked. Even further, comments left on a digitally published text will expand not only its meaning but indeed the text itself through the ongoing give-and-take of discussion in that text's margins.

We are thus presented with another point of potential anxiety for the author considering digital publication, as the relationship between this give-and-take and the text that it alters is itself a nervous one. While the reviews of a published book may well affect its reception, they don't change the text itself; similarly, articles that respond to or argue with previously published articles don't leave traces on the original text. We are very much accustomed to drawing boundaries around our texts, understanding them to be separate from those of other authors. In fact, our understanding of authorship is in part contingent upon such separation; the name of the author imprinted on a text serves as a kind of contract with the reader, indicating that the text has been at least primarily, and preferably wholly, written by that individual, and thus that text must be clearly separable from the texts that it cites or those by which it is cited.[17] The interconnections of the network, however, make some of those boundaries between texts a bit fuzzy, and that fuzziness can be quite troubling to our understanding of the relationship between our work and that of others. As Bloch and Hesse (1993, 7) note in thinking about the complex structures of future textual collections, "for some, this conception of the library as an ever-expanding web of intellectual freeplay is, again, the source of profound anxiety, rooted in the fear of losing a cherished liberal conception of cultural author-ity: the self-contained individually authored text, whose author can be held accountable to a reading public." What, exactly, will we be given credit for—or held accountable for—when our texts form part of a larger network, when other authors' responses appear within the same frame as our own writing? How will the multivocal nature of such texts transform our sense of authority?

It's obvious, but still bears pointing out, that such anxieties will be most pronounced in those fields, predominantly within the humanities, in which single authorship is the norm. As Christine Borgman (2007, 219–20) points out, "The humanities are at the opposite extreme from the sciences, where 'collective cognition' is valued. They have the lowest rates of coauthorship and collaboration of the disciplines, with the higher rates of collaboration occurring in digital projects. E-Research is expected to promote collabora-tion in the humanities, due to the size of projects and the range of expertise required." Certainly such large-scale projects as those Borgman imagines will necessitate a form of multiple authorship like that in common practice in many of the natural and social sciences, just as most projects that focus on the production of media other than print (film, video, etc.) have long required substantive collaboration. As these new kinds of projects become increasingly common within the academy, we will be required to rethink the ways that we give credit for such projects; scholars have frequently encoun-tered obstacles to having non-print work given appropriate credit, and many scholars in the humanities also report difficulty having their coauthored publications taken seriously as part of their record of production.[18] And, as Bethany Nowviskie pointed out in a paper delivered at the 2009 Modern Language Association Convention, these collaborations are frequently led by library and technical staff, whose intellectual property rights in the work they produce are often severely restricted by university policies that under-stand all of their production as "work for hire"; it is incumbent on the fac-ulty who collaborate with such staff members to ensure that they receive the appropriate credit for and control over their work.

Beyond such obviously collaborative endeavors, we need as well to reconsider the individualism with which we approach our authorship with respect to projects for which we would continue to consider ourselves "sole authors." If, as Poster (2001, 68) suggests, digital writing "separates the author from the text, as does print, but also mobilizes the text so that the reader transforms it, not simply in his or her mind or in his or her marginalia, but in the text itself so that it may be redistributed as another text," networked writing will require us to forge a new understanding of the relationship between the author and the reader, and between the reader and his or her own authorship practices. To some extent, all of the texts published in networked environments will become multi-author by virtue of their interpenetration with the writings of others; our task will be, first, to acknowledge the ways that our work has always been collaborative, relying upon texts that precede and follow, and second, to understand the collective not as the elimination of the individual, but rather as *composed of* individuals—not as a hive mind within which we all become drones, but as a fertile community composed of multiple intelligences, each of which is always working in relationship with others.

These relationships may be partnerships; dozens of articles, written by scholars from across the disciplines, have pointed to the benefits of collaborative authorship. Many of these articles, however, particularly those originating outside of the field of rhetoric and composition, point toward "increased productivity" as a primary benefit of collaboration, a phrase that should either raise specters of old Soviet jokes about new tractors and five-year plans or remind us of Readings's assessment of the university's drive to produce competitive quantities of intellectual capital.[19] Other benefits, however, resulting from the combination of collaborators' different knowledge bases as researchers and strengths as writers, include the potential for "increased creativity and deepened analysis of research questions and data" (Mullen and Kochan 2001, 130)—not just *more* work, in other words, but *better* work, and a more enjoyable work process: "Researchers who collaborate with others to accomplish mutual aims can experience a fertile synergy that enhances the work of all" (p. 128), in no small part by reducing the loneliness and isolation of writing itself.[20]

However, the kinds of collaboration I'm interested in need not necessarily result in literal coauthorship; given what Lisa Ede and Andrea A. Lunsford (2001, 355) refer to as the "socially constructed nature of writing—its inherently collaborative foundation," even the work that appears to take place in isolation nonetheless remains part of a fundamentally social process, as each author writes with and against the writings of others. The shift that I'm calling for may therefore be less radical than it initially sounds—less a call necessarily for writing in groups than for a shift in our focus from the individualistic parts of our work to those that are more collective, more socially situated. In some sense, when we write, we are entering into conversation with the scholars with whom we work, both those whom we have read and those who will read us; focusing on this social mode of conversation, rather than becoming obsessed with what we, unique individuals that we are, have to say, may produce better exchanges. One need not literally share authorship of one's texts in order to share the process of writing those texts; the collaboration that digital publishing networks may inspire could parallel, for instance, the writing groups in which many scholars already share their work, seeking feedback while the work is in process.

That mode of sharing work, however, takes on a new resonance in the network, as the responses to the text appear in the same form, and the same frame, as the text itself. Moreover, the openness of such digital practices produces concerns for many writers about sharing material too soon. It's no accident that both Tim and Laura indicated in their conference papers that one of the most significant anxieties produced by the thought of writing-in-public is that of being "scooped"—of giving away our ideas, such that they no longer remain "ours," before we've had a chance to mark our authorial imprint upon them. Of course, authorship has always been, in part, a practice of giving ideas away; one of the key notions behind the "death" of the author is the recognition that, at the moment of publication, the author cedes all control over the text and the meanings drawn from it to its readers, as well as to future authors' characterizations of the text. Electronic publishing, particularly of the sort that shifts its focus from final, closed products to open-ended processes, will require creating new understandings of the movement of ideas from one author to another, of associating texts and ideas with authors, and of accounting for the ways that we influence and are influenced by our colleagues, as we read and comment upon their texts, and as they incorporate our readings and comments.[21]

That we cling to a profound individualism in thinking about scholarly productivity, however, is relatively easy to see: as Ede and Lunsford point out, no matter how much we might claim to privilege collaboration, the multi-author dissertation remains literally unthinkable; when it comes to assessment, every tub, as it were, must sit on its own bottom. And so, the many texts published in recent decades calling for reform, for the acceptance, if not the privileging, of collaboration in the humanities—including Ede and Lunsford's *Singular Texts/Plural Authors*, David Damrosch's *We Scholars*, and so on—have gone more or less unheeded. Network-based publishing technologies, however, add a new impetus for scholars to revisit these issues, to face down our individualism, as the network's interconnections among texts reveal the porous boundaries of their authorship, making collaboration all but unavoidable.

From Originality to Remix

In contemplating the movement of texts and ideas across what previously seemed firmly delineated authorial boundaries, there is an additional level of concerns that do not revolve solely around the notion of having to share the "credit" for authorship of a text that is open to communal interpretation, analysis, and revision. Digital publishing of necessity bears profound implications for our assumptions about the originality that authorship implies. These two facets of conventional authorship—individuality and originality—are complexly intertwined: insisting that a dissertation, for instance, must consist of one's "own" work is to insist that it make an original contribution to the field; the bottom that every tub sits on must not simply be its own, but uniquely its own. The links and interconnections facilitated by the digital network, however, profoundly affect the shape of the texts that are distributed through it. If, in digital scholarship, the relationships between the authors whose ideas we draw upon (now traditionally cordoned off from our own ideas via quotation marks and citations) and the texts that we produce in response are made material—if the work of our predecessors is in some sense contained within whatever increasingly fuzzy boundaries mark the outlines of our own texts—how can we demarcate what constitutes our own contribution to the discourse? How can our texts possibly remain unique, discrete, original in an environment so thoroughly determined by the copy?

The notion of authorship in modern literary culture historically has held originality among its key values. As Raffaele Simone (1996, 241) argues, the closed text that we associate with print carries with it several key assumptions; one of these assumptions, which appears to be a common-sense, baseline prerequisite for publication, is that the text is finished: "the text is presented to the reader in the final version intended by the author, or at least in a single, final, and *ne varieteur* form." Finished, in this sense, implies not simply completion but perfection, existing without the kind of flaw that would make possible the requirement of the text's retraction. In addition, however, the text, "assumed to be *perfectum*, has also to be original, and the well-educated reader takes it for granted that this is the case. The reader assumes that the text derives wholly or mainly from the author's ideational effort and that the author has distinguished himself or herself from the work carried out by others, even if he or she cannot disregard the existence of texts by others" (p. 242). It's thus not enough that the text be finished; it also has to be new, springing entirely from the head of the author, and always distinguishing itself from the writing of other authors. As we have already noted, however, digital technologies force us to reconsider these presuppositions with respect to the published text; writing within the network may be published and yet incomplete, remaining open to addition and revision. Further, the openness of the digital text implies potential openness in our attribution of authorship, while the closed text carries with it

> the presupposition of the *pre-eminence of the author*. If the text is closed, it generally has an author (or a definite number of authors). Not only is the author the pure and simple generative source of the text but he or she also acts judicially, as it were, because he or she assumes specific rights and duties by the pure and simple fact of making him or herself author of that text. (Simone 1996, 240)

The ownership rights that come with the attribution of authorship of a closed text include the reservation to the author of the ability to reopen and revise a text, but those rights are accompanied by a number of responsibilities, including the obligation to "distinguish the original parts (= resulting entirely from his or her own invention) from those which are not original (= resulting from the invention of others)" (ibid.). The combination of these two assumptions—that the only author of a text is its named author, and that the author has scrupulously given credit for any borrowings—together produce the borders of our notion of plagiarism, an idea that "cannot be applied to the author who copies him or herself; only by plagiarizing someone else does plagiarism exist" (p. 241).

The specter of plagiarism makes clear that some of our anxiety about originality in our writing has to do with the dangers presented by its potential failure: we as scholars, as the producers of closed texts, are permitted to interact with the texts of others only in a passive, clearly designated fashion—and, by extension, others can only interact with our texts in a similar manner. This is one of the most crucial assumptions of the print-based modern literary system. But as the dominant mode of text delivery shifts from the read-only structure of print to the read-write structure of digital technologies, can this assumption of authorial primacy, and its attendant pressures toward pure originality, continue to make sense?

It's important to note that the kind of closed text that produces the presuppositions about authorship Simone describes has not always been the norm; numerous other modes of textual production—Simone points to the compilation, the miscellany, and the commentary—have at various times come into popular circulation, and have even at particular historical moments become the dominant form that authorship practices have taken. These forms, in which the words of others achieve preeminence over the voice of the author him- or herself, indicate not only that our notion of authorship is "not native and does not originate together with the texts (not even the written ones)," instead waxing and waning with changing historical circumstances, but also that, under certain of those circumstances, originality presents itself not as a virtue to be sought but as a danger to be avoided: "Theoretic and doctrinal innovation is created only through small increases, *per additamenta*, through additions, always gradual and suitably apportioned. If the text is original and evinces its own claim to originality, it risks being untenable. Originality is dangerous" (Simone 1996, 246, 247–48). The preferred act of authorship, under such circumstances, is that of bringing together the words of others, such that their juxtapositions, harmonies, and dissonances might produce an argument by implication.

I do not suggest that we are now in an era in which originality has once again become dangerous; our very language reveals through its connotations our preference for the original over the derivative. On the other hand, I do suggest that we no longer inhabit a world in which originality reigns unchallenged. Challenges to the premium placed on originality have been raised by theorists of authorship for some decades, dating back to Roland Barthes: "We know now that a text consists not of a line of words, releasing a single 'theological' meaning (the 'message' of the Author-God), but of a multi-dimensional space in which are married and contested several writings, none of which is original: the text is a fabric of quotations, resulting from a thousand sources of culture" (Barthes 1967/86, 52–53). Barthes refers here not simply to literal miscellanies or other compilations drawing together pieces of many texts, but to all writing; every text is "a fabric of quotations," whether its author is conscious of such borrowings or not, as the language that we use is never our creation, but rather that which has created us. Similarly, the development by Julia Kristeva (1986), during the same period, of the notion of "intertextuality" suggests that even the most ostensibly "original" of texts is in fact rife with references to other texts, and that it is impossible for a reader to approach any given text without reference to everything she has previously read or seen.

Such intertextuality becomes even more pronounced in the era of digital networks, as the structure of the hyperlink causes every text in the network to become part of every text that links to it, and thus each text is completed by every other, and becomes raw material for every other. Scholars of hypertext have long explored the ability of the link to make manifest the previously implicit relationships among texts, but more recently, scholars in media studies have explored another form of authorship within digital culture that consciously focuses on bringing together that "fabric of quotations" under the umbrella of the "remix" or the "mashup." Within the sphere of music, these forms have roots in the Jamaican culture of the late 1960s and early 1970s and attained broad penetration through the sampling practices of hip-hop artists from the 1970s forward. The phenomenon of the audio mashup may have achieved its greatest prominence with the 2004 release of Danger Mouse's *The Grey Album*, a coupling of Jay Z's *The Black Album* with *The Beatles*, more commonly known as the "White Album."[22] More broadly, however, remixes and mashups of multiple media forms have become a significant feature of Internet-based fan culture, as inexpensive and widely available audio- and video-editing tools and a proliferation of digitally available texts have encouraged the grassroots production of new kinds of content from the raw materials of the media.[23]

The question remains, however, whether such remix culture might fruitfully influence our own scholarly authorship practices. If, as Simone (1996, 249) puts it, the moment is coming when "the protective membrane of the texts [we produce] will decompose and they will once more become open texts as in the Middle Ages with all the standard concomitant presuppositions," we would be well served in considering the ways that our authorship practices might be affected. We might, for instance, find our values shifting away from a sole focus on the production of unique, original new arguments and texts to consider instead curation as a valid form of scholarly activity, in which the work of authorship lies in the imaginative bringing together of multiple threads of discourse that originate elsewhere, a potentially energizing form of argument via juxtaposition. Such a practice of scholarly remixing might look a bit like blogging, in its original sense: finding the best of what has been published in the digital network and bringing it together, with commentary, for one's readership. But it might also resemble a post-hoc mode of journal or volume editing, creating playlists, of sorts, that bring together texts available on the web in ways that produce new kinds of interrelationships and analyses among them.

The key, as usual, will be convincing ourselves that this mode of work counts as *work*—that in the age of the network, the editorial or curatorial labor of bringing together texts and ideas might be worth as much as, perhaps even more than, the production of new texts. As we've already seen, in contemplating peer-to-peer review, the greatest labor involved in transforming the Internet into a venue for the publication of serious scholarship may well be that of post-publication filtering—seeing to it that the best and most important new work receives the attention it deserves. Moreover, much of the writing we currently produce serves this same function, if in different form: recuperating overlooked texts, reframing past arguments, refuting earlier claims. Today, in the current system of print-based scholarship, this work takes the form of reviews, essays, articles, and editions; tomorrow, as new mechanisms allow, these texts might be multimodal remixes, mashing up theories and texts to produce compelling new ideas.

From Intellectual Property to the Gift Economy

The notion of the scholarly remix, however, raises some quite serious questions about the "ownership" of ideas—which is to say intellectual property—and its relationship to our authorship practices. If we come to accept remix as a mode of scholarly authorship, a form of academic *bricolage*, how will the relationship between the *bricoleur* and the texts he or she uses be understood? And what kind of relationship will be assumed to exist between the *bricoleur* and the products of his or her work?

As numerous recent explorations of the history of copyright and intellectual property have demonstrated, the original reasoning behind this legal protection of authors' rights over the distribution and use of their texts was the assumption that such protections would reserve to authors the ability to benefit financially from their labor, if there were benefits to be gained, thereby encouraging new invention and production.[24] Retaining ownership of intellectual property has, through the defense of copyright, come in fact to seem a prerequisite for continued production; why would anyone innovate if they couldn't benefit from the results of that innovation? However, as studies of intellectual property law also demonstrate, over the course of the twentieth and early twenty-first centuries copyright has increasingly come to be assigned to corporations, rather than being retained by the individuals whom the principle was in theory meant to protect.[25] In addition, as the term of copyright has repeatedly been extended long beyond the life of the author and is now straining to approximate the life of the corporation, its purpose has been radically eroded. Despite the rhetoric suggesting that the illegal downloading of music represents theft from artists, in fact, it's argu-

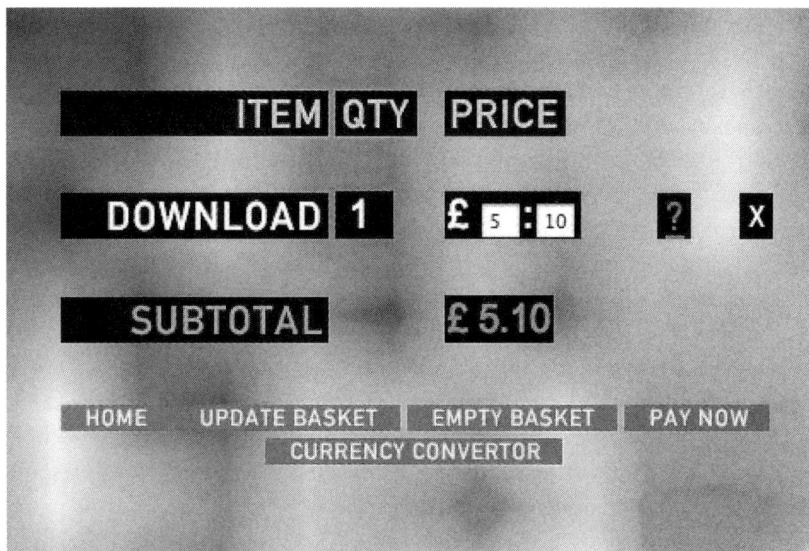

Fig. 2.2. Radiohead's "pay what you will" sale of *In Rainbows* (inrainbows.com)

able that illegal downloading more closely represents theft from corporations who have already appropriated the property of artists, by using increasingly arcane distribution channels to require them to work within a system that does not have their interests at heart (see Love 2000). This made sense, perhaps, when the costs of media production were such that only large organizations could afford to produce and distribute new material; now that such production is affordable, all one need do is straighten out the distribution channels, and then more of the profits will go directly to the artists.

Or so the theory goes. A number of musicians have experimented with such new modes of distribution, including, most famously, Radiohead, who released their *In Rainbows* album as a "pay what you will" download in 2007 (see fig. 2.2). Sixty-two percent of downloaders, perhaps unsurprisingly, paid nothing for the music, but the other 38 percent paid an average of $6 for the album. These statistics led a number of publications, including *Fortune* magazine, to declare the experiment a failure.[26] However, as other commentators pointed out, it's estimated that more than 2 million people downloaded the album, and at an average of $6 for 38 percent of those downloads, the result would be revenue of $4.56 million; compared with the $1 from each sale of a traditionally distributed album that goes to the artist, Radiohead may have more than doubled their income on the album. But even more remarkably, after the album was available for download for more than three months, it was also made available on iTunes, where it sold 30,000 copies during the first week, and it was also produced as a physical CD, selling another 1.75 million copies, plus 100,000 copies of a deluxe box set ("Exclusive").

It's arguable, of course, that only a band of the stature of Radiohead could have successfully pulled off an experiment like this one; others are still dependent on the channels of promotion and distribution provided by the music industry. But that industry is beginning—if all too slowly—to recognize the need for change, and other media companies are beginning to follow suit, gradually realizing that content is no longer king, and that, paradoxically, one can earn more by giving it away (Doctorow 2006a, 2006b). And that's the key point that I want to make with respect to scholarship, as digital publishing forces us to rethink what it means for us to "own" the texts we produce. Scholarly authors, after all, already exist in a fairly attenuated position with respect to copyright's original purposes; it's only the rare academic who earns much of anything directly from the publishing he or she does,[27] and the incentives that we have to produce—obtaining and maintaining academic positions, primarily—by and large include the financial in only an indirect sense. Clinging to a principle designed for the marketplace when our own mode of exchange doesn't adhere to marketplace values seems rather beside the point. Instead, we might usefully ponder the mode of exchange that best suits academic culture, and what rights authors must retain within that mode of exchange. We should carefully consider what the potential value in "giving it away" might be—not least that, as Radiohead found, and as author Cory Doctorow (2006b) has demonstrated across his own career, "releasing electronic texts of books drives sales of the print editions." If the purpose of scholarship is to be read, understanding its distribution as partially driven by a gift economy only makes sense.

One might look to the free and open-source software community for a model of such a gift economy; as Chris Kelty has explored, it's of course an imperfect community, but one that might teach us much about how to orient our work. Kelty introduces the concept of the "recursive public" to talk about this community, defining it as "*a public that is vitally concerned with the material and practical maintenance and modification of the technical, legal, practical, and conceptual means of its own existence as a public*" (Kelty 2008, 3); digital publishing tools might provide the scholarly community the opportunity to become precisely such a recursive public, one that understands itself as working toward a common goal, and that is explicitly focused on improving the communication systems that foster its work. By and large, programmers working on free and open-source software projects do so less out of any sense of altruism than out of the desire to work with better tools. So with scholarship: we already contribute our work to a community of scholars out of a primary desire for better knowledge; if we focus on the commons-based aspect of that community, giving our work away in a manner that acknowledges that its primary purpose is to be reused and repurposed, we have the potential to contribute to the creation of both better tools and a stronger sense of the scholarly public.[28]

Even within such a gift economy, however, numerous mechanisms remain through which authors can maintain some kinds of control over what becomes of their texts and ensure that they receive appropriate credit for their work. Most famous among these is Creative Commons licensing, which allows an author or other creator of intellectual content to specify precisely what rights to the material she is giving away; the license can allow the full reuse of the text while requiring attribution, or it can restrict reuse to non-commercial purposes, or it can even require that any resulting texts be shared in the same fashion as the original.[29] If we are to move scholarly communication back toward its basis in the gift economy, I'd argue, scholars must begin adopting Creative Commons licenses for their work, thus defining for themselves the extent to which they want future scholars to be able to reuse and remix their texts, thereby both protecting their right to be credited as the author of their texts and contributing to a vibrant intellectual commons that will genuinely "promote the Progress of Science and useful Arts."[30]

The point, finally, is not to promote one particular form of licensing for scholarly work over another, but rather to suggest that we might fruitfully separate our notions of authorship from their association with ownership, or at least to question that linkage, in order to think about more productive ways of distributing and sharing that work with the people we most want to read it.

From Text to . . . Something More

Across this chapter, I've focused on the degree to which a shift to networked publishing environments will require scholars to think about authorship in ways that diverge somewhat from our current assumptions and yet are latent within them: we need to think less about completed products and more about texts-in-process; less about individual authorship and more about collaboration; less about originality and more about remix; less about ownership and more about sharing. None of this is to say that the former structures will disappear, but rather that they'll be complicated by the modes of communication that network technologies privilege.

Aside from these somewhat abstract assumptions about the nature of authorship, however, the most obvious change that digital publishing encourages, the one that many academics leap to first when talking about the ability to publish via the web, is the expansion of our toolset. Digital technologies in scholarly publishing will allow us to begin to shift our thinking about the mode of our work away from a uniform focus on the traditional text-only formats, encouraging us instead to think about the ways that our work might interact with, include, and in fact *be* something more than just text.

This is not to suggest that everyone should be making YouTube videos instead of writing argumentative essays. In fact, as Clifford Lynch (2001) has argued, there's a value in ensuring that most of our production in this new network age retains its recognizable, traditional form:

> Recently there has been a lot of thinking about how to devise intellectual successors to the scholarly monograph that specifically exploit the online environment. One key idea is that while the definitive and comprehensive version of the work will be digital, there will also be a sensible (though impoverished) "view" of the work that can be reduced to printed form as a traditional monograph. This is critical in providing scholarly legitimacy in an intensively conservative environment that still distrusts the validity of electronic works of scholarship, and will thus be important in encouraging authors to create these new types of works. It allows authors to exploit the greater expressiveness and flexibility of the digital medium without alienating colleagues who haven't yet embraced this medium.

As Lynch here suggests, ensuring that our new texts have a sort of reverse-compatibility with the structures of a fundamentally conservative academy has been important in the early stages of the transition to digital publishing; print has served scholars well for the better part of six hundred years, and however quickly the world around us seems to be changing, the academy may do well to be cautious in its embrace of the next new thing. However, if we continue to focus our attention exclusively on the production of digital texts that can be translated, in whatever "impoverished" way, into print, the range of our potential innovation will remain quite narrow. The relative slowness of such change might be put in perspective by drawing attention to the fact that Lynch made the claim above in 2001, and yet we remain in exactly the same position, with precious little in the way of forward movement toward thinking about new possible structures for the successor to the scholarly book; we are still required to think of those successors in models that are analogous to print, when we might more productively start thinking of them as being far more multimodal.

What do I mean when I say "multimodal"? It's something more than simply multimedia; it's not just a new relationship between text and image, or image and audio, or other forms of representation. Those other forms are already embedded in many of the texts that we produce, and scholars have always been required to move ideas from one form to another in the process of writing. Art historians, for instance, have long translated the visual into the textual in the process of analyzing it, and recently the somewhat reduced costs of print production have enabled a more widespread inclusion of visual materials, without translation (or, rather, with a different form of translation), in the scholarly text. But such inclusion largely remains a mode of illustration rather than production; as Stuart Moulthrop (2005) has argued, academics cling tenaciously to an "old separation of media, whereby all things not of the letter must be exchanged for letters in order to enter the system of learning." We can thus write *about* images, but not *in* images; we can write *about* video, but not *in* video. As Moulthrop goes on to suggest, the clear separation among forms during previous eras of media transition made this possible; there was never a threat that the film about which I wrote could somehow bleed into the words with which I wrote about it:

> Earlier so-called communications revolutions wrought only partial transformations: the increased emphasis on the image in photography and film; the recovery of orality in telegraphy, telephony, and radio; the creation of mass consciousness through broadcasting. Though they began to challenge writing as the primary foundation of culture, these media did not affect the conditions of writing itself. This was good news for academics. It was possible to study just about any medium through the miracle of *content*—by which we meant, written representations of our experience of the other medium—without having to become much more than auditors or spectators. Among other things, this allowed the academy to draw a bright line between production work in various media (mere *techne*) and the writing of criticism and theory (the primary work of scholars).
>
> With the coming of cybernetic communication systems—hypertext, the World Wide Web, soon now the Semantic Web—the conditions of all media are strongly transformed, and writing is clearly included.

Now, when my computer translates my words into the very same digital substance in which sound, image, and other modes of representation exist, we encounter the potential for a radical change that doesn't just break down the boundaries between text and video—for instance, allowing me to embed illustrative clips within the analysis I produce of them (this is the case that Moulthrop covers by saying that "Writing is still writing, even with funkier friends")—but instead changes the fundamental nature of the analysis itself.

Resistance to allowing scholarly production to take non-textual form runs deeply in many fields, particularly those that have long reinforced the divide between *criticism* (art history, literature, media studies) and *practice* (studio art, creative writing, media production). But one of the explicit goals of many media studies programs over the last ten years has been finding a way within the curriculum to bridge the theory-practice divide: to give our production students a rigorously critical standpoint from which to understand what they're doing when they're making media; to give our critical studies students a hands-on understanding of how the forms about which they're writing come into being. And yet it remains only the rare scholar who brings criticism and production together in his or her own work—and for no small reason: faculty hired as conventional scholars are only rarely given credit toward promotion for production work; faculty hired to teach production are not always taken seriously as scholars. In fields such as media studies, we are being forced to recognize, one tenure case at a time, that the means of conducting scholarship is changing, and that the boundary between the "critical" and the "creative," if it exists at all, is arbitrary. My colleague Alex Juhasz, for instance, has written critically about YouTube but has also done a tremendous amount of work *on* YouTube, work that is inseparable from the critical analysis. Eric Faden, in a slightly different vein, is a film scholar working almost exclusively in the form of the video essay. In the coming years, more and more scholars in fields across the humanities will be taking up such unorthodox means of producing scholarship, in order to make arguments in forms other than the textual. Other scholars, including Tim Anderson and Tom Porcello, are working on audio *in audio form*, and in digital media studies, the list of scholars both writing about and producing interactive work includes Ian Bogost, Mary Flanagan, Noah Wardrip-Fruin, and too many others to name here.

Numerous possibilities exist for these future forms of argument across the humanities: exciting historical work is already being done in digital form, through the production of interactive archives and exhibits; visual anthropology has long used documentary film production in ways that other scholars in the field might adopt. Scholarly analysis, in other words, can take the form of video, producing a visual response to a cultural object or phenomenon; it might take the form of audio, layering sound in order to focus our attention on that which we ordinarily miss in the world around us; it might take the form of an interactive game, in which we encounter an interpretation of a scenario in the rules that govern it. It's not too much of a stretch, after all, to argue that if authorship practices have changed, the very nature of writing itself has changed as well—not just our practices, but the result of those practices.

But there's something more. At the beginning of this chapter, I made a number of claims about the significance for the process of academic writing of the technological shift from typewriter to word processor. However, that shift changed not only whose hands were on the keyboard, as well as the ways the thoughts that wind up in our texts come together, but also the very thing we wind up producing. A mildly tendentious example, perhaps, but I think a significant one: rather than putting ink onto paper, when my fingers strike the keys, I'm putting pixels onto a screen[31]—and, it cannot be said clearly enough, the pixels on the screen *are not my document*, as anyone who has experienced a major word processor crash can attest. The image of my document on the screen of my computer is only a representation, and the text that I am actually creating as I type does not, in fact, look anything like it, or like the version that finally emerges from my printer. The document that is produced from all this typing is produced only with the mediation of a computer program, which translates my typing into a code that very, very few of us will ever see (except in the case of a rather unfortunate accident) and that even fewer of us could read. On some level, of course, we all know this, though we're ordinarily exposed to the layers of code beneath the screen's representations only in moments of crisis; computers that are functioning the way we want do so invisibly, translating what we write into something else in order to store that information, and then retranslating it in order to show it back to us, whether on screen or in print.

It's important to remain cognizant of this process of translation, because the computer is in some very material sense cowriting with us, a fact that presents us with the possibility that we might begin to look under the hood of the machine, to think about its codes as another mode of writing, and to think about how we might use those codes as an explicit part of our production. As Moulthrop (2005) says, "[W]hen [John] Cayley opens the definition of writing to include programming, he registers a change in the status of the letter itself—crucially, a change that flows into writing from cybernetic media." If "the letter itself," the smallest unit of our discourse, has been thus transformed by the computer that encodes and represents it to us, it's arguable that we need to begin wrestling with that encoding process itself, to understand code as a mode of writing, to become literate in markup/computer languages as well as human languages.

The thought of looking under the hood like this, of being asked to understand not simply another publishing format, but another language entirely, will no doubt result in new kinds of anxieties for some authors. Perhaps we don't all need to become comfortable with code; perhaps literacy in the computer age can remain, for most of us, at the level of the computer's representations to us, rather than at deeper layers of the computer's translations. I raise the question of reading code, however, as a means of asking us to consider what a text is, and what it can be, in the digital age. If we have the ability to respond to video with video, if we can move seamlessly from audio files to images to text as means of representing music, it may behoove us to think about exactly what it is we're producing when we write, how it is that these different modes of communication come together in complex document forms. And, as the next chapter will argue, we need to think about textual structures at multiple levels, in order to develop new digital structures that can begin to do some of the work that the codex form has long done.

3

Texts

> [T]here are still many tricks that electronic technology is quite incapable of performing; still many structural, practical, and interpretative problems embedded in the new systems; still many radical and continuing limitations on the supposed electronic management of knowledge.
>
> —Ian Donaldson, "The Destruction of the Book"

> Books, the centuries-old foundation of textuality, can now be seen as overshadowed by a metatextuality that extends progressively to the whole complex of modes of representing the world, to all the different media, while continuing, nevertheless, to function as a referent. It is for this reason that the difficulty of perfecting and framing the methods for leafing through "pages" on screen witnesses both an effort to reconform the book as a nonbook, and at the same time the book's permanence.
>
> —Patrick Bazin, "Toward Metareading"

If, as I argued in the preceding chapters, peer review in a digitally networked environment might most productively become a process of peer-to-peer review, and if online authoring will require us to think differently about the relationships among individual authors, we might expect that moving the machinery of publishing online would similarly demand or result in some greater connectivity in the forms that our published texts assume. To some extent, this goes without saying: the very essence of the web lies in the hyperlink, and texts on the web seem destined to be connected via links of one form or another. In this chapter, however, I press a bit harder on what those connections might mean and how they might affect the kinds of texts we produce, the ways we distribute them, and the ways that they are, finally, read. In exploring those connections, I want to think less about the technology of the link per se than about what D. F. McKenzie (1999) has called "the sociology of texts," which is to say the ways that texts of all varieties interact, both with one another and with their readers. In thinking through the sociology of texts, we need to consider "the human motives and interactions which texts involve at every stage of their production, transmission, and consumption" (15). Because the dominant print-based forms of today's scholarly communication have been with us for so long, many of those motives and interactions have become invisible to us; texts simply are the way they are, or, when we do consider them more deeply, they are the ways that print requires them to be.

In what follows I will explore the kinds of interactions fostered by the current forms of scholarship—which have developed in concert with print's technologies of production, distribution, and use, but which aren't in any inescapable sense determined by those technologies—and how network-based communication might inspire new kinds of interactivity in our scholarship. When I talk about "interactivity" in this sense, however, I don't mean the kinds often associated with computer-based texts, which are imagined to be digital forms of the "choose your own adventure" text. Lev Manovich (2001, 55) has compellingly debunked what he refers to as "the myth of interactivity" in new media, pointing out that the term as used in this sense is tautological, "stating the most basic fact about computers." Instead, I'm interested in a more communicative sense of interaction across texts, between texts and readers, and among readers. These forms of interaction exist even in what seems like the static, discrete textual forms made possible by print, but the affordances of network-based communication present the potential for heightening and highlighting them in ways that could prove extremely powerful for the future of scholarship.

Although this chapter explores the new kinds of textual structures that network-based publishing might inspire, it doesn't attempt to take on *all* such structures. Most notably, I'm not primarily focused on the kinds of multimodal scholarship that I discussed at the end of the previous chapter, though I think that such new forms, especially as they're being pioneered in venues such as the online journals *Kairos* and *Vectors*, could have an enormous impact on the ways that we produce and support scholarly arguments. Multimodal texts, which make rich use of images, audio, video, and other forms of computer-processed data, enable authors to interact in new ways with their objects of study, and to create rich models of complex processes and ideas. In this chapter, however, I focus most of my attention on the kinds of scholarly texts that are primarily composed of *text*, in no small part because the new digital form that we're seeking might continue the work that the book has done for us for the last five centuries. What I hope to explore in the pages that follow are the possibilities for a new digital form that's as comfortable, engaging, information-rich, flexible, and inviting as the book itself has been—but that extends beyond the covers of the individual text to take advantage of the interactive possibilities that the network presents.

In order to begin exploring that new textual structure, it would be useful first to think carefully about what exactly the book has been, how its affordances have affected the organization of knowledge, and how our interactions with it have shaped our assumptions about the relationships between author, text, and reader that it mediates. During the December 2006 Modern Language Association convention in Philadelphia, Peter Stallybrass presented a paper whose title indicated that it would focus on the relationship between textual studies—or the application of material culture approaches to the study of textual production—and the book.[1] At the very outset of his presentation, however, Stallybrass overturned several basic assumptions about that form's production often unconsciously held by both literary scholars and textual critics. In asking who, exactly, it is that produces the thing we know as the book, he made a somewhat startling claim: *Authors* do not write books, he argued, but rather sentences or, on a larger scale, texts. Similarly, *printers* do not produce books, but rather pages. The primary argument that Stallybrass's paper sought to make was about the need for textual studies scholars to think in terms of pages, both bound and unbound, in order to escape what he called "the tyranny of the book."[2] While any such escape from tyranny in criticism is undoubtedly a good thing, our attention in *this* project needs to remain on the book, as it is the endangered form that we must either save or replace.

In setting up his argument about the need for textual scholars to focus on the page, however, Stallybrass suggested, almost as an aside, that the book is a production, finally, of the binder. This is a point I'd like to dwell on a bit, as it suggests that the bookness of the book derives less from its material composition—ink-on-paper—than from its organization, which in the case of print takes the form of sequenced, bound, and cut leaves. As Stallybrass (2002, 42) notes, conventional wisdom holds that the development of that form—specifically, the shift from the scroll to the codex—enabled "the capacity for random access," allowing a reader to turn immediately to any particular point in a text, thus facilitating the reader's active engagement in and manipulation of the textual object. Turning our material focus from print to binding as the source of bookness holds significant implications for scholars working on new, electronic modes of textuality, and in particular, on the future of the book. For if this is the case—that the formal properties of the book that have the greatest impact on our reading experience are derived not from print, but rather from the codex—researchers working on new ways of transforming ink-on-paper to pixels-on-screens may be addressing the wrong problem, or at least the wrong aspect of a knottier problem than it has at times appeared. As Johanna Drucker (2008, 217) has suggested, it's all too easy for the problem of the digital future of the book to get caught up in how the book *looks* rather than how it *works*; in order to imagine a new digital form for the book, we need to focus on what, and how, it communicates.

The task, in other words, is on some level to forget about the arrangement of pixels on the screen and instead focus on our experience of larger-scale structural or organizational matters. This is not to say that interface design isn't important; as scholars including Stan Ruecker and Alan Galey (2009) have recently argued, design is itself a hermeneutic process, always presenting an interpretation of the ways digital projects communicate. It's also evident that the absence of careful design can interfere with the reader's ability to engage with digital text. Stallybrass (2002) notes the irony, for instance, in what appears to be the computer's regression from the kinds of manipulation that the codex made possible, as many digital texts reimpose the limitations of the scroll on our reading practices. Despite having greater capacities for random access to texts via searching and other modes of linking, the web's reliance on scrolling text too often fails to take account of the ways that cognitive practices of reading are spatially organized. See, for instance, Geoffrey Nunberg's footnoted observation in "The Places of Books in the Age of Electronic Reproduction": "One ancillary effect of this homogenization of the appearance of electronic documents is to blur the sense of provenance that we ordinarily register subconsciously when we are reading. As a colleague said to me not long ago, 'Where did I see something about that the other day? I have a clear mental picture of a UNIX window'" (1993, 37n31). Stallybrass similarly notes the dislocation that results from the inability to stick one's finger between the pages of an electronic text to mark one's place. None of this is meant to imply that digital publishing ought to mimic the spatial arrangement of bound pages; if anything, too much current thinking about the design of digital texts is predicated on the structure of the book rather than any natively networked structure. Rather, I suggest that those of us working on the future of publishing online need to think in terms that are not just about page design, but rather about larger-scale textual structures, and about readers' interactions with and through those structures.

In what follows, I will explore a few projects focused on stretching the boundaries of textual structures in digital scholarship, exploring the ways these projects conceive of the possibilities for a web-native replacement for the codex form. An early draft of a portion of this chapter was posted for comment and discussion using one of these technologies, CommentPress; I later revised the article based upon the comments I received and republished it in CommentPress on MediaCommons, as well as in a more traditionally linear format in the *Journal of Electronic Publishing*.[3] This experiment allowed me, in some sense, to practice what I am preaching, but it also permitted some insight into the limitations of current web-based publishing technologies, as well as into some of the issues that publishing organizations face in the deployment of these technologies. None of the projects I discuss in this chapter should thus be imagined as a conclusion to the issues I'm exploring, but instead as various modes of exploration, ways of approaching the issues involved in electronic publishing from a broader structural perspective. At stake is not the success or failure of any particular technology, but rather our ability to produce a reading experience that provides net-native principles of organization as compelling as those of the codex, but with the extraordinary flexibility and multiplicity of the digital. Only in significantly broadening our sense of the text beyond the structures that have developed in print, I argue, will we be able to forge a new form for scholarship that will thrive electronically.

Documents, E-books, Pages

As I've suggested, much recent research on new systems of digital textuality has fallen into the trap of attempting all too literally to reproduce the printed page on digital screens through innovations in hardware or software—whether through various "e-book" readers such as Amazon's Kindle or computer-based document types such as the PDF (Portable Document Format) originated by Adobe. Many of these technologies have been reasonably successful, perhaps most notably the PDF, which has made possible the widespread distribution online of materials that either were originally in print or that are intended to wind up in print once again. Except for their mode of distribution, however, there's almost never anything particularly "net-native" about PDF-based texts, with little in their form that makes use of the digital environment in which they exist. These documents are, until printed, like paper under glass: mostly unmarkable, resisting interaction with an active reader or with other such documents in the network. More recent iterations of PDF software do allow users to annotate documents, but even so, such annotations remain superficial—the ability to add "sticky notes" or to mark in the margins of a static document is useful, but no deeper interaction with the text, its author, or its other readers is possible. Various modes of e-book hardware and software, ranging from the Expanded Books of the early 1990s Voyager Company through today's platforms such as the Kindle, have focused on becoming more genuinely digital in mode by providing readers with a set of tools that can be brought to bear on the text, including bookmarking, annotation, hyperlinking, and the like, all of which are simultaneously aimed at allowing the reader to traverse the text in ways that would be difficult, if not impossible, in print, while also providing the ability to mark the text so lamented by bibliophiles in contemplating on-screen reading.[4] Thus far, however, no e-book format, whether, in Clifford Lynch's (2001) terms, device-based or text-based, has been terribly successful at luring readers away from pages and toward screens.[5]

One of the problems with both the e-book reader and the portable document format—as well as, for that matter, the more generic HTTP/HTML-based web technologies that have produced billions upon billions of web pages—is visible in their very vocabulary: despite whatever innovations exist in "pages," "documents," or "e-books," we remain tied to thinking about electronic texts in terms of print-based, or, more specifically, codex-based, models. As Drucker notes, "Such nomenclature seems charged by a need to acknowledge the historical priority of books and to invoke a link between their established cultural identity and the new electronic surrogates" (2008, 216). The book and other forms of print have been critically important to the development of Western culture over the last six hundred years; they are so deeply ingrained in the ways we think that it becomes hard to imagine alternatives to them.[6] However, simply translating texts from paper to screen misses the point. There's a reason, after all, why so many of my students print the PDFs that I teach in my classes before they read them, and why the response of many readers to e-book formats is to talk about the smell of paper, the use of a pencil, or the comfort of reading in bed; each of these e-book forms loses many of the benefits of print in the process of trying to retain them.[7] While these technologies have demonstrated that the format of ink-on-paper can successfully be translated into pixels-on-screens, they've done so at the cost of remaining trapped in what Paul Levinson (1997, 126), following Marshall McLuhan, has referred to as "rear-view mirrorism," the difficulty we have defining new technologies except in terms of older ones. Take, for instance the example of the car: the first major insight of its inventors was the flash that one might produce a carriage that was able to move without the horse; had the thinking about such an invention remained at the phase of the "horseless carriage," however, many of the later developments in automotive design would have been impossible.[8]

In the same fashion, many of our attempts to produce a new form of electronic textuality have yet been unable to escape the structures of thought associated with the printed book, resulting, as Drucker (2008, 216) points out, in forms that "often mimic the most kitsch elements of book iconography while for the longest time the newer features of electronic functionality seemed not to have found their place in the interface at all."[9] These elements of the book mimicked in the e-book of course have their own histories; print-based features such as the title page, for instance, or the table of contents, or running page headers, or even something as simple as page numbers, took decades to coalesce, and as Kindle users are discovering, they don't translate easily to new environments. Worse, attempting to make those translations in any direct sense may prevent us from really seeing the ways the new format might best function; we are being distracted by our attempts to simulate "the way a book *looks*" from the more crucial problem of "extending the ways a book *works*" (p. 217). Once we've genuinely managed to make that turn, developing wholly new textual structures, today's concept of the "e-book" will no doubt sound naïve, a remnant of our tenuous toe-dipping into digital publishing.

Hypertext

Some part of that naïveté arises from the term's very indication that we have not yet found the net-native structure that will be as flexible and inviting to individual readers as the codex has been. The absence that the "e-book" highlights is not the means of moving from imprinting ink on paper to arranging pixels on screens, but the means of organizing and presenting digital texts in a structural sense, in a way that produces the greatest possible readerly and writerly engagement, that enables both the intensive development of an idea within the bounds of the electronic text and the extensive situation of that idea within a network of other such ideas and texts. Developing this format is of vital importance, not simply because the pleasure it can produce for readers will facilitate its adoption, but because it promises to have a dramatic impact on a wide range of our interactions with texts. As Roger Chartier has argued,

> If texts are emancipated from the form that has conveyed them since the first centuries of the Christian era—the codex, the book composed of signatures from which all printed objects with which we are familiar derive— by the same token all intellectual technologies and all operations working to produce meaning become similarly modified. . . . When it passes from the codex to the monitor screen the "same" text is no longer truly

the same because the new formal mechanisms that deliver it to the reader modify the conditions of its reception and its comprehension. (Chartier 1993, 48–49)

Those conditions of reception and comprehension, and the intellectual technologies that will be put to use in the production of further, future texts, are the true stakes of imagining new structures within which new kinds of digital texts can be published.

Hypertext is one of the few modes of radical experiment in textual form to which the digital has thus far given birth. This networked data structure, the invention of which is generally credited to Ted Nelson and Douglas Englebart, created the possibility of dramatically reorganizing text in networked ways, delinearizing and interlinking the text both within its own boundaries and in relation to other such texts. Numerous literary authors and critics saw the future in early hypertext publishing, envisioning a means of creating a new, more active relationship between the reader and the text. On the one hand, such thinkers pointed out the ways that hypertext's technologies succeeded in making manifest what had always been latent in the reader's encounter with print: "Hypertext only more consciously than other texts implicates the reader in writing at least its sequences by her choices" (Joyce 2000, 131).[10] In this, hypertext became the fulfillment of the ideal form of the codex. On the other hand, hypertext also promised a radical restructuring of worldview, of "intellectual technologies," as Chartier suggests, by lending its readers a new set of metaphors through which to build a whole new epistemology. Thus, J. David Bolter suggested early on that hypertext's structure might affect not just the ways we understand texts, but the ways we understand the world in its entirety:

> There is nothing in an electronic book that quite corresponds to the printed table of contents. . . . In this sense, the electronic book reflects a different natural world, in which relationships are multiple and evolving: there is no great chain of being in an electronic world-book. For that very reason, an electronic book is a better analogy for contemporary views of nature, since nature today is often not regarded as a hierarchy, but rather as a network of interdependent species and systems. (Bolter 1991, 105)

In leaving behind the codex, in eliminating the "great chain of being" enforced by the book, such critics suggested, hypertext would enable a new enlightenment to dawn, resulting in, among other things, the leveling of the

for directions click yes (y)-- to start press Return

©1987 Michael Joyce
The Eastgate Press Edition 1990
PO Box 1307
Cambridge, MA 02238

Fig. 3.1. Opening screen, Michael Joyce's *Afternoon* (screenshot from the author's collection)

previously hierarchical relationship between author and reader, elevating the reader to full participation in the production of the text's meaning.

But—and this is one of the dirty little secrets of electronic textuality, one that doesn't get spoken terribly often—hypertext can often be difficult to read. And to teach: the vast majority of my students have visceral reactions against hypertext every time I introduce them to it. Some of what they hate, of course, may be attributed to the general appearance of datedness that most of the classic hypertexts now have, given that the most crucial Storyspace-composed texts haven't been ported to OS X-native formats, thus requiring that they be run in "Classic" mode, a mode no longer available since the release of OS 10.5 and one that was clunky even when it was available under OS 10.4 (see fig. 3.1).[11] But when pressed to think beyond the slowness, the small window, the pixelated fonts, what my students most often voice is their sense of disorientation, their lostness within the world of the text. They stab randomly at it, trying to find their way somewhere; they wander aimlessly, trying to make sense of their paths; they finally give up, not at all sure how much of the text they've actually read, or what they should have taken from it. As critics including Christopher Keep (1999, 165) have pointed out, the disorientation produced by hypertext's apparent immateriality can have powerful physical and metaphysical effects: "Hypertexts refigure our perception of ourselves as closed systems: sitting before the computer monitor, mouse in hand, and index finger twitching on the command button, we are engaged in a border experience, a moving back and forth across the lines which divide the human and the machine, culture and nature." This "back and forth" cannot be experienced neutrally, as it suggests a profound dislocation of the self in the encounter with the machinic other.

The negative response to hypertext among contemporary students often gets dismissed as a kind of reactionary technophobia resulting from tradition-bound understandings of textuality, and not without reason; we've taught them, and they've learned well, to value the organizational strategies of the book. Students of mine, in fact, who've been willing to rough it through the confusions of a text like Thomas Pynchon's *Gravity's Rainbow* have felt stymied by Michael Joyce's *Afternoon*, unable to discern from the text the most basic rules for its comprehension. But I'm unconvinced that the problem that this generation of students has with hypertext is entirely a retrograde one; one of the other issues that they point to, in their complaints about the hypertext form, is feeling manipulated. Hypertext isn't really interactive, they argue; it only gives the *illusion* of reader involvement—and certainly only the illusion that the hierarchy of author and reader has been leveled: *clicking*, they insist, is not the same as *writing*. In fact, hypertext caters not to the navigational and compositional desires of the reader, but to the thought processes of the author. Hypertext, after all, was originally imagined in Vannevar Bush's classic 1945 essay "As We May Think," not as a technology through which readers would encounter a single text, but as a means for researchers to organize their thoughts about multiple texts and share those thoughts with other researchers. Similarly, Nelson (1965, 84) describes "the original idea" of his Xanadu project as having been the production of "a file for writers and scientists." The "we" doing the thinking in both Bush's and Nelson's visions was the author and his descendants, not average readers. Insofar as hypertext attempts in its form to more accurately replicate the structures and processes of human thought, it is the processes of the *author's* thought that are represented, often leaving the reader with the task of determining what the author was thinking—thus effectively reinscribing the author-reader hierarchy at an even higher level.

Such a focus on authorial desire wasn't a necessary element of early interactive texts; in addition to the Storyspace-style hypertexts such as *Afternoon*, the personal computing environments of the late 1970s and early 1980s gave rise to a number of "interactive fiction" titles such as *Adventure* and *Zork*. These texts, part narrative and part game, provided an often dungeon-like space that users explored, solving puzzles, fighting battles, and unlocking new parts of the textual world for further exploration. Such interactive fiction relied on a parser that took textual inputs from a user, read them for comprehensible commands (such as "go north," "open window," or "take rock"), and selected the appropriate outputs. While a text like *Zork* arguably bore less in common with narrative in any traditional sense than it did with games, particularly of the Dungeons & Dragons role-playing variety, the mode of interactivity that it relied upon was far closer to the hypertextual ideal of reader-as-coauthor than that of hypertext itself.

Given the original publication dates and platforms of *Zork* and *Adventure*, they should be equally difficult to access today as are *Afternoon* and the other Eastgate-published hypertexts. However, as Dennis Jerz pointed out (2009), Infocom, the primary publisher of interactive fiction in the early 1980s, designed a virtual machine through which those titles run; all that is required to operate the virtual machine on any new platform is a new interpreter for that platform, and the fans of interactive fiction, many of them technologists, have over the years produced the new interpreters that have kept *Zork* and *Adventure* alive even on today's newest operating systems and devices. Had early hypertext such as *Afternoon* run in such a virtualized, interpretable environment, its user base might have been able to help the publisher keep the texts alive. But it's also worth suggesting that the deeper level of interactivity of the writing user of interactive fiction, as opposed to the clicking reader of hypertext, might have contributed to the creation of that actively invested user base in the first place.[12]

Experiments in hypertext thus may have pointed in the general direction of a digital publishing future, but were finally hampered by difficulties in readerly engagement, as well as, I would argue, by having awakened in readers a desire for fuller participation that hypertext could not itself satisfy. For this reason, I suggest that if we are going to make any real headway in bridging the gap between our evident abilities with respect to arranging pixels on screens and the difficulties that remain with organizing texts in digital environments—in moving away from thinking about electronic publishing as a problem revolving around the future of *print* and instead thinking of it as a problem related to the future of the *codex*—we need to think differently about the networked relationships among our texts, and among the readers who interact with them. Enormous amounts of research have been done on the means of situating text within a digital network—on making text transmissible, comfortably readable onscreen, and so forth. All of this is necessary, of course, and no doubt a precursor to the problems on which several contemporary projects are focused: the need to situate text within a network that is not just digital but interactive, fostering communication that is not just one-way, from author to reader, but multi-directional, from reader back to author, among readers, among authors, across texts. This network is fundamentally social in its orientation; as John Seely Brown and Paul Duguid (2000, 18) have convincingly argued, the ends of information are always human ends, and thus the communication of that information must always follow social purposes; similarly, Drucker (2008, 221) reminds us that the book is not, and has never been, separable from the interactions we have with it. In building the scholarly communication network of the future, a network that can foster the discursive exchange and development of ideas among peers that is ostensibly the purpose of all scholarship, we need to create structures that foreground those social interactions that we have with and through texts.

Database-Driven Scholarship

One key element in building such a network will be a shift in our understanding of the relationship between the individual text and the many other texts to which it might potentially connect. Lev Manovich has convincingly argued in *The Language of New Media* (2001) that the constitutive features of computerized media forms include the modularity of the media elements they involve, the automated processes that can be used to bring them together, and the variable nature of the texts that such processes create. If this is so, it stands to reason that digital publishing structures designed to facilitate work within the database logic of new media, in which textual and media objects can be created, combined, remixed, and reused, might help scholars to produce exciting new projects of the kind that I discussed near the end of the last chapter. Such a platform, for instance, might fruitfully allow authors to create complex publications by drawing together multiple preexisting texts along with original commentary, thus giving authors access to the remix tools that can help foster curation as a sophisticated digital scholarly practice. Curated texts produced in such a platform might resemble edited volumes, whether by single or multiple authors, or they might take as yet unimagined forms, but they would allow users to access and manipulate a multiplicity of objects contained in a variable, extensible database, which could then be processed in a wide range of ways, as well as allowing users the ability to add to the database and to create their own texts from its materials.

Numerous such databases exist, of course; extensive digital projects focused on the creation of archives and repositories have developed since the early days of popular computing. The oldest and most famous such archive may be Project Gutenberg, founded by Michael Hart in 1971. Hart's philosophy in beginning the production of this archive was that "anything that can be entered into a computer can be reproduced indefinitely" (Hart 1992); perhaps more importantly, anything so entered can also be processed in a wide variety of ways. The potential value of creating a full archive, in "Plain Vanilla ASCII," of the wealth of texts available in the public domain is evident: these texts can not only be read on a wide variety of platforms, but also repurposed in a range of other projects. The scholarly value of Project Gutenberg, however, may be open to question; as Hart has noted, "Project Gutenberg has avoided requests, demands, and pressures to create 'authoritative editions.' We do not write for the reader who cares whether a certain phrase in Shakespeare has a ':' or a ';' between its clauses. We put our sights on a goal to release etexts that are 99.9% accurate in the eyes of the general reader" (ibid.). Scholars, however, do care about the authoritativeness of the objects with which they work, and therefore a range of authoritative digital archives of work by and about a number of authors has been created, including *The William Blake Archive*, *The Walt Whitman Archive*, *The Swinburne Project*, and so on. These projects are grounded in the large-scale digitization of published and unpublished texts, images, and other materials related to the work and lives of these authors, creating extensive searchable databases of digital objects that potentially can be reused in a wide range of scholarly projects.

The problem in developing such new forms of publication as these databases, however, is what Jerome McGann (2005, 112) has referred to as one of the crises facing the digital humanities: such "scholarship—even the best of it—is all more or less atomized"; the various digital texts and collections that have been created are "idiosyncratically designed and so can't talk to each other," and there are no authoritative, systemic, searchable bibliographies of these projects that enable scholars to find the digital objects they'd like to reuse.[13] In response to these problems, McGann and the Applied Research in 'Patacriticism group at the University of Virginia began developing NINES, the Networked Infrastructure for Nineteenth-century Electronic Scholarship, as "a three-year undertaking initiated in 2003 . . . to establish an online environment for publishing peer-reviewed research in nineteenth-century British and American studies" (p. 116). NINES has since become an aggregator for peer-reviewed digital objects published in a range of venues. This project, which has received significant funding from the Mellon Foundation, was established as a means of averting atomization in the digital humanities, bringing separate projects into dialogue with one another. The NINES goals, as described on the site ("What Is NINES?"), are:

- to serve as a peer-reviewing body for digital work in the long 19th-century (1770–1920), British and American;
- to support scholars' priorities and best practices in the creation of digital research materials;
- to develop software tools for new and traditional forms of research and critical analysis.

Among the tools that NINES has developed are Juxta, a system for online textual collation and analysis, and Collex, which forms the core of the NINES site today. Collex is an aggregator tool that searches multiple scholarly databases and archives, with fifty-eight federated sites represented, including library and special collection catalogs, repositories, journals, and other projects; Collex allows a user to find objects in a wide range of such locations and then to "collect" and tag such items, structuring them into exhibits (see fig. 3.2).

Collex's tagging function serves to add user-generated metadata to expert-created data within the various collections and archives that NINES draws together, but the key aspect of this "folksonomy" arises when the user then reshares the tagged objects; as Kim Knight (2006) has argued, "Collex's folksonomical characteristics only take on interpretive importance as the community of users develops and collections and exhibits are shared." As NINES/Collex developer Bethany Nowviskie has noted (2007, 1), however, one of the project's primary focuses is on precisely such an "expansion of interpretive methods in digital humanities," through the connection and juxtaposition of digital objects and the production of commentary on and around them. The potential impact of such curatorial work could be enormous, as scholars find new ways to discover, manipulate, connect, and comment upon digital research objects. One problem facing the system, however, is that, as Madeleine Clare Elish and Whitney Trettien (2009, 6) point out, "in reality, the information that NINES aggregates is quite shallow, most of it only metadata, or information about information." Most of the "objects" that NINES is currently able to retrieve in a search are simply citations or catalog entries rather than the objects themselves. However, as access to primary objects alongside this metadata is increased, Collex's usefulness as a research and publishing tool will no doubt grow.

Other such collection- and exhibit-building projects are in production as well. Most notably, the Center for History and New Media is developing Omeka, a simple but extensible open-source platform that, once installed,

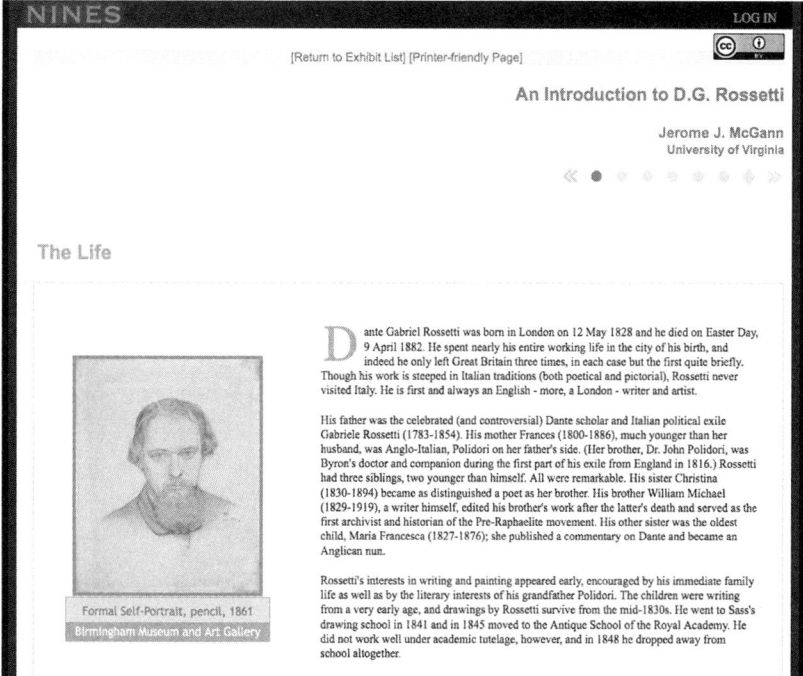

An Introduction to D.G. Rossetti

Jerome J. McGann
University of Virginia

The Life

Dante Gabriel Rossetti was born in London on 12 May 1828 and he died on Easter Day, 9 April 1882. He spent nearly his entire working life in the city of his birth, and indeed he only left Great Britain three times, in each case but the first quite briefly. Though his work is steeped in Italian traditions (both poetical and pictorial), Rossetti never visited Italy. He is first and always an English - more, a London - writer and artist.

His father was the celebrated (and controversial) Dante scholar and Italian political exile Gabriele Rossetti (1783-1854). His mother Frances (1800-1886), much younger than her husband, was Anglo-Italian, Polidori on her father's side. (Her brother, Dr. John Polidori, was Byron's doctor and companion during the first part of his exile from England in 1816.) Rossetti had three siblings, two younger than himself. All were remarkable. His sister Christina (1830-1894) became as distinguished a poet as her brother. His brother William Michael (1829-1919), a writer himself, edited his brother's work after the latter's death and served as the first archivist and historian of the Pre-Raphaelite movement. His other sister was the oldest child, Maria Francesca (1827-1876); she published a commentary on Dante and became an Anglican nun.

Rossetti's interests in writing and painting appeared early, encouraged by his immediate family life as well as by the literary interests of his grandfather Polidori. The children were writing from a very early age, and drawings by Rossetti survive from the mid-1830s. He went to Sass's drawing school in 1841 and in 1845 moved to the Antique School of the Royal Academy. He did not work well under academic tutelage, however, and in 1848 he dropped away from school altogether.

Formal Self-Portrait, pencil, 1861
Birmingham Museum and Art Gallery

Fig. 3.2. Introduction to a NINES exhibit (nines.org)

enables the creation, organization, and publication of archival materials in a wide range of formats, producing sophisticated narratives by combining digital objects with text about them. Omeka's ease of use and granular publishing structure resemble that of a blog engine, leading Dan Cohen (2008) to describe the project as "WordPress for your exhibits and collections." Like Collex, Omeka is developing means of accessing and ingesting materials from existing repositories of digital texts and objects, thus potentially enabling scholars to repurpose those objects in engaging ways. While the "exhibit" has not been a standard mode of scholarly production in fields outside art history, we might consider the new kinds of scholarly inquiry such a mode of curation could inspire. As more of our work within the humanities comes to engage with mediated primary materials such as visual representations and digital archives, the more we might fruitfully create new forms of networked arguments driven by the juxtaposition of digital objects and their analysis.

Furthermore, the availability of digital objects is producing new kinds of research questions. In addition to the collection and exhibit software discussed above, a wide range of tools is being developed to support what has been called "data-driven scholarship" in the humanities; these include SEASR (Software Environment for the Advancement of Scholarly Research), which allows scholars to perform sophisticated forms of textual analysis, process the results of that analysis, and create engaging visualizations of the data that the analysis returns. Other tools such as Pliny allow scholars to create rich annotations for the objects they are studying and then organize those annotations in ways that highlight the relationships among the objects. Annotation, organization, analysis, and visualization represent new, computer-native modes of academic work, all of which permit scholars to find and analyze patterns at a scale previously impossible. One problem tools such as these face, however, is uptake; as a report from a meeting titled "Tools for Data-Driven Scholarship: Past, Present, Future" notes, "the vast majority of scholars who are not directly involved with the creation of digital tools and collections are not adopting these new applications and resources in the number one might anticipate this far into the digital revolution" (Cohen et al. 2009). To some extent, the report indicates, failures in uptake have to do with lapses in communication; scholars are too often unaware that such tools exist.[14] Even when traditional scholars do find these tools, there's often lingering uncertainty about what exactly one might *do* with them and why—what they'll accomplish, what the resulting project will look like, what it will tell us that we haven't yet seen. Those questions can be answered only when digital humanists engage and experiment with such computational tools, and thereby give rise to new kinds of scholarly questions.

Each of the projects discussed above is focused on the interactions among texts that the modularity, automatization, and variability of computer-based media might enable. What hasn't yet been fully realized in many of these projects, however, is the key aspect of interaction between the reader and the text; despite all of the wonderful work being done on NINES, through Omeka, and in a range of other exciting digital tools, that work remains largely author-centric. Given the discursive purposes of scholarship, it might be useful to explore the ways that, long before the development of the digital network, the circulation of texts operated within and was driven by the social networks of their readers.

Reading and the Communications Circuit

Scholars working on areas of material culture studies such as the history of the book, as well as those literary critics focused on reader reception, have long included among their interests the social networks formed by readers and their effects on the dissemination and the reception of texts. Leah

Price (2004, 309–10), in an essay reviewing the vast number of approaches to the study of reading as a cultural activity, notes that some scholars trace an historical trajectory from "the open spaces of antiquity (gardens, porticoes, squares, streets) to the closed sites of the Middle Ages (churches, monks' cells, refectories, courts)," while the act of reading also "carved out privacy within communal institutions such as the coffee shop, the public library, and the railway carriage," both trends suggesting an increasing privatization of the act of reading. However, Price also notes that even at its most solitary, reading has always had communal aspects. These social aspects of reading have been explored by scholars ranging from Robert Darnton (1982), who focuses on books' circulation as a manifestation of a "communications circuit," to Elizabeth Long (1993), who argues that, in Price's words, "readers need others to set an example, to provide a sounding board for reactions to texts, to recommend and criticize and exchange books" (Price 2004, 306), to Stanley Fish (1980), who has argued most famously for the role of "interpretive communities" in shaping readers' potential responses to texts.

Texts have thus never operated in isolation from their readers, and readers have never been fully isolated from one another, but different kinds of textual structures have given rise to and interacted within different kinds of communications circuits. Newspapers and pamphlets, as most famously studied by Jürgen Habermas (1989) and Benedict Anderson (1991), developed their influence in close concert with the rise of a coffee-house culture in which the events and polemics of the day were discussed and debated, giving birth not simply to a Habermasian sense of the "public sphere," but to a sense of the public inhabiting that sphere, the "imagined community" of the nation.[15] Books, similarly, moved within a set of social and communal structures that greatly affected their reception and comprehension, including libraries and reading groups, which not only assisted readers in the selection of texts but also provided space for their discussion. That said, the technology of the book, which fostered the notion of the text as the discrete, unique, authentic product of an individual author—what Joseph Esposito (2003) has referred to as "the myth of the primal book"—similarly fostered a sense of the discrete reader with whom it interacted, shifting the predominant mode of reading from a communal reading-aloud to a more individualized, isolated, and silent mode of consumption.[16]

This isolated mode of reading overwhelmingly dominates our understanding of book-consumption today, and particularly the form done by scholars. The library model of textual circulation, once understood to be a communal enterprise, now comes to seem profoundly individualistic: books are checked out and read by one person at a time, in retreat from interaction with the world. Indeed, when we imagine scholarly interactions with the bulk of printed texts today, particularly within the humanities, the primary images that arise are of isolation: individual scholars hunched over separately bound texts, each working individually, whether in their separate offices or in the silent reading rooms of the major research libraries. Of course scholars need to read and reflect in relative silence and retreat in order to understand and process the texts with which they work, as well as to produce more texts from those understandings. But the isolated aspect of this mode of reading has come to dominate our sense of the practice of reading as a whole, and in so doing the scholar has come to partake of the myth of individual genius, in which the great man produces noble ideas wholly from his own intellectual resources.[17] As Walter Ong has suggested,

> Writing is a solipsistic operation. I am writing a book which I hope will be read by hundreds of thousands of people, so I must be isolated from everyone. While writing the present book, I have left word that I am "out" for hours and days—so that no one, including persons who will presumably read the book, can interrupt my solitude. (Ong 2002, 100)

Such an understanding of the operation of scholarship ignores the ways that the communal lingers in the circuit, if only in submerged ways; the scholar alone in his or her office with a book is never wholly alone, but is always in conversation with that book's author,[18] and the products of this scholar's readings are likewise intended to contribute to an ongoing conversation with other thinkers in the field. This conversation takes place at an often glacial pace, as years elapse between thought and utterance, in the form of the book's publication, and between utterance and response, in the form of reviews of or responses to that book, but it is a conversation nonetheless.

This perspective on the practices of scholarly discourse is meant to suggest that, in attempting to reproduce the book form electronically, technologists have for too long focused on the isolated practices of reading—the individual reader, alone with a screen—rather than the communal engagement in discussion and debate to which those practices are, on some level, meant to give rise. Scholars operate in a range of conversations, from classroom interactions with students to conference discussions with colleagues; they need to have available to them not simply the library model of texts circulating among individual readers, but also the coffee-house model of public reading and debate. This interconnection of individual nodes into a collective fabric is the strength of the network, which not only physically binds individual machines, but also can bring together the users of those machines, at their separate workstations, into a communal whole.

There's nothing particularly revolutionary in this insight; "The network can create virtual connections among otherwise isolated individuals!" is little more than the kind of utopian thinking that's colored Internet studies since Howard Rheingold's *The Virtual Community* was first published in 1993. My interest in thinking about the relationship between the social network and the structure of online texts should not be read as suggesting that such wired community will solve all of the problems of contemporary scholarly publishing. I do argue, however, that understanding the ways that texts circulate within and give rise to communities will be a necessary component of any successful electronic publishing venture. Given that the strength of the network with respect to the circulation of text is precisely its orientation toward the commons—that many readers can interact with the same text at the same time—developers of textual technologies would do well to think about ways to situate those texts within a community, and to promote communal discussion and debate within those texts' frames. Developers of new textual technologies and publishing systems must recognize that, on the one hand, simply publishing texts online, finding ways to reproduce the structures of the book in digital form, is insufficient, because the network cannot, and should not, replicate the codex; and that, on the other hand, simply moving toward a more internally networked form of publishing will likewise not revolutionize the circulation of texts, as the emphasis remains on the individual text, the individual author, the individual mind. The processed book, as Esposito (2003) has argued, cannot remain isolated from other texts: "By being placed within a network, where it is pointed to and pointed from, where it is analyzed and measured and processed and redistributed, a book reveals its connections to all other books." And, as Richard Lanham (1992, 203) noted in an early review essay on studies of electronic textuality, these connections have the potential to alter "the whole idea of scholarly originality, research, and production and publication"—but such transformations can only succeed if the medium's interactivity and nonauthoritative structures are fully mobilized in our new textual forms.[19] It's no paradox that my students resist hypertext while embracing Facebook; the generation celebrated by *Time* magazine as the "Person of the Year" in late 2006—"you" (Grossman 2006)—expects that the reader will likewise be allowed to write.

The speedy rise to popularity of academic blogging, and in particular in the success of a range of scholarly group blogs such as *The Valve* in literary studies (Holbo et al.), *Crooked Timber* in political philosophy (Bertram et al.), *Cliopatria* in history (Bady et al.), and *Language Log* in linguistics (Lieberman et al.), indicates that scholars, and not just students, desire such interaction. Many scholars feel over-isolated, longing for new modes of collaboration and discussion, and such blogs have enabled a kind of conference-without-walls in which new ideas and texts can be discussed in something closer to real time. Moreover, contrary to the sense of some more curmudgeonly folks that the kinds of casual writing done on scholarly blogs can only detract from one's ability to produce "serious" work by stealing time and focus or by encouraging speed at the cost of deliberativeness, in fact, many academic bloggers argue that their blogging and the discussions on various other blogs have helped them produce more substantive work. By revitalizing discourse among peers, blogs have helped revive the coffee-house model of textual circulation.

But this coffee-house model still largely revolves around the contemporary equivalent of newspaper and pamphlet publishing, rather than the longer, more deliberative form of the book. One question that remains is whether the library model of the circulation of single-author, long-form texts meant to be consumed in relative isolation over longer periods of time might similarly benefit from the kinds of interaction that blogs produce, and if so, how. The library in such a model would become not simply a repository, but instead fully part of a communications circuit that facilitates discourse rather than enforcing silence. Many libraries are already seeking ways to create more interaction within their walls; my institution's library, for instance, hosts a number of lecture series and has a weekly "game night," each designed to help some group of its users interact not simply with the library's holdings, but with one another. Games may seem a frivolous example of the contemporary academy's drive to cater to the younger generation's relatively nonintellectual interests, but it is in fact hoped that patrons who use the library in such a fashion will not only be more likely to use it in traditional ways— more likely, for instance, to feel comfortable approaching a research librarian for help with a project—but also more empowered to collaborate with one another, breaking the library's stereotypical hush.

Libraries are interested in establishing themselves as part of a scholarly discursive network, and for that reason emphasizing the development of electronic publishing technologies based on an individualist sense of book circulation—on the retreat into isolation that accompanies our stereotypical imaginings of the library—threatens to miss the point entirely, ignoring the ways that the book itself has always served as an object of discussion, and thus overlooking the real benefits of liberating the book's content from the codex form. Network interactions and connections of the types provided by blog engines can revitalize academic discourse not just in its pamphlet/coffee-house mode, but also in its book/library mode, by facilitating active reader engagement with texts, promoting discussion within the text's own frame, and manifesting the ways that each individual text is, and has always been, in dialogue with numerous texts that have preceded it, as well as others yet to come.

CommentPress

A number of projects underway attempt to reimagine reading as a socially situated process. Among the most significant of these is CommentPress, a blog-based publishing engine developed by the Institute for the Future of the Book, which seeks to promote dialogue within and around long-form texts in two primary ways: first, by structuring those texts around chunks that can be interlinked in linear and non-linear fashions, and that can take advantage of the ability to link to (and receive links from) other such texts in the network; and second, by allowing those chunks of texts to be commented on and discussed at various levels of granularity, from the whole document to the individual paragraph. The goal of CommentPress stems from the desire

> to see whether a popular net-native publishing form, the blog, which, most would agree, is very good at covering the present moment in pithy, conversational bursts but lousy at handling larger, slow-developing works requiring more than chronological organization—whether this form might be refashioned to enable social interaction around long-form texts. ("About CommentPress" 2007)

Such interconnections and discussions are possible in large part because CommentPress builds upon a popular blogging engine, WordPress. As I noted in the last chapter, blogs are arguably the first successful web-native mode of electronic publishing, and their rapid spread and relative robustness suggest that their tools might be applicable to a range of other potential digital publishing modes. The conventional structure of a blog privileges immediacy—the newest posts appear first on the screen, and older posts quickly lose currency, moving down the blog's front page and eventually falling off it entirely, relegated to the archives. This emphasis on the present works at cross purposes with much long-form scholarship, which needs stability and longevity in order to make its points. But, as I've argued elsewhere, such scholarship might adopt from blogs their community-oriented structure, in which posts are generally made to elicit comment, and in which responses from other authors produce links on the original posts to which they refer (see Fitzpatrick 2007a). CommentPress allows commenting technologies to be usefully appropriated to a number of forms of scholarly publishing, ranging from the article to the long-form monograph, making manifest the recognition that readers of scholarly texts are nearly always themselves authors in other venues.

I have worked with the Institute for the Future of the Book for the last several years, most notably on MediaCommons, an electronic scholarly network focused on media studies that hopes to reground the purposes of scholarly publishing in the desire for communication among a group of peers. The Institute has conducted a number of experiments focused on new textual structures, seeking to devise ways to publish long texts online in engaging, readable formats. These experiments, by and large, have sought to enable conversation in and around digitally published texts. As Bob Stein suggested to a reporter from *The Chronicle of Higher Education*, the electronic text can powerfully overcome the codex's isolation: "[B]est of all would be if readers could talk to each other, and if readers could talk to the author, because the reason for a book is to afford conversation across space and time, and so why shouldn't some of that conversation take place literally within the book itself?" (Young 2006) CommentPress is one of the primary tools through which the Institute hopes to facilitate some of that conversation.

The deep origins of CommentPress lie in a project with McKenzie Wark who, in preparing the manuscript for his 2007 book *Gamer Theory*, was persuaded to collaborate with the Institute in putting a draft of the text online. Because of the text's structure, the online version (titled *GAM3R 7H30RY* so that Wark could distinguish Google hits mentioning the online text from those mentioning the print book) easily adapted itself to publication through a blogging engine. However, Wark and the Institute early expressed an interest in subverting one of the basic structures of the blogging hierarchy: rather than keeping each chunk of the "original" text up top, with comments relegated to a spot further down the screen, Wark and the Institute's developers collaborated on a design (see fig. 3.3) that placed the text and the comments side-by-side, emphasizing the conversational principle that they hoped the publication would foster.[20] *GAM3R 7H30RY* lent itself to being published in this fashion in part because the text was already "chunked," written in a rigidly algorithmic structure, with 9 alphabetically sequential chapters, each

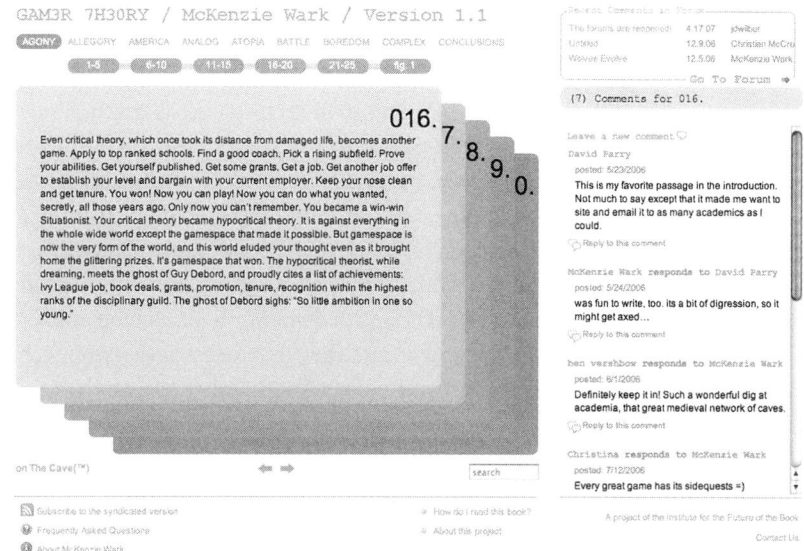

Fig. 3.3. McKenzie Wark, *GAM3R 7H30RY* (futureofthebook.org/gamertheory)

containing 25 paragraphs, with a strict 250-word limit per paragraph; as the paragraphs themselves were often aphoristic, many of them stood alone well, and reader comments thus could be closely associated with each paragraph of the text. However, the translation of what was originally intended to be a traditional codex book into this non-linear structure nonetheless created some complications: each paragraph looked a bit more free-standing than it really was; a reader couldn't simply enter and exit the text at any random point; readers often left questions or comments on early chunks about issues that were addressed in later parts of the text. Moreover, publishing Wark's text online was extraordinarily labor-intensive, as the interface required too much manual tweaking to be readily adaptable for more general publishing purposes.

The next phase in the Institute's development of CommentPress was its publication of Mitchell Stephens's article "Holy of Holies: On the Constituents of Emptiness" (2006) as what they termed a "networked working paper," imagining this paper, as their blog entry announcing its publication suggested, as "small steps toward an n-dimensional reading/writing space" (Vershbow 2006b). This new experiment was in part designed to help develop means for publishing texts that aren't as quite so self-chunking as Wark's manuscript was, so that a reader could simultaneously have a sense of the text's whole and pay close attention to its individual parts. In the design for "Holy of Holies," the Institute gave each paragraph its own comment stream, allowing the comment area to the right of Stephens's text to become dynamic, changing as the user selects the comment icon next to each paragraph (see fig. 3.4). Each section of the text likewise allows for more general comments, which can be found by selecting the comment icon next to the section title; all comments that have been made on any section can be read by clicking on the "All Comments" tab above the comment window. Moreover, clicking on the small icon to the right of a commenter's name highlights the paragraph to which the comment is attached. The 104 comments Stephens received on the paper were by and large substantive, and they included a number of technical comments that allowed the Institute to continue developing the templates for publications with this kind of fine-grained commenting ability.

The Institute's next such venture was in certain ways the most ambitious, and in others, the most traditional: the Institute teamed up with Lewis Lapham of *Lapham's Quarterly* to publish a commentable version of the *Iraq Study Group Report*. This version of the CommentPress templates carried over from "Holy of Holies" the ability of readers to discuss full sections of the text as well as comment at the more fine-grained paragraph level, but added two important innovations: first, a space for general comments about the report as a whole, and second, and more importantly, the ability to read comments organized not just by section but also by commenter, enabling a reader interested in the responses of another particular reader to see those comments as a group. The Institute followed this with a treatment of President Bush's televised address to the nation responding to the report, interweaving the transcribed text of the address with streaming video of the speech, opening both the content and the delivery to discussion.

Interestingly, the entire *Iraq Study Group Report* received a total of 92 comments, fewer than did Mitchell Stephens's much shorter—and arguably much less pressing—paper. The reasons in no small part have to do with the structure of the two social networks into which the texts were released: Stephens put his paper into CommentPress as a means of presenting it to a working group at the Center for Religion and Media at New York University, a group organized around the discussion of texts like Stephens's, so the technology to some degree facilitated the interactions and exchanges members of the group already wanted to have. However, the majority of commenters on the paper were not affiliated with the working group but had been following Stephens's blog, hosted by the Institute, on which he had for some months been thinking out loud about the process and progress of his research. These read-

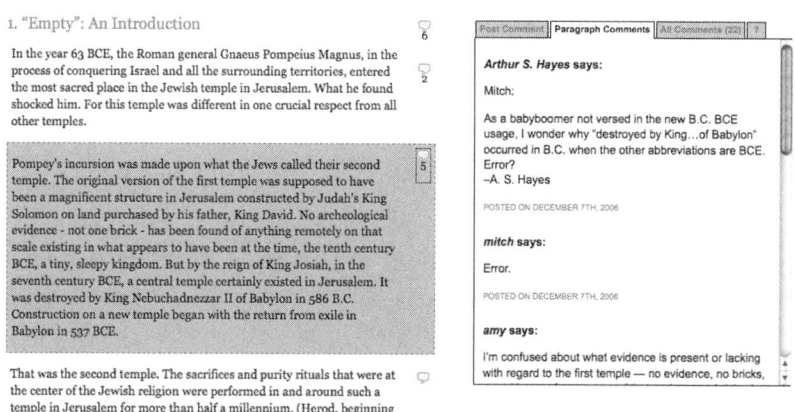

Part 1. "Empty": An Introduction

1 2 3 4 5 6 7 8 9 10 11 12

The Holy of Holies:
On the Constituents of Emptiness

1. "Empty": An Introduction

In the year 63 BCE, the Roman general Gnaeus Pompeius Magnus, in the process of conquering Israel and all the surrounding territories, entered the most sacred place in the Jewish temple in Jerusalem. What he found shocked him. For this temple was different in one crucial respect from all other temples.

Pompey's incursion was made upon what the Jews called their second temple. The original version of the first temple was supposed to have been a magnificent structure in Jerusalem constructed by Judah's King Solomon on land purchased by his father, King David. No archeological evidence - not one brick - has been found of anything remotely on that scale existing in what appears to have been at the time, the tenth century BCE, a tiny, sleepy kingdom. But by the reign of King Josiah, in the seventh century BCE, a central temple certainly existed in Jerusalem. It was destroyed by King Nebuchadnezzar II of Babylon in 586 B.C. Construction on a new temple began with the return from exile in Babylon in 537 BCE.

That was the second temple. The sacrifices and purity rituals that were at the center of the Jewish religion were performed in and around such a temple in Jerusalem for more than half a millennium. (Herod, beginning in 19 BCE, built a version that may truly have qualified as magnificent.)

Post Comment | **Paragraph Comments** | All Comments (22) | ?

Arthur S. Hayes says:

Mitch:

As a babyboomer not versed in the new B.C. BCE usage, I wonder why "destroyed by King...of Babylon" occurred in B.C. when the other abbreviations are BCE. Error?
–A. S. Hayes

POSTED ON DECEMBER 7TH, 2006

mitch **says:**

Error.

POSTED ON DECEMBER 7TH, 2006

amy **says:**

I'm confused about what evidence is present or lacking with regard to the first temple — no evidence, no bricks,

Fig. 3.4. Mitchell Stephens, "The Holy of Holies" (futureofthebook.org/mitchellstephens/holyofholies/)

ers not only were interested in the same subject matter as Stephens—as were the members of the working group, many of whom resisted online discussion—but were ready to use the technologies to facilitate that conversation.

By contrast, Lapham's project brought together what the site referred to as "a quorum of informed sources (historians, generals, politicians both foreign and domestic)," as well as a number of writers and reporters, all of whom had a vested interest in the material, but most of whom were unaccustomed to working in such a mediated or interactive vein. (In fact, more than a third of the comments on the report came from one participant, novelist and political writer Kevin Baker, who maintains an extensive web presence.) Other mitigating factors have to be considered, of course; for one thing, the *Iraq Study Group Report* had, at least initially, a closed commenter base, as opposed to Stephens's paper, which was open to community input. Moreover, the timing of the report's release by the study group—December 6, 2006—meant that the Institute's commentable version went online precariously close to the holidays. And even worse, by the time the commentable version was released, the Bush administration had already dismissed the report, making discussion of its proposals a significantly less compelling exercise. I would hold, however, that the readiness for online interaction is the most compelling reason for the relative quiet on the Iraq report's discussion channel; Stephens's commenters were, by and large, not just attuned to the issues he presented, but actively engaged in other online reading and writing practices, which prepared them to be active contributors.[21]

All this is to say that no technology, whether CommentPress or another system, will be a panacea; even the most ingenious new structures for publishing a text online will not automatically get any randomly selected group talking. Technologies like these can, however, facilitate discussions among readers who are both motivated and prepared to have them.

And academics, unsurprisingly, often want to talk. After their first successful experiments with this new format for discussion-oriented publishing, the Institute began receiving numerous requests from academics and other authors hoping to use the template to publish their papers. They agreed in a few cases, helping Cathy Davidson and David Theo Goldberg (2007) publish a HASTAC (Humanities, Arts, Science, and Technology Advanced Collaboratory) working paper, as well as using a modification of the template as the engine behind the first release of MediaCommons's ongoing video discussion feature, *In Media Res*. This growing demand spurred the Institute to compile the various hacks and templates that, to this point, they had been tweaking manually into a releasable, documented, open-source theme easily installable and usable with any WordPress installation. CommentPress 0.9, a development release, was first made available to testers on July 21, 2007. The following day, I used my web hosting provider's one-click install function to load a new installation of WordPress, installed and set up the CommentPress theme, loaded in the text, and did a bit of tinkering with formatting and the like, taking a draft of the article on which this chapter is based from a Word document to "published" (including, arguably, founding the publisher) in under three hours (see fig. 3.5).

The original releases of CommentPress provided two "skins" from which users could select: one more traditionally blog-like, in which excerpts from posts appeared in reverse-chronological order on the site's front page, but full post pages provided paragraph-level commenting parallel to the original text; and one for "documents," which presented a table of contents on the front page linked to each of the document's sections. In either skin, comments were readable in multiple modes: clicking on a small dialogue bubble to the right of a paragraph revealed comments on that paragraph, while a combination page/bubble icon to the right of a page's title showed comments on the whole page. Readers could also browse all comments, organized either by commenter or by section of the text; browsing in this way provided links back to the portion of the original text on which the com-

Fig. 3.5. Kathleen Fitzpatrick, "CommentPress" (screenshot from the author's collection)

ments were made. In the months following the beta release of Comment-Press, the Institute updated and advanced the software to release 1.4, adding features such as a widget-ready theme that allowed users to customize the sidebar of a text quickly and easily. Moreover, because CommentPress was released as an open-source project, users were able both to get the tool quickly into use—it was adopted, for instance, for a web-based version of the Ithaka Report, "University Publishing in a Digital Age" (Brown, Griffiths, and Rascoff 2007)—and to repurpose and redistribute it in ways that could enrich the possibilities the project presents for electronic publishing.

My experience of using CommentPress left me quite enthusiastic about the form; I was able to get the kinds of feedback on my article draft that I required, as well as to have a record of the responses the draft produced. The draft received a total of fifty-nine comments, just over a third of which were my own responses to issues raised by other readers. Those issues ranged from the factual to the interpretative, and in every case pressed my thinking about the article forward. In fact, though the *Journal of Electronic Publishing*, which published a revised version of the article (Fitzpatrick 2007d), offered to have it peer reviewed, I felt strongly enough about the reviews the article had already received to stick with the open process; rather than send the finished version to blind reviewers, I republished it in CommentPress as well, receiving another twenty-five or so comments from a second group of readers. The kinds of feedback that I received helped me clarify that article's argument as it continued to develop into this text.[22]

In my experience, then, CommentPress became a useful tool not just for quickly and engagingly publishing a text, and for seeking feedback while a text is in draft form, but for facilitating an open mode of review. As I discussed briefly in chapter 1, Noah Wardrip-Fruin similarly used a CommentPress-derived tool to facilitate the blog-based review of the manuscript for his book, *Expressive Processing*; his reflections on the process not only pointed out that "the blog commentaries will have been through a social process that, in some ways, will probably make me trust them more" than the traditional blind peer reviews he also received (Wardrip-Fruin 2008), but also that the blog-based review uncovered one of the manuscript's weaknesses in an unexpected way. One of the reviewers, Ian Bogost, noted on his own blog that he had trouble following the manuscript's argument through the series of posts that comprised it, attributing that difficulty to the blog form's serialized structure (Bogost 2008).[23] As it turns out, however, the traditional peer reviewers noted issues in following the argument across the text as well: "What had seemed like a confirmation of one of our early fears about this form of review—the possibility of losing the argument's thread— was actually a successful identification, by the blog-based reviewers, of a problem with the manuscript also seen by the anonymous reviewers" (Wardrip-Fruin 2009a). In the end, the blog-based review provided Wardrip-Fruin with more feedback, and with feedback that he trusted more, based upon the community out of which it arose.

Wardrip-Fruin also notes, however, that the preexistence of the community was an absolute necessity for this project; while the Institute for the Future of the Book "sought to build new communities from scratch, via widespread publicity, for their projects" such as *GAM3R 7H30RY*, he argued, "this cannot be done for every scholarly publication—and a number of fields already have existing online communities that function well, connecting thinkers from universities, industry, nonprofits, and the general public" (Wardrip-Fruin 2009a). Making use of such an already existing community was necessary for the richness of discussion that *Expressive Processing* received. Similarly, a commenter on the revised version of my article noted that "in order to get the 'liveliness of conversation and interaction' required, some kind of community has to exist. Maybe in the form of an established scholarly web site, journal portal, or blog" (Hillesund 2007). Without such a community available and willing to discuss published texts, interaction will inevitably lag; one of the key tasks in building such technologically networked publishing environments will be maintaining the social networks they are meant to connect.

CommentPress ran into a series of problems early in its life, however, due in part to its dependence on the stability of the WordPress software on which it was based, as well as its reliance on the particular developer who originally wrote the plugin. The October 2007 release of WordPress 2.3, which heavily revised some key aspects of the codebase, effectively broke CommentPress; current CommentPress users were required to refrain from updating their WordPress software, and new users were obliged to find an older release in order to create CommentPress sites. In the meantime, however, the developer of CommentPress had moved on to another project. The Institute was finally able to release a WordPress 2.3–compatible update for CommentPress in January 2008, but the project's momentum had been severely compromised in the interim. Since that time, however, CommentPress has undergone two parallel development paths: the original developer has updated the code, re-releasing it as "digress.it," while the Institute has, following another successful project, overhauled the code as well, and in late 2009 released CommentPress 3.1 (see "digress.it").

In its most recent experiment, the Institute published the entire text of Doris Lessing's 1962 novel *The Golden Notebook* online, engaging seven women to read and discuss the text in the margin (see fig. 3.6). This project produced robust discussion not just among the seven primary readers, but also among a wide range of other readers who participated in the connected forum. This division between readers who could comment in the margins and those who could only discuss in the forums became one of the most heated topics under consideration; as the project announced on its front page,

> How come only the seven women can comment in the margins?
> Good conversations are messy, non-linear and complicated. The comment area, a chronological scrolling field[,] just isn't robust enough to follow a conversation among an infinite number of participants. Seven may even be too many. (Lessing 2008)

As one commenter noted in the forum, she understood why the "two-tiered structure" was necessary to "prevent chaos," but was unhappy with the distinction that resulted: "Grad school all over again I guess" (marthaquest 2008). The Internet hates walled gardens, and thus one of the clear challenges faced by a conversational publishing system like CommentPress is precisely that of managing the potential for chaos in large-scale open discus-

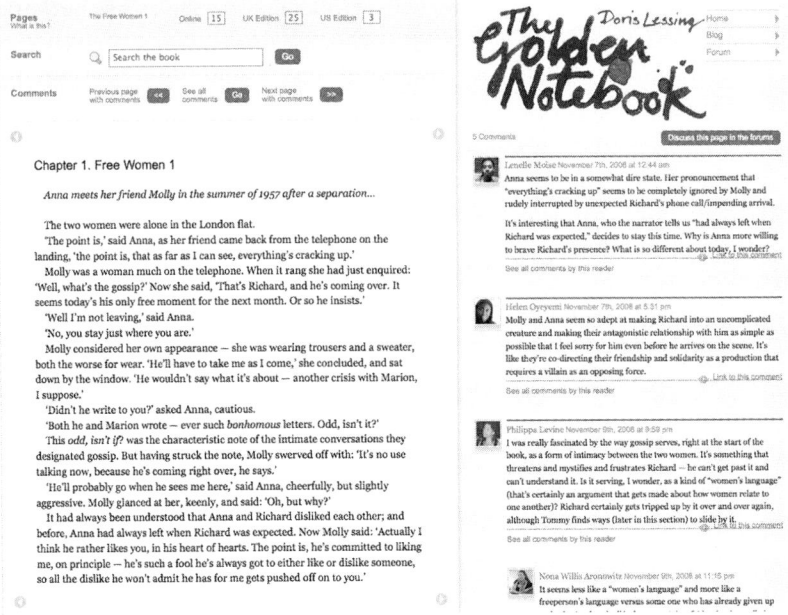

Fig. 3.6. Page from the Institute for the Future of the Book's publication of Doris Lessing's *The Golden Notebook* (thegoldennotebook.org)

sions. And while CommentPress has gone some distance toward imagining social interaction within and around texts, the fact that it still relies upon scrolling text windows suggests that, though we're beginning to solve the larger-scale structural problems of native digital textuality, we still have miles to go before our interactions with the screen have the ease of our interactions with the book.[24]

The new kinds of interactions we need to develop affect authors as much as readers. Authors who publish via CommentPress need to develop the hosting skills required for such a conversational publishing strategy to succeed; as their texts are under discussion, they need to be present without being omnipresent, responding as called upon to reader comments, but without dominating and therefore closing down the discussion. As Wardrip-Fruin (2009a) notes, "[T]he flow of blog conversation is mercilessly driven by time. While it is possible to try to pick up threads of conversation after they have been quiet for a few days, the results are generally much less successful than when one responds within a day or, better yet, an hour." Authors will therefore be required to manage the labor involved not simply in producing the text, but also in publishing it and in engaging with its audience, and our expectations with respect to faculty workload will have to reflect that labor: "[G]enerally pursuing blog-based review with time for full conversational engagement would require a shift in thinking around universities. It isn't uncommon for authors to request release time for book writing and revisions, yet it has almost never been requested in order to participate more fully in community peer review. I hope that will change in the future" (ibid.). As authors begin increasingly to publish in networked environments, we won't be quite so able to walk away from a text in manuscript form and leave its dissemination and discussion to others; we'll need to commit to being present in a text, for a time, and to engaging with the publishing process. This mode of participation is only one of the ongoing challenges involved in maintaining new digital publishing systems once they're built; new forms such as CommentPress will require significant investments of labor, not just in the development, installation, and implementation of the technologies themselves or in the design and release of texts through them, but in the post-publication maintenance of the texts. Publishing systems like CommentPress thus won't relieve institutions of the infrastructural demands posed by current analog press and library systems; if anything, as I discuss in the next chapter, they'll produce new kinds of requirements for preservation of the texts published through them.

That said, CommentPress demonstrates the fruitfulness of reimagining the technologies of electronic publishing in service to the social interconnections of authors and readers. The success of the electronic publishing ventures of the future will likely hinge on the liveliness of the conversations and interactions they produce, as well as the new writing that those interactions inspire. CommentPress grows out of an understanding that the chief problem in creating the future of the book is not simply placing the words on the screen, but structuring their delivery in an engaging manner; the issue of engagement, moreover, is not simply about locating the text within the technological network, but also, and primarily, about locating it within the social network. The publishing platform of the future might bring together the modes of interaction between readers and texts that CommentPress fosters with the modes of interaction among texts that are produced by the database-driven scholarship of projects such as NINES. Such a platform would allow not only for ease of reading and for engaging discussion, but also for the curation and remix of existing texts and digital objects into more new, exciting kinds of texts, finally resulting in a digital mode of publishing that doesn't just rival but indeed outdoes the codex. This new publishing structure would invite the reader in, acknowledge that the reader's engagement with the text is a mode of social interaction, and recognize that the reader is, in many cases, a writer too. This publishing structure would also demonstrate an understanding that all publication is part of an ongoing series of public conversations, conducted in multiple time registers, across multiple texts. Making those conversations as accessible and inviting as possible should be the goal in imagining the textual communications circuit of the future.

4

Preservation

Access to data tomorrow requires decisions concerning preservation today.
> —Blue Ribbon Task Force on Sustainable
> Digital Preservation and Access

Despite real technical obstacles, digital preservation is ultimately a challenge demanding social (above and beyond the purely technological) solutions.
> —Matt Kirschenbaum, *Mechanisms*

Having explored the ways that authorship, authority, and interaction will of necessity change as we establish and come to depend upon new networked publishing systems, we must also think carefully about how those systems, and the texts that we produce within them, will live on into the future. Absent a printed and bound object that we can hold in our hands, many of us worry, and not without reason, about the durability of the work that we produce. Having opened a word-processing document only to find it hopelessly corrupted, watched a file seemingly evaporate from our computers, or possibly even suffered a massive hard disk failure, we are understandably nervous about committing our lives' work to the ostensibly intangible, invisible bits inside the computer. So goes the conventional wisdom of inscription and transmission: the more easily information can be replicated and passed around, the less durable its medium becomes. The post-Gutenberg form of print-on-paper provided vast improvements in our cultural ability to reproduce and distribute texts, but it's undeniable that stone tablets promise to last far longer. And so it is with the shift from print into the digital: what we gain in ease and speed of copying and transmission, we apparently lose in permanence; the ephemeral nature of digital data threatens our cultural and intellectual heritage with an accelerated cycle of evanescence.

To an extent, this conventional wisdom is correct: we do need to think seriously about how we preserve and protect the key digital documents and artifacts that we are in the process of creating. As I explored in the introduction, early hypertexts such as Michael Joyce's *Afternoon* (1987/90) provide a case in point; the hardware and software environments necessary to opening these files are largely out of date, and many licensed users of these texts find themselves unable to read them. This is the kind of scenario that sets off warning bells for many traditional scholars; the idea of a book's protocols suddenly becoming obsolete—the ink fading from the page, the pages refusing to turn—are unthinkable, and seemingly similar obsolescence in digital environments only reinforces the worst suspicions about these new "flash in the pan" forms.

However, I want to counteract these assumptions from two directions. The first is simply to note that books are often far more ephemeral than we often assume. Bindings give way and pages are lost; paper is easily marked or torn; and many texts printed before the development of acid-free paper are gradually disappearing from common usefulness (Baker 2009).[1] But over the centuries libraries and archives have developed a vast infrastructure to support the preservation of print, including space within our institutions (such as the book bindery contained within most research libraries), budgets dedicated to the mission of conserving our print resources, and perhaps most importantly, staff members whose labor is specifically dedicated to preservation. If books were as permanent as we often assume, we wouldn't have needed this infrastructure designed to protect them.[2]

Second, and by contrast, bits and the texts created with them can be far more durable than we think; as Matt Kirschenbaum (2008) has convincingly demonstrated, once written to a hard disk, even deleted data is rarely really gone beyond the point of recovery. It's important to stress that this durability is of data written to *hard disk*; removable media such as tapes, floppy disks, and CDs or DVDs tend to be much more fragile. That having been said, all web-based data is, somewhere, and often several somewheres, written to hard disk. And in fact, it's the Internet that transformed the digital text that was most clearly intended to enact and embody the ephemerality of the digital form—William Gibson's poem "Agrippa," published in 1992 on diskette as a self-displaying, self-consuming, one-read-only artifact—into one of the most durably available texts in network history, by virtue of the ways that it was shared and discussed. The difference between preserving texts in electronic form and those in print thus does not hinge entirely on the ephemerality of the newer medium itself, given what Kirschenbaum calls "the uniquely indelible nature of magnetic storage," citing the testimony of computer privacy experts like Michael Colonyiddes who argue that "[e]lectronic mail and computer records are far more permanent than any piece of paper" (Kirschenbaum 2008, 51). Rather, the difference has to do with our understandings of those media forms, the ways we use them, and the techniques that we have developed to ensure their preservation. We have centuries of practice in preserving print—means of collecting and organizing print texts, making them accessible to readers, and protecting them from damage, all standardized across many libraries with frequently redundant collections. But it *took* centuries to develop those practices, and we simply do not have centuries, or even decades, to develop parallel processes for digital preservation. We now must think just as carefully, but much more quickly, about how to develop practices appropriate to the preservation of our digital heritage.

The paradox, as Kirschenbaum demonstrates, is that digital storage media are frequently far more durable than we think; it's the ways that we understand and treat stored data that produce the apparent ephemerality of digital artifacts. *Afternoon* still exists, after all, in many different forms and locations; what has been lost is not the text, or even that text's legibility, but our transparent ability to access that text. To read *Afternoon* on a contemporary Macintosh, we need access to an emulator, a software package that re-creates the conditions under which *Afternoon* and other such early hypertexts were run when they were originally released. Numerous emulators exist for various hardware and software configurations, and some of them are in fact produced by the original manufacturers to keep their systems reverse-compatible; Rosetta, for instance, is an emulator produced and distributed by Apple as a part of Mac OS X, allowing contemporary Intel-based processors to run software written for older PowerPC machines. But Rosetta does not allow those processors to run programs that were originally written for systems older than OS X; those programs were until recently accessible through "Classic" mode, an OS 9 emulator contained within OS X systems prior to 10.5. Since the release of OS 10.5, no emulator within which one can run OS 9 programs has been available. Apple's desire—and one generalized throughout the computer industry—to move users to newer systems by deprecating older ones (thus minimizing the number and range of systems for which they are required to provide support) suggests that we will need to look to sources other than the manufacturers in order to ensure access to older systems. And in fact many emulators for older systems have been created by fans of now-outdated texts and platforms, such as the range of Z-machine interpreters to which I referred in the last chapter, which allow contemporary users to interact with a number of text-adventure games such as *Zork* and *Adventure*, which date back as far as the late 1970s. Another example is Mini vMac, a

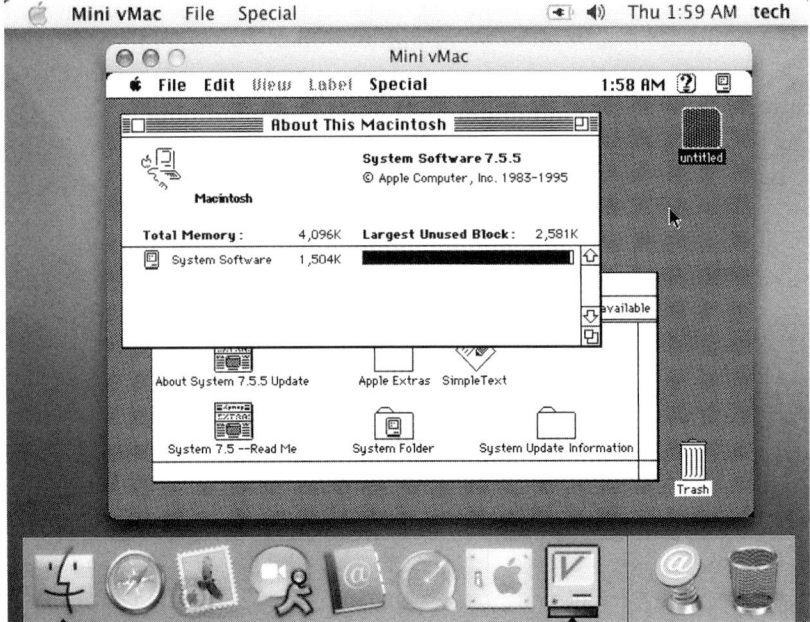

Fig. 4.1. Screenshot of the emulator MinivMac (pcwin.com)

program that emulates the environment of a Mac Plus (circa 1986–90) within a window of a contemporary OS X machine (see fig. 4.1). As Nick Montfort and Noah Wardrip-Fruin (2004) note in their white paper on preserving electronic literature, "As long as some strong interest in work from certain older platforms remains, it is likely that emulation or interpretation of them will be an option—new emulators and interpreters will continue to be developed for new platforms." The wide availability of such emulators and their ability to resurrect decades-old software and texts on contemporary systems suggest that our concerns about the digital future should be focused, not on fears about the medium's inherent ephemerality, but rather on ensuring that the digital texts we produce remain accessible and interpretable, and that the environments those texts need to operate within remain available.[3]

My suggestion that digital media texts and technologies are less short-lived than we think should not be interpreted to mean that we can be cavalier about their preservation, or that we can put off decision-making about such issues for some more technologically advanced future moment. As a recent report from the Blue Ribbon Task Force on Sustainable Digital Preservation and Access suggests,

In the analog world, the rate of degradation or depreciation of an asset is usually not swift, and consequently, decisions about long-term preservation of these materials can often be postponed for a considerable period, especially if they are kept in settings with appropriate climate controls. The digital world affords no such luxury; digital assets can be extremely fragile and ephemeral, and the need to make preservation decisions can arise as early as the time of the asset's creation, particularly since studies to date indicate that the total cost of preserving materials can be reduced by steps taken early in the life of the asset. (Blue Ribbon Task Force 2008, 9)

Although the appeal to the fragility and ephemerality of digital assets is a bit of a red herring, I would certainly agree that we cannot save money now by deferring preservation practices until they're needed; planning for the persistent availability of digital resources as part of the process of their creation will provide the greatest stability of the resources themselves at the least possible cost. In order to make such advance planning possible, however, we must genuinely "understand the nature of what is being collected and preserved, and where the most significant challenges of digital preservation finally lie" (Kirschenbaum 2008, 21), a set of understandings that will require the collective insight and commitment of libraries, presses, scholars, and administrators. These understandings will likely also be subject to a great deal of flux; Clifford Lynch compellingly argued in 2001 that we did not then "fully understand how to preserve digital content; today there is no 'general theory,' only techniques." These techniques, which include hardware preservation, emulator creation, and content migration, have begun to coalesce into something of a theory, but we have a long way to go before that theory is sufficiently generalized that we can consider the problem solved. And perhaps that theory will never be as fully generalized as it has become for print, in part because of the multiplicity of systems on which digital artifacts run, and in part because, as computer users know all too well, technologies, formats, and media will continue developing out from under us, and so techniques that appear cutting-edge today will be hopelessly dated some years from now. We absolutely must not throw up our hands at that realization, however, and declare the problem intractable; we can and should take steps today to ensure that texts and artifacts produced and preserved under today's systems remain interoperable with or portable to the systems of tomorrow.

While questions surrounding digital preservation present us with a range of thorny technical issues, I argue, following Kirschenbaum, that their solutions are not predominantly technical in nature. In fact, the examples presented by the emulators mentioned above may help us recognize that what we need to develop in order to ensure the future preservation of our digital texts and artifacts may be less new *tools* than new *socially organized systems* that take advantage of the number of individuals and institutions facing the same challenges and seeking the same goals. The digital projects that run the greatest risk of being lost are those founded and developed by individual scholars who, when they move on to new projects, leave the resources they've created in limbo. But as we have seen, a range of fans and collaborators have kept titles like *Zork* and *Adventure* alive for thirty years, across a vast range of platforms and operating systems, by responding to a communal desire for those texts and sharing the tools necessary to run them. Preservation, I will suggest in what follows, presents us with technical requirements but overwhelmingly social solutions; scholars who collaborate with one another, or with larger institutions, will be more likely to produce digital work that will be preserved.[4] D. F. McKenzie (1999, 4) argued that the book "is never simply a remarkable *object*. Like every other technology it is invariably the product of human agency in complex and highly volatile contexts." Context is equally important, and equally volatile, in shaping our understanding of the production, circulation, and preservation of digital texts. In this understanding, the library, for instance, is not simply a building (or a computer server) in which texts are housed, but a social space through which texts circulate, and within which communal efforts toward preservation will find the greatest success.

As a report by the Council on Library and Information Resources notes (2008, 8), however, it is likely that "the library of the 21st century will be more of an abstraction than a traditional presence"; substantive changes in the library and how it works with the academy have already begun. For that reason, in contrast to the other chapters in this text, in which I argue that we as scholars need to make a concerted effort to change something about our institutions and the ways we work within them, I am here instead describing an incompletely understood series of changes already more or less underway within our libraries. It should not come as any surprise that librarians are, for the most part, way ahead of most of the academy on these issues; as Richard Lanham (2006, 135) has noted, the library in its preservation function "has always operated with a digital, not a fixed print, logic. Books, the physical books themselves, were incidental to the real library mission, which was the dispersion of knowledge." Thus the transformations of many MLS (Masters of Library Sciences) programs into MLIS (Masters of Library and Information Sciences) programs might be seen as emblematic of the ways in which the library and its professionals have long since begun to grapple with the new systems that digital communication and its preservation require. But to successfully face the challenges before them, librarians need broad support from across the academy; scholars and administrators alike must understand something of how digital library systems work and how we might best work within those systems to ensure that the digital collections we use in our research and the digital objects that we produce as a result of that research will be persistently and usefully available into the future. My advocacy, then, is in service of changing *our understanding* of the library and how it functions, in order that we might conceive of our projects in ways that best work within the library's developing information systems, and so that we can help support the library as it moves into the digital age.

There is, of course, no lack of resistance, particularly among the faculty, and especially within the humanities, to the ways in which the library is changing. Many of these changes, unfortunately, are worth being concerned about, as they stem less from modernization than from contemporary budget crises. Within many institutions, including my own, the library has begun both deaccessioning print copies of journals to which we have digital access and moving large portions of the remaining print collections to off-site facilities. These are developments that the faculty would do well to be concerned about; thinning and storing a collection should always be undertaken in a thoughtful, well-considered way. In the case of deaccessioning of print materials, for instance, caution demands that at least one clean print copy remain available somewhere within a library consortium in the event that a text needs to be redigitized, and care needs to be taken that contracts with digital journal providers allow for post-cancellation access to texts released while a library maintains its subscription.[5] Similarly, in moving print materials off-site (a necessity for many overcrowded libraries, if their collections are to continue to grow), careful consideration must be given to the ways those materials will be protected and accessed. As faculty, we have a stake in ensuring that these changes are managed in the best ways possible—but throwing up roadblocks in front of such changes would be counterproductive, either causing the library to become unable to grow and develop or reducing the faculty's future input into such development. Instead, we need to figure out how best to work with the library in order to ensure that the richness of our scholarly archives—whatever their medium—is preserved and protected.

The need for faculty input into the preservation of digital resources is even more pressing; though the bulk of the work of preserving digital texts will fall to the library, we all have a share in it, and we all must be aware of the issues. The recent Blue Ribbon Task Force report (2008, 21) exploring the options for economically sustainable digital preservation concluded that "the mantra 'preserve everything for all time' is unlikely to be compatible with a sustainable digital preservation strategy. The mechanism for aligning preservation objectives with preservation resources is *selection*—determining which materials are 'valuable enough' to warrant long-term preservation." This somewhat fatalistic vision, suggesting that we as scholars will need to compete to make sure our resources are seen as "valuable enough," runs counter to two well-ingrained scholarly principles: that we cannot know today what will be important tomorrow and, as a result, that everything has potential intellectual value. Storage is inexpensive, and choices can be made in the process of developing digital resources that will help make their preservation easier. Even more, we can and should begin to mobilize community resources so that many stakeholders with a wide range of investments help support the preservation of the objects we are now building. As Montfort and Wardrip-Fruin (2004) argue:

> Preservation is always the work of a community. Ultimately, preserving electronic literature will be the work of a system of writers, publishers, electronic literature scholars, librarians, archivists, software developers, and computer scientists. But today, and even once such a system is in place, the practices of authors and publishers will determine whether preserving particular works is relatively easy or nearly impossible.

This chapter focuses on such community-oriented systems and practices; each of the sections that follow takes on one key aspect of the requirements for the digital library by exploring representative projects or technologies. In the process, I look at three issues with respect to preservation: the need to develop commonly held *standards* for markup, so that texts are produced in a format that will remain readable in and portable to new platforms as they arise; the need to provide sufficiently rich *metadata* for our texts, such that the objects we create will be flexibly findable through search engines and other means, including developing stable locators that allow texts to be retrievable into the future, regardless of the changing structures of our institutional websites; and the need to provide continued *access* to digital objects, ensuring that texts remain available when we seek them out. Although I focus on a few particular projects in each of these areas, I want to be clear that this chapter is not advocating for any particular technical solution to the issues facing the library in its drive to preserve our developing digital cultural heritage; I am more interested in the fact that each of the technical systems I here describe is at heart a *social* system that develops from a collective, community-derived set of concerns and procedures and requires community investment in order to succeed. As Kirschenbaum (2008, 21) has argued, "The point is to address the fundamentally social, rather than the solely technical mechanisms of electronic textual transmission, and the role of social networks and network culture as active agents of preservation." Each of the projects I discuss provides a means of investigating the social networks that are developing around issues of preservation, and how those developing social practices can help us understand preservation not as a matter of protecting ephemeral media but rather of making adequate and responsible use of what are in fact surprisingly durable forms of communication.

Standards

One of the first issues we must consider in thinking about the durability of digital texts is the format in which those texts are produced and encoded. A format that adheres to commonly agreed-upon standards can enable long-term access to the text, while one that uses a nonstandard protocol can create difficulties. This is not to say that all texts must or even should conform to the same structures and formats; any text contains its own peculiarities, and the possibilities presented by digital publishing only expand the range of potential forms and formats. But certain kinds of standardization are helpful for ensuring that a text is at least commonly readable across as many platforms as possible, and for as long as possible.

We employ standards in this way across our lives, where they often appear wholly naturalized but in fact represent the imposition of certain kinds of socially determined regulations that provide us with a stable and reliable experience of the phenomenon in question; the electrical system that provides power to our homes and offices, for instance, does so through a set of standards for voltages and interfaces, and nearly anyone who has traveled abroad can testify to the problems that can result from using an appliance that does not conform to the local standards. Even time itself had to be standardized; the development of phenomena such as time zones didn't take place until the spread of the railroads demanded a commonly accepted schedule. Textual standards exist for many of the same reasons, making nearly any given newspaper, journal, or book we pick up, from any publisher in any city, instantly comprehensible to us (at least in format, if not in the particulars of its content). The phenomena that operate all but invisibly to make the pages of a book readable to us today, including spacing between words, punctuation, regularized spelling, paragraphing, page numbers and headers, tables of contents, and so forth, took centuries to develop. Digital texts, by contrast, proliferated quickly, and their producers were concerned enough about sharing them that the problem of standards arose quite early in their lifespan.

Certain kinds of standards have long been available in web publishing; standards for HyperText Markup Language (HTML), for instance, are developed by the World Wide Web Consortium (W3C), which under the direction of World Wide Web inventor Tim Berners-Lee issues protocols and guidelines designed to ensure robust web interoperability. Such "vendor-neutral" interoperability ensures, among other things, that web pages are and will remain interpretable by any major browser.[6] As Nick Montfort and Noah Wardrip-Fruin (2004) advise authors of electronic literature, "Validating a page or site, using a service like the W3C Validator or the validator built into BBEdit, ensures that all browsers that comply with World Wide Web Consortium standards, now and in the future, will deal with the page correctly." This is not to say that HTML hasn't changed over time, or that browsers are somehow *required* to conform to the W3C's recommendations, but the web's general stability is the product of voluntary cooperation among a broad variety of W3C member organizations, including hardware and software manufacturers who recognize the value of ensuring that their products comply with what the broader industry considers its "best practices," so that they might be adopted by as wide a range of users as possible.

One of the ways that the standardization of HTML works is through a separation between issues that relate to a web document's *structure* and those that relate to its *design*. This separation is in part a legacy of HTML's parent language, Standard Generalized Markup Language (SGML). The latter relies on an interpreter-agnostic set of tags that describe the structural characteristics of a text and its component parts, ignoring entirely the way that any given browser or system will present those tags. HTML similarly provides tags that describe the structure of a text, such as **\<h1\>** to designate a top-level heading, **\<p\>** to designate paragraphs, **\<blockquote\>** to designate block quotations, and so forth. None of these tags specify anything about the appearance of the data they contain on the computer screen; **\<h1\>** demarcates a heading, but says nothing about the font or size of that heading. Thus, to emphasize text within a paragraph, HTML provides the **\<em\>** tag, which generally renders as (but does not specify) italics; emphasis is structural, while italics is about appearance.[7] Also inherited from SGML is the fact that most such tags come in pairs that indicate the beginning and end of the data they contain; **<h1>Introduction</h1>** thus produces a level-one heading that reads "Introduction," formatted in whatever way the browser's defaults indicate, and everything after that will belong to some other part of the document's structure.

As HTML was first being developed in the early 1990s, the only existing web browsers were entirely text-based, and thus it made sense to limit HTML to controlling document structure rather than presentation. With the 1993 introduction of Mosaic, the first web browser capable of displaying inline images, things became much more complex; suddenly browsers were able to manage a much wider and more idiosyncratic range of tags and to interpret them much more loosely, resulting in web pages that would look vastly different, or potentially even be uninterpretable, on different browsers. (This period led to the introduction of the **<blink>** tag and other such web design abominations.) In order to rein in the chaos, in mid-1994 Dan Connolly produced a draft specification for what would come to be HTML 2, circulating it within "the Internet community" for discussion, incorporating much of the feedback that he received, and finally producing a Document Type Definition for HTML 2 (Raggett 1998).[8] Later that year, the W3C was founded in order to provide for the continued community-based management of HTML and its specifications for the broadest possible interoperability.

HTML, however, is a document type specifically meant for use in creating hypertext, and as such does not provide for all types of documents a scholar or publisher might want to create.[9] HTML's parent language, SGML, has roots in generic coding techniques for document processing developed in the late 1960s, though SGML as a formal specification wasn't officially recognized by the International Standards Organization until 1986. SGML was developed in order to standardize the markup through which document processing took place, allowing digital documents to be shared across platforms and ensuring that their markup would contain "not only formatting codes interpreted by computer itself, but also descriptive human-legible information about the nature and role of every element in a document" (Darnell 1998). This human legibility, a product of the fact that SGML documents are produced in plain text, is particularly important for ensuring that documents remain accessible, as such plain-text formats "can be edited, read, and inspected on many platforms. This accessibility remains even if the program that created it, or the program that was meant to interpret it, is no longer available (or exists in a radically different and incompatible version)" (Montfort and Wardrip-Fruin 2004). But this accessibility is also produced through the careful use of a set of tags specified in a Document Type Definition (DTD), which is a schema that lays out the syntax of a particular class of document; HTML is thus not an independent language, but rather a DTD, or an application of SGML, which specifies the codes that may be used to markup hypertext web documents.[10] SGML, and its more recent and now far more widespread descendant XML (for eXtensible Markup Language), are thus *metalanguages* that provide the specifications for the creation of more particular languages, including HTML.[11] What makes XML so significant is precisely its extensibility; as a metalanguage, it allows users to create whatever tags or entities their particular applications require, as long as those tags are defined in the application's schema or DTD. A range of validators for such applications are readily available, both online and in desktop clients, such that coders can ensure that the documents they produce conform to the schema they are employing, thus ensuring that their texts adhere to the standards that any interpreter of that document will employ.

The extensible standards of XML have become particularly important in an age in which the vast majority of web pages, and particularly large, complex websites, aren't hand-coded HTML but are in fact rendered by various content management systems such as blog engines. What we experience on the web as individual pages often do not exist as independent, static, archivable documents, but are instead dynamically generated in the interaction between web programs written in a range of scripting or programming languages (most frequently PHP, but including others such as Javascript, ASP, and Ruby) and a database (most commonly MySQL). Any such web application, whether a blog engine such as WordPress, a content management system like Drupal, a wiki engine such as MediaWiki, or any of a range of others, will employ a set of standards that govern how it renders the information stored in the database in a form readable by a web browser. It's important to note, however, that those standards are nearly always particular to the engine in use, and in many cases proprietary to the company that produces and sells the software. Such proprietary, or closed, standards present the potential for "trapping" the user's data in an unusable form, should the engine that renders the individual pages become outdated, or should the scripting language or database structure not be supported into the future.[12]

For this reason, among others, it's important for the longevity of web-based projects that their developers use software that adheres to open standards rather than proprietary ones.[13] Open standards, such as those supported by the W3C, should not be confused with open-source software, which is a means of software distribution that allows users certain kinds of access to and interactions with its source code. One author has compared open standards with the interoperability of the telephone jack: whoever your carrier, and whoever the manufacturer of your handset, plugging one into the other will always produce the same results.[14] But the phone system itself is not open source; if it were, users would be able to access, tinker with, and redistribute the system's underlying architecture, which might produce some interesting results! Nonetheless, open standards and open-source software are related in important ways, not least of which is that they are both supported by development communities committed to their sustainability. For this reason, the data structures of an open-source system such as WordPress are likely to remain supported or at least migratable well into the future, where the closed data structures of proprietary systems such as Blackboard may not.[15] In a system such as WordPress, however, perhaps more important than the openness of its source code is its use of open standards that can produce XML-based "feeds" of the data it manages, feeds which are then broadly reusable and interoperable with a range of web-based systems. In this sense, the openness of open standards is arguably deeper than that of open-source software, as it allows for robust data portability.

Even the most open publishing systems require clear standards, however, as the chaos of late 1990s HTML suggests, and questions remain about who will be responsible for setting those standards, and how those standards will achieve community buy-in. In order to explore how such standards come into being, and how they might come to be commonly accepted within digital scholarship, I now turn to the Text Encoding Initiative (TEI). Work on TEI began in 1987 with a meeting at Vassar College; prior to this time a number of separate text digitization and encoding projects were underway at several different institutions, and the scholars involved were looking for ways to manage "the proliferation of systems for representing textual material on computers" (Mylonas and Renear 1999, 3). As Lou Burnard (2000), one of TEI's editors, framed their concerns, "Scholarship has always thrived on serendipity and the ability to protect and pass on our intellectual heritage for re-evaluation in a new context; many at that time suspected (and events have not yet proved them wrong) that longevity and re-usability were not high on the priority lists of software vendors and electronic publishers." A group of thirty-two scholars thus came together to explore the development of a set of standards to support the exchange and interoperability of the texts they produced. The meeting resulted in what have come to be called the "Poughkeepsie Principles," a document that would steer the development of guidelines for future text encoding. As set forth in TEI's "The Preparation of Text Encoding Guidelines," these principles include commitments to creating "a standard format for data interchange in humanities research," to drawing up recommendations for syntax and usage within the format, to producing a metalanguage for describing text encoding schemas, and to creating "sets of coding conventions suited for various applications." The production of these guidelines was to be undertaken by three sponsoring organizations, the Association for Computers in the Humanities, the Association for Literary and Linguistic Computing, and the Association for Computational Linguistics, which together appointed a steering committee for the project to be led by two editors and contributed to by several working groups focused on specific issues. The first draft of the TEI guidelines (labeled "P1") was released in June 1990; following an extensive process of revision, the first official version of the guidelines ("P3") was released in May 1994. In all, well over a hundred scholars participated in the production of the TEI Guidelines during the first ten years of the project, which marks TEI as "an exemplary achievement in collaboration, one on a scale fairly rare in the history of the humanities" (Mylonas and Renear 1999, 4).

Such a large-scale enterprise required careful and committed management, however, particularly in order to survive beyond its early stages. In 1999, two of the principal institutions involved in the TEI project, the University of Virginia and the University of Bergen in Norway, submitted a proposal to the TEI executive committee for the formation of a membership-oriented parent body, which became incorporated in late 2000 as the TEI Consortium. The goal of the Consortium was two-fold: first, "to maintain a permanent home for the TEI as a democratically constituted, academically and economically independent, self-sustaining, non-profit organization," and second, "to foster a broad-based user community with sustained involvement in the future development and widespread use of the TEI Guidelines" ("TEI: History"). Since the founding of the Consortium, TEI has undergone some significant transformations. The first drafts of the guidelines were SGML-based; beginning with P4, TEI was entirely revised to be fully XML-compliant. The guidelines have since been further revised to version P5, and the Consortium has also produced TEI customizations such as TEI Lite, a streamlined version of the tagset that is sufficient to support the vast majority of users, and a number of TEI-oriented tools, including Roma, which allows users to create customized validators for their particular applications. TEI is used widely in digital humanities publishing projects (see "TEI: Projects Using the TEI" for an extensive listing) and has generally become accepted as a community-driven standard for text encoding, included as part of the "best practices" embraced by groups such as the Modern Language Association's Committee on Scholarly Editions and the National

Endowment for the Humanities. Even more, "[T]echniques pioneered by the Text Encoding Initiative have been taken up into wider development of technical and engineering standards supporting networked communication" (Mylonas and Renear 1999, 7); in fact, methods used by the TEI were incorporated into the development of XML itself.

Descriptive rather than procedural, demarcating logical structure rather than visual presentation, and thus both hardware- and software-independent, TEI's "lasting achievement," as Burnard (2000) has pointed out, is "not in its DTD, but in the creation of the intellectual model underlying it, which can continue to inform scholarship as technology changes." That intellectual model, in which markup is understood fundamentally as a descriptive act focused on the logical structure of a document rather than its physical appearance, allows TEI to be customized to nearly any use, and allows the texts marked up with TEI to be repurposed in numerous ways, not only for digital and print republication, but also for intensive text-mining and analysis. The current TEI Guidelines fill a more than 1,300-page manual containing an "exhaustive tag library" (Lazinger 2001, 150) and complete specifications for syntax. According to one scholar, however, the "complexity of the TEI is, in a sense, only apparent. For the most part only as much of the TEI as is needed will be used in any particular encoding effort; the TEI vocabulary used will be exactly as complex, but no more complex, than the text being encoded" (Renear 2004, 234). This is made possible by TEI's reliance on the DTD-model; every TEI project must begin with the construction of a TEI schema that details the tags and usages available within the project. Every document in the project then becomes an instance of that document type, which it declares in a comment that precedes the text; this declaration provides for the document's proper validation. The text itself then begins with a header that serves to "describ[e] an encoded work so that the text itself, its source, its encoding, and its revisions are all thoroughly documented," thus serving as "an electronic analogue to the title page attached to a printed work" (Sperberg-McQueen and Burnard 2009, 17), providing both metadata and instructions for the document's use. Because this header information, as well as the rest of the marked-up document, is both human- and machine-readable, and because it is platform-agnostic, capable of being parsed by any number of browsers and other applications, TEI promises a great deal of longevity for the projects encoded with it.

TEI is not and cannot be a singular solution to all of the preservation issues that will present themselves as digital scholarly publishing moves forward. One of its primary shortcomings derives from its complexity, even if that complexity is only apparent: the overhead required in terms of both time and expertise in order to begin the process of marking up digital texts in TEI can be prohibitive, and the development of more user-friendly authoring tools may be required to facilitate the standard's uptake.[16] Moreover TEI's grounding in text *encoding* means that it is focused on the digitization of previously printed texts, or the digital formatting of otherwise print-like texts, as the X-Lit Initiative of the Electronic Literature Organization points out:

> Many technical solutions are being developed by humanities computing scholars and information-science researchers to ensure that digital media will have a longer "shelf life." However, as the shelf metaphor might indicate, these solutions (for example, the Text Encoding Initiative's TEI schema or the library METS metadata standard) are often currently better suited for print, or print-like, static works that have been digitized than for born-digital artifacts of electronic literature with dynamic, interactive, or networked behaviors and other experimental features. (Liu et al. 2005)

Genuinely "born-digital" texts that take robust advantage of the multimodal potential of the network will require other solutions. The TEI may point the way, however, in its reliance on the common, portable standards of XML; other, similar projects may need to be developed in order to deal with changing publishing circumstances, but the flexibility of XML and its related languages might provide the basis for such new formats. For instance, the Electronic Literature Organization's Preservation/Archiving/Dissemination conceptual project, X-Lit, imagined "developing a rich representation for electronic literature" regardless of the original format of that literature, as an application of the XML standard, allowing "the representation of media elements (including text, graphics, sound, and video) as well as a description of the interactive and computational workings of an e-lit piece. Such a standard would also provide a way to document the physical setup and material aspects of an e-lit work," thus ensuring that such texts "will be human-readable and machine-playable long into the future" (Montfort and Wardrip-Fruin 2004). In parallel, the Variable Media Network has brought together digital artists and museums in an effort to preserve artwork produced in "ephemeral" media; one of the outcomes of this project is the Media Art Notation System (MANS), developed by Richard Rinehart, which uses an application of XML, the Digital Item Declaration Language, to create fine-grained descriptions of complex digital objects.[17] As with the TEI, perhaps the most significant aspect of projects like X-Lit and the Variable Media Network is their community-driven basis: first, their grounding in the work of professional organizations with a common if complex set of concerns for the preservation of digital work, and second, their adherence to an open standard, one that will no doubt change in the future but that has a broad enough user base to ensure reverse compatibility for any such changes. As more publishers and publishing centers produce growing numbers and kinds of digital texts across the academy, such issues of community support for the standards they employ will become increasingly important for securing the future of those texts.

Metadata

An especially important feature of both TEI and the Media Art Notation System is that, through their markup, they aim to preserve not just the *content* of the texts they encode, but enough information *about* that content to re-create the experience of using those texts in the future. This metadata might include, in the case of TEI, information about the authorship, publication history, provenance, structure, and format of the text being encoded; in the case of Media Art Notation System, it might include information about the hardware and software environment within which the text was composed and that it requires to run. In each case, it might also include appropriate bibliographic information that will allow a text to be catalogued, searched, and cited by future scholars. Given the proliferation of digital texts, it's increasingly clear that we need much more robust and extensible metadata than we have ever had before; not only do we need better ways of organizing and finding materials today, but we need to allow for the different means of storage and retrieval that will no doubt develop in the future. As Christine Borgman (2007, 88) has argued, access is not simply a matter of a document being available; it also "depends on the ability to discover and retrieve documents of interest, and then follow a trail through the scholarly record." That trail is built of metadata.

As the previous paragraph suggests, there are many kinds of metadata, some of which provide information about a text's production context, others about the particular form in which a text appears, and still others about what has been done with the text since its production. Metadata can thus provide a map of sorts to a large set of data, enabling a user to find patterns that make sense of the data, or to find her way to the particular pieces of data she needs. In this sense, while much of what goes into a document's metadata is objectively verifiable information, the production of the set of metadata, as the production of any map, is always an interpretive act, indicating what the mapmaker has found to be significant about the terrain.[18] One of the problems that metadata poses for the future of digital publishing lies precisely in the difficulty of making maps of future terrain; we never have enough information at present about what will be important in the future, and this truism is particularly applicable to technological developments. We therefore need to develop structures for organizing information, and metadata to describe those structures, that will remain flexible and extensible into the future.

In thinking through the issues surrounding our uses of metadata in digital publishing, I'm mostly concerned with the sorts of citational metadata used by scholars to record, maintain, and communicate findable references to the texts they use. This form of metadata falls under the category of the bibliographic, including information about the document, its production, and where it is stored, so that searching a digital database will produce results about the document as well as links or other information that allow the document to be retrieved. One might think that such organizational systems have been made unnecessary by the development of the search engine—now that we can search our documents for whatever information we like, why would we need to impose such systems upon them? The first reason is that all search engines rely on metadata in some form; full-text searching of the vast quantity of information now available to us is unwieldy at best, and thus most search engines rely upon the existence of information about the information they're searching. The question is rather what metadata search engines are using. This returns us to a point that I made in discussing the issues surrounding filtering systems in chapter 1: any such filtering system is only as good as its algorithm. We know surprisingly little about the algorithms used by most search engines, however, and what we do know doesn't exactly inspire confidence. Between the mid-1990s and the mid-2000s, as Borgman (2007, 90) has pointed out, most search engines tended to ignore user-created metadata such as keywords embedded in HTML-encoded web pages, "despite the massive investments of libraries and publishers in describing the contents and subject matter of scholarly books and journals," because in the early days of the web such metadata was subject to extreme abuse. Website producers often loaded the <**meta keywords**> tags of their HTML headers with redundant and misleading keyword information in order to drive search engines to return links to their pages regardless of the search's actual object. This metadata version of spam, which often loaded search results pages with links to porn sites, led to the tag being almost entirely deprecated by about 1997.[19] With the advent of more trusted systems, such as the Dublin Core Metadata Initiative, which provides community-derived standards for metadata terms, and the Open Archives Initiative Protocol for Metadata Harvesting (OAI-PMH), which allows data providers to make their metadata available to various web services, publishers are increasingly able to provide search engines with reliable metadata.[20]

Again, though, what metadata search engines *actually* rely upon remains an open question. Google's search results, for instance, depend more on the ways other pages link to a text than on the actual content of that text. Most famous is its "PageRank" system, which analyzes links to particular web pages as a means of determining the "importance" of any given page; the more inbound links to a particular page, the higher its PageRank, and the more inbound links to the pages that link to that particular page, the greater weight given to their links in determining the importance of the original page. Links, in other words, are treated as votes, though some votes carry greater weight than others. Google's algorithm is thus heavily determined by popularity, and given the mushiness of popularity as an arbiter of relevance, particularly within scholarly work—not to mention its potential for manipulation, as seen in the rash of "Googlebombing" that swept the Internet in the early 2000s—we might do well to be cautious about relying on the search engine as our primary means of finding the texts we need.[21] This is true even when the subset of what's being searched is specifically scholarly material; Google Scholar remains a problematic research resource both because of the uncertainty surrounding the sources that it indexes—Google does not publish a list of the journals or databases that Google Scholar crawls, though its coverage is undeniably skewed toward the hard sciences—and because it uses citation analysis as one means of determining relevance. Similarly, as Geoff Nunberg (2009) has pointed out, the reliance on machine-generated metadata in the production of the Google Books corpus has led to a "metadata train wreck," an embarrassment of misdated, misattributed, and miscategorized texts. In other words, Google, Google Scholar, and Google Books are already relying upon metadata in producing their search results; it's just not the kind of metadata that we might be most interested in, or that might produce the best results.

As the archives of our scholarship are increasingly stored in digital formats and accessed through search engines that interact with the metadata we use to describe the texts they contain, it becomes much more important for us to develop trustworthy metadata. Such metadata should enable us to classify our digital texts reliably, giving us confidence that the right texts, and not just the most popular ones, will surface when we search for them. These modes of classification may not bear much in common with the hierarchical, ontological systems long in use. As Clay Shirky (2005) has argued, traditional ontologies such as library classification systems work best when the corpus they describe is limited and the producers and users of the ontology are a coordinated group of experts; we can trust that new books entered into a library's cataloging system will be correctly classified because of the finite nature of the data the system organizes and the expertise of those doing the organizing. Such ontologies, Shirky argues, are much less effective when the corpus is large, unstable, or blurrily defined, and when the users are a dispersed group of amateurs. This describes much of the work produced on the Internet, and it will increasingly come to define our scholarly publishing systems, as our digital networks decentralize them, moving them outside traditional institutional and disciplinary frameworks. Because we cannot define in advance the ways that users will employ or want to access the texts we produce—because we can neither know the future nor account for the multiplicity of user perspectives—we need to supplement our expert-produced ontologies with user-generated tagging.

I say "supplement" rather than "replace," because, contra Shirky, certain kinds of expert knowledge will of necessity continue to govern the systems through which scholarly knowledge is organized. Some of the metadata we need to describe our texts, after all, can be objectively determined—author name, title of text, publisher, date—but that information is not always immediately apparent, as Google Books' misattributed and misdated texts indicate. Expert-produced ontologies are key to the disambiguation of apparently identical terms (which "John Jones" is the author of this text? Which date on the copyright page is the original date of publication?). Moreover, certain kinds of expert classifications or subject headings will no doubt still be useful to us, even though the "keywords" that apply to a text might differ from user to user, as readers differ in their senses of a text's important aspects. We can and should thus authoritatively produce certain kinds of metadata, but other kinds cannot be so centralized. For this reason, in the classification systems of the future our metadata needs to be not simply extensible but also *customizable*, drawing upon the best of expert production as well as what is in current web parlance referred to as "crowdsourced" information, so that we can account for the ways that users actually interact with texts.[22] As an example, we might look at the ways that many online library catalogs are beginning to employ not just traditional modes of classification such as Library of Congress subject headings, but also some form of user tagging. My own institution's library catalog is linked to LibraryThing, drawing in the tags that actual readers of a given text have used to categorize it within their own virtual libraries. The current implementation of this link allows users of my library's online catalog to browse by clicking on a user tag and discovering the texts to which users have applied that tag; as of this writing, however, this tag browser does not allow users to add tags to the library's catalog, nor does it associate tags with users. These two bits of functionality would result in a far more effective crowdsourced system of metadata generation by enabling scholars to apply tags to texts, use those tags in the process of filtering their search results, and see how other scholars with whom they work have tagged texts.

For instance, Zotero, an open-source extension for the Firefox web browser produced by the Center for History and New Media at George Mason University, allows users to "collect, manage, and cite" their research sources, as its home page indicates. Beyond this, however, Zotero takes advantage of the social aspects of network-based research, allowing users to create profiles on the site, to synchronize their libraries between their local machines and the website, to share their libraries with other users and follow their libraries in return, to join groups of scholars working on similar issues, to create collective libraries within those groups, and so on. In this fashion, Zotero users can maintain detailed metadata for their own research sources, enabling them to quickly produce bibliographies and other citation information within their writing, but they're also able to see what other scholars are reading. Moreover, Zotero assists its users in making their own websites and other publications Zotero-readable by providing metadata-generating plugins for popular content-management systems such as WordPress.[23] Future plans for the service include making it more commons-oriented, including the development of a recommendation engine that will suggest new texts based on those the user already has in her library ("Development Roadmap" 2010). Through tools such as this one, scholars will be able to help produce and maintain the kinds of citation-oriented metadata required to find important digital resources.

Beyond the problem of finding references to appropriate documents when we search for them, we face another difficulty: ensuring that the texts themselves can be retrieved. Libraries are founded upon the notion of stable, unique object locators, an idea that first became clear to me as an undergraduate, when my university's library was caught in the middle of a transition from the Dewey Decimal System to the Library of Congress Classification System for shelving its books; half the collection was shelved one way, and half the other, and there seemed to me to be no rhyme or reason to the ordering of blocks of shelves on particular floors. In order to find any given text, you needed to know not only how to search the card catalog system—and yes, I am old enough that I mean the *card catalog* system—but also how to look up the locator found there on the library's shelving map. With a few of the usual exceptions (mis-shelved books, books awaiting reshelving, books that were checked out[24]), if you knew how to read the metadata, your search would lead you directly to the book, despite what seemed like a chaotic, if not wholly random, arrangement of texts.

In digital publishing, being able to rely on our locators requires that the links to the texts for which we are searching work; in theory, those links take us directly from the catalog to the text. The web, however, is notoriously prone to "link rot," such that "hard-coded," static links to specific URLs, or Universal Resource Locators, quickly break. A 2005 study found that that the half-life of links included in articles in *D-Lib Magazine*, an online journal focused specifically on issues regarding digital libraries, was about ten years, meaning that after that span of time half of the links no longer functioned (McCown et al. 2005).[25] This presents a significant enough problem for scholarship that the Modern Language Association, in its most recent update of its bibliographic format, deprecated the inclusion of URLs in citations, saying that these links were too fluid to serve as permanent referents, and that searching the web for current links would be more reliable.[26] And they're not wrong: projects move, server structures change, and software upgrades or platform migrations produce entirely new URL models. When we reach a point, however, at which having *no* information about a text's location is preferable to having *some*, because the some we have is more likely to be wrong than right, something has clearly gone wrong.

The mobility of digital resources, which the rewritable nature of the web promotes, is extremely problematic for libraries and archives. As Marlene Manoff (2009, 3) notes, "The function of bibliographic control is to insure that every item has its unique place in an organizational arrangement that allows for systematic searching, discovery and retrieval. But the web plays havoc with the notions of control, order, fixity and hierarchy that are at the heart of the bibliographic enterprise." The answer, however, is neither to mandate fixity on the part of a fluid medium nor to eliminate links and references in our citations. Rather, we need to focus on the implementation of more robust ways of determining where our desired resources are and of creating links to them that will not break even as the resources grow, develop, and move. Our digital publications thus must employ a system of bibliographic identification that allows object identifiers to resolve dynamically into the correct URL as materials move.[27]

The Handle System is a key project working toward this goal. Handle was conceived and developed beginning in 1994 by researchers at the Corporation for National Research Initiatives (a not-for-profit organization that is also, among other things, the publisher of *D-Lib Magazine*); the system provides the specifications for assigning and resolving persistent identifiers for digital objects on the Internet, enabling "a distributed computer system to store names, or handles, of digital resources and resolve those handles into the information necessary to locate, access, and otherwise make use of the resources" (Sun, Lannom, and Boesch 2003). While traditional URLs focus entirely on location, combining the name of a particular web server (regulated by the Domain Name System, or DNS) with the local name of a document, thus tying that resource to a specific filepath on a specific server, handles are unique and persistent references for the *name* of a digital object, rather than its location.[28] A document's handle can remain the same even as the document moves, so long as the metadata in the Handle System associating that document name with a particular URL is updated. Thus links to the document, structured as handles rather than URLs, will continue to function regardless of the document's actual location. Moreover, Handle, unlike DNS, is a fully distributed system; the handle that names a particular document includes a reference to a "naming authority," or a local instance of the Handle System that resolves the object's name, followed by the name itself. The global Handle namespace is thus the sum of all local namespaces, registered with the global system and governed by local naming authorities. A user's request for a particular handle is sent by the global Handle System to the appropriate local naming authority, which then resolves the handle into the correct URL.

While there are over a thousand handle services running today, a key implementation of the service is found in the Digital Object Identifier (DOI) system, which is in use in many scientific and scholarly publications and which has registered over 40 million handles (see Handle System 2009). The DOI system, which is governed by a not-for-profit foundation initially funded by its member organizations,[29] is an application of Handle focused specifically on intellectual property, adding much more robust metadata about each digital object, including information about access rights, display formats, encryption, and the like, in addition to the more bibliographic forms of metadata discussed above (Rosenblatt 1997). The identifier in the DOI system refers, as in Handle, to a particular object, but based upon the object's metadata, the identifier might resolve to one of a number of potential URLs; for instance, a journal article may be mirrored on multiple servers or may be available in multiple formats, and thus the DOI would direct the user to the most appropriate copy for the user's location and browser. The most extensive implementation of DOI is CrossRef, founded in 2000 by a group of leading scholarly publishers who formed a non-profit, independent organization, Publishers International Linking Association, to oversee the project. Today nearly 3,000 publishers and scholarly societies around the world use its services, for which they pay an annual fee as well as transaction costs for each DOI registered with CrossRef. Library affiliates of CrossRef can use its system to provide links from citations or database records to the digital objects in question (see CrossRef.org, "Fast Facts").

DOI and CrossRef thus provide a means of creating and resolving persistent, unique handles for and links to digital texts published online; they also provide the potential for access control to particular documents based on copyright restrictions and the user's subscription information. Used in conjunction with OpenURL, which "provides a standardized format for transporting bibliographic metadata about objects between information services" (Van de Sompel and Beit-Arie 2001), thus providing for "context-sensitive linking" (Paskin 2010), DOI handles can resolve to the most appropriate copy of a digital object, using information about a user's institutional affiliation. If, for instance, the user's library has a subscription to a particular journal, the DOI can resolve into full access to the article from an appropriate provider; otherwise, it can resolve into a link through which the user can request the article or get more information about the library's holdings.

Handle, DOI, CrossRef, and OpenURL are each produced by a group of interested parties, whether researchers, publishers, or librarians; are governed by not-for-profit corporations or foundations; and are designed with openness and extensibility in mind. The projects are therefore complementary rather than competitive, solving more problems together than they can independently. Of course, simply *having* systems such as these won't do us much good unless those systems are *used*; as creators of new digital objects, whether as authors or as publishers, we must insist on the use of persistently resolvable object identifiers in our links and appropriate metadata in our archives, to ensure that the resources we use and create in our research remain searchable and addressable in the future.

Access

None of the metadata and locator systems discussed above, however, preserve the digital objects themselves. In addition to ensuring that our digital objects conform to durable, community-derived standards, so that they remain readable on the platforms of the future, and providing appropriate metadata, so that they can be found, we also must ensure that the digital files themselves continue to exist so that they can be accessed. Although, as

I argued in the introduction to this chapter, the hard disk is a more durable medium of inscription than we often give it credit for being, things can nonetheless go wrong; trusting your hard drive so much that you fail to back it up could be a costly mistake.[30] Even more, as we move increasingly toward distributed, "cloud"-based storage systems, we can find ourselves at the mercy of a service provider's continued viability; should they suddenly go out of business, the files they house could become inaccessible.[31] Preserving our digital future requires careful attention to the digital objects themselves, and ensuring that our access to them is uninterrupted.

Some have claimed that preservation and access work at cross purposes, an idea that carries over from a conflict inherent in traditional physical archiving (in which public access to and use of an object may directly interfere with that object's preservation);[32] in fact, however, "digital preservation is inseparable from questions of access" (Kirschenbaum 2008, 189). This is so not only because the process of preservation is different in the digital realm from that in print—as Kenneth Thibodeau (2002) points out, the process of digital preservation depends upon access for its success[33]—but also because the very point of digital preservation is ensuring future usability. For this reason, among others, we need to think carefully about questions related to access as we consider our preservation practices.

The issue surrounding access that has gotten the most play in debates about digital scholarly publishing is the question of open-access publishing; as the topic has been covered admirably in books such as John Willinsky's *The Access Principle* (2006) and Gary Hall's *Digitize This Book!* (2008), I won't belabor the issue here. Suffice it to say that the ethical issues surrounding open-access publishing have been clouded by the circulation of much misinformation about the practice—for instance, that the only road to open access is an author-pays model; there are many other models for increasing access to published materials, as Willinsky and Hall both demonstrate.[34] One key model is the institutional repository, which allows authors to self-archive their work. These repositories, often set up through university libraries, are an important step toward establishing open access to the products of scholarly research, and as Hall and others have convincingly argued, depositing our work in open-access archives like these is a matter not just of pragmatics but of ethics. Many publishers also now support the self-archiving of journal articles, at least in pre-print, if not post-print, form.

Nonetheless, there are some problems associated with relying on the institutional repository (or even the disciplinary repository, such as the arXiv pre-print server); preservation requires access, but access is not enough to ensure preservation. As noted by the authors of the report "E-Journal Archiving Metes and Bounds," published by the Council on Library and Information Resources, "Open 'archives' are primarily concerned with providing open access to current information and not with long-term preservation of the contents" (Kenney et al. 2006, 24). While some repository systems such as DSpace provide tools that promote such long-term preservation, many libraries' digital archives may not provide the mechanisms necessary for ensuring uninterrupted access to the materials they contain in the event of catastrophic system failure, nor do all of them have in place the ability to migrate or emulate their contents on newer platforms as needed. Moreover, while such archives currently contain the contents of published articles, they often do not contain *the published articles themselves*. Some journals still don't allow for self-archiving, of course, and those that do typically allow it only in "pre-print" form, meaning that the manuscript as submitted to a publisher prior to the peer-review process may be deposited in an institutional archive, or at best in "post-print" form, the final manuscript submitted after the review and revision process. Very few publishers allow the final typeset article as published to be archived in open-access form. Given that research and citation practices in the humanities and social sciences still require the published version of a text to be consulted, we must ensure that our repositories contain those published versions before we can fully rely upon them as a means of preserving the scholarly record. Repositories are an important step toward preservation, but they do not get us all the way there.

In order to fully preserve that scholarly record, we need to consider how our publications, which are increasingly delivered in digital form, are distributed and stored, how our libraries subscribe to such publications, and how that content is handled, both by publishers and by libraries. In the past, a library's subscription to a journal resulted in the delivery of a printed copy that was physically housed in the library and which the library continued to own even if the subscription were canceled or the journal ceased to publish. In today's digital publishing systems, however, that "delivery" is more often the provision of access to files on a publisher's server than it is of the actual files themselves; the library may never "possess" those texts at all, and should the subscription be canceled or the journal cease publication, that access may suddenly disappear. The question of persistent access to such licensed materials was most crucially raised by Donald Waters, reporting on a meeting of digital library specialists and university administrators sponsored by the Mellon Foundation, pointing out the risks involved:

When research and academic libraries license electronic journals, they do not [get] to take local possession of a copy as they did with print. Rather, they use content stored on remote systems controlled by publishers, and economies of scale in electronic publishing are driving control of more and more journals into fewer and fewer hands. Although some—but certainly not all—licenses now recognize that libraries have permanent rights to use electronic journal content, these rights remain largely theoretical. If a publisher fails to maintain its archive, goes out of business or, for other reasons, stops making available the journal on which scholarship in a particular field depends, there are no practical means in place for libraries to exercise their permanent usage rights and the scholarly record represented by that journal would likely be lost. (Waters 2005, 1)

Waters advocates the creation of a cooperative means of ensuring long-term access to such digital materials in the event of publisher failure or other forms of loss, and to specify the kinds of services that such an archiving solution might provide, before going on to insist that *"research and academic libraries and associated academic institutions must effectively demand archival deposit by publishers as a condition of licensing electronic journals"* (p. 3). This need for archival deposit cannot be satisfied by the "legal deposit" requirement of the national libraries, as noted in the "Metes and Bounds" report:

First, and most important, while most of the laws are intended to ensure that the journals will be preserved, there is less clarity as to how one can gain access to those journals. In almost all cases, one can visit the national library and consult an electronic publication onsite. It is unlikely, however, that the national libraries will be able to provide online access to remote users in the event of changes in subscription models, changed market environments, or possibly even publisher failure. (Kenney et al. 2006, 21–22)

Similarly, the report argues, archival deposit cannot be satisfied by a publisher's assurances of persistent access: "The question, of course, is whether one can trust the publisher or distributor to keep older content accessible and unchanged, especially after the publisher stops distributing a title or the library stops subscribing to it. Hence, the second option found in many licenses: the requirement that publishers will give libraries copies of the files that constitute an e-journal" (p. 7). Libraries that actually possess the files that constitute the digital scholarly record stand a far better chance of ensuring that the record is preserved.

By this argument, libraries must share in the responsibility for preservation by ensuring that the files they need remain accessible in the event that publishers fail to do so. However, the difficulties involved in each and every library creating and maintaining a full archive of the materials to which it subscribes would be insurmountable, while institution-specific, or even consortium-specific, archiving projects would produce too much duplication of effort that might be better distributed and shared. The Mellon Foundation has thus taken the lead, first by funding a series of prototype projects and then more substantially funding the establishment of two large cooperative projects focusing on the production and maintenance of digital journal archives. The first of these projects, centered at the Stanford University Libraries, is LOCKSS (or Lots Of Copies Keeps Stuff Safe). LOCKSS describes itself as an "international community initiative" (LOCKSS, "Home"), bringing together hundreds of university libraries worldwide. Each library installs the open-source, freely available LOCKSS system on an inexpensive desktop computer, which is then referred to as a "LOCKSS box." This LOCKSS box crawls the websites of publishers who have given the system access, capturing the presentation files (as opposed to the source files) of the journals to which the library subscribes. The LOCKSS box then maintains communication with the full network of other such boxes, comparing the content it has collected with other libraries' archives and repairing any difference or damage that is found; as the project's name suggests, the redundancy of its distributed files creates a safety net for the material. The archives that are created via LOCKSS are referred to as "light archives," meaning that their files are immediately accessible when needed (as opposed to a "dark archive," which remains inaccessible except under certain specific circumstances). Additionally, the LOCKSS system "preserves the content in its original format and dynamically migrates the content to a newer format, if required, when a reader requests the preserved content" (LOCKSS, "How It Works"); migration-on-access allows the files to be preserved in their original presentation formats (thus meeting archival requirements), while providing a means of preventing those formats from becoming technologically obsolete that absolves individual libraries of migration responsibilities.

The LOCKSS project is emblematic of a community-driven preservation program; the hardware is inexpensive, the software is free, and the network is self-correcting. The system is maintained, and the direction for its future development set, by the subscribing members of the LOCKSS Alliance. Alliance members thus have more input over the system's functioning than do unpaid users, and they have the ability to "collect and preserve premium content not available to the general LOCKSS community" ("LOCKSS Alliance"). The basic functionality of the system, however, is made available to any interested library. As Don Waters (2002, 91) has described it, an archive such as this one, like Robert Frost's wall, is of necessity a communal endeavor, but it's also the endeavor that builds the community: "what makes good neighbors is the very act of keeping good the common resource between them—the act of making and taking the time together to preserve and mend the resource." LOCKSS is thus grounded in the alliance it has forged among libraries, recognizing that strength of preservation rests in the numbers of and connections among entities doing the preserving. Moreover, the LOCKSS Alliance has begun a second cooperative project named CLOCKSS (for Controlled LOCKSS), through which a select number of member libraries archive not just the journals to which they subscribe, but *all* journal content to which publishers allow access, both presentation files and source files, thus seeking to provide what the CLOCKSS website calls a "sustainable, geographically distributed dark archive with which to ensure the long-term survival of Web-based scholarly publications for the benefit of the greater global research community." In the case of a select number of "trigger events" (such as a publisher going out of business or a publication being discontinued), CLOCKSS will make its archives of that preserved material available not just to its members but to the *entire* scholarly community.[35] CLOCKSS will not, however, provide post-cancellation access to its archives, and is thus not a substitute for the local archive provided by LOCKSS.

The second such preservation project originally funded by the Mellon Foundation is Portico, a centralized system that produces dark archives of electronic journal literature. A project of Ithaka, the parent organization of J-STOR, Portico is now governed by an advisory committee of librarians and publishers and supported by library subscriptions and publisher contributions. Portico archives the publisher source files for all approved content, "normalizing" them into a standard archival format that will permit their long-term management (see "Portico's Archival Approach"). This initial migration can be followed by future migrations as technological formats become obsolete. Like CLOCKSS, Portico's archives remain dark until the occurrence of a trigger event; unlike CLOCKSS, those archives are then opened only to Portico subscribers.

The differences between LOCKSS and Portico are thus in part the difference between a co-op and a subscriber service, with very different implications for the libraries involved. As Karen Schneider wrote in *Library Journal*:

LOCKSS is attractive to libraries already comfortably maintaining servers and open source software; for these institutions, Portico's proprietary software and annual licensing fees are less appealing. Librarians using Portico counter that LOCKSS has fewer publishers participating (one librarian at an institution with a large e-journal collection reported that LOCKSS had 12 percent of its titles and Portico 33 percent) and stress Portico's ease of use, as Portico maintains the content on its own servers. (Schneider 2007)

The two projects also espouse different archiving and migration philosophies, as LOCKSS maintains the original presentation files while Portico maintains standardized content in nonproprietary formats.[36] A study published by the Joint Information Systems Committee (JISC) in 2008 comparing the performance of the two systems, among a range of other such programs, acknowledges that the preservation landscape presents "a confusing and not wholly reassuring picture to those professionals trying to make sense of what is happening and looking for simple, clear-cut guidelines" (Morrow et al. 2008, 7). LOCKSS provides immediate availability of publisher files that suddenly become inaccessible, but it has lower publisher buy-in than Portico because some publishers feel their intellectual property rights threatened by having content archived in multiple locations. By contrast, Portico, with its centralized, dark archives, has far greater publisher participation, but has a much higher threshold for the release of its files, and thus subscribers may face a potentially longer delay before archived material can be made available. LOCKSS requires a relatively small investment from libraries, primarily for staff and equipment, but it does need some ongoing technical maintenance; Portico eliminates the need for such in-house maintenance, but does so by imposing significant annual subscription costs on libraries (Morrow et al. 2008, 16–18). Donald Waters has suggested that Mellon's decision to fund the startup of both projects was meant "to give the marketplace of scholarly institutions an opportunity to vote with their own investments" (quoted in Schneider 2007). However, the JISC report concludes that neither project as yet provides complete insurance against the potential disappearance of the digital scholarly record: "None of the current initiatives is likely to yet fulfil [*sic*] all the access and archival needs of a modern library" (Morrow et al. 2008, 7). That said, the report strongly suggests that both approaches "deserve support," and that libraries should invest in "well thought through and sustainable archiving solutions" (ibid.).

Of course, these programs are for the most part journal-specific, and the more digital our publishing systems become, the more we're going to need to think about these same questions with respect to digital books, as well as a wide variety of forms of born-digital scholarship.[37] As Borgman has pointed out, and as the 2009 incident in which Amazon remotely deleted legally purchased copies of several unauthorized editions of George Orwell's novels from users' Kindles confirms, the business model for e-book publishing remains in flux; sales of digital monographs

> may follow the leased bundles models of journals. Libraries and individuals could subscribe to digital books, much as they subscribe to movies with Netflix. Rather than borrow or purchase individual titles, they may have access to a fixed number of titles at a time, or "check books out" for a fixed period of time. These models raise a host of questions about relationships among publishers, libraries, and readers with regard to the privacy of reading habits, the continuity of access, preservation, and censorship. (Borgman 2007, 113)

Some subset of that "host of questions" was raised by Clifford Lynch as far back as 2001:

- Can you loan or give an e-book (or access to a digital book) to someone else as you can a physical book? To what extent do digital books mimic (and perhaps even improve upon) physical books, and to what extent do they break with that tradition? What other constraints on usage (for example, printing) exist?
- Do you own *objects* or *access*? If your library of e-books is destroyed or stolen, can you replace it without purchasing the content again simply by providing proof of license or purchase? One very interesting service is a registry that allows you to replace your e-books if you lose your appliance.
- From whom are you really obtaining content—the e-book reader vendor, a publisher, or some other party? Who has to stay in business in order to ensure your continued ability to use that content? What happens if the source of your content goes out of business?
- Can you copy an e-book for private, personal use? If you own two readers, can you move a digital book from one to the other without having to purchase it again?
- Do you have the right and the ability to reformat an e-book or a digital book in response to changes in standards or technologies or do you need to repurchase it? What happens when you upgrade or replace your e-book reader with another one? What happens when you replace the PC that might house your "library"? What happens if you replace one brand of e-book reader with another, perhaps because your reader vendor goes out of business?

- Do you have to obtain e-books on a pay-per-view or other limited time rental basis or do you buy a perpetual license to the content, or ownership of a copy?
- What are the policies of the content provider with regard to your privacy and to usage monitoring? What limitations does your book reader technology place on the ability of a content supplier to collect usage data?

Few of these questions have been adequately answered, and the answers that we do have are unsatisfying, mostly pointing to increasing levels of digital rights management and decreasing user control. Other questions have continued to crop up alongside these: What plans exist for archiving multimodal scholarship? Are our open access journals and repositories adequately backed up? What provisions are being made for preserving access to data sets and other digital source material? Such questions about access will no doubt proliferate as new modes of scholarly work expand; it seems clear, however, that whatever long-term solutions to problems of preserving digital scholarly content arise will of necessity be *social* in origin, requiring the input and commitment of many individuals and institutions in order to succeed.

Cost

These solutions will also require significant investments of time and money on the part of institutions and individuals. As the JISC report notes, "Any e-journal preservation process is going to cost money. The costs include, among other things, storage hardware systems, processing and retrieval software (all of which require regular maintenance and updating), and people to watch over and develop the systems and services" (Morrow et al. 2008, 11). This is true for all forms of digital scholarship, of course, and the more process-intensive born-digital forms will, if anything, require more such attention. Preservation thus has significant budgetary implications for libraries and their broader institutions, as indicated by the report of the Blue Ribbon Task Force:

> To accommodate the new resource requirements imposed by the long-term stewardship of digital assets, it is likely that many organizations, at least in the short-run, will need to shift funds from one allocation to another within an effectively fixed budget. For example, a library might reduce its investment in services and infrastructure surrounding its print collection in order to release resources to support increased investments in the long-term stewardship of its digital collections. (Blue Ribbon Task Force 2008, 16)

As the report also indicates, these investments must be ongoing, as preservation "*is not a one-time cost*; instead, it is a commitment to an ongoing series of costs, in some cases stretching over an indefinite time horizon" (p. 18). It cannot be funded in a one-off, ad hoc fashion, but must instead be understood infrastructurally: "Organizations must secure sufficient resources to sustain their digital preservation activities beyond the next budget cycle or the end of a grant award" (p. 12). Some institutions may hesitate to begin preservation programs in part due to anxiety about their projected costs, but as Brian Lavoie and Lorcan Dempsey (2004) have noted, the projections that have been undertaken to this point may have overestimated those costs, given their focus on the upfront expenses of starting up a new preservation program. That said, ongoing preservation will require ongoing resources, and figuring out where those resources will come from—and what might need to be cut in order to make room for preservation—will not be easy.

In making such choices, institutions will be required to weigh the costs of preservation less against its benefits than against the risks presented by failing to ensure persistent access to digital resources. Traditional cost-benefit analysis could lead institutions to focus on the "what's in it for us" aspect of preservation, leading them to withhold resources that seem better spent on meeting the institution's own needs. By contrast, real risk assessment might force institutions to recognize their responsibilities to something beyond themselves: the risks involved are posed not institution by institution, but to the entire scholarly enterprise, suggesting that the responsibility for mitigating such risks accrues to everyone, *even if everyone cannot meet that responsibility equally*. As Waters (2002) has pointed out, preservation must be thought of as serving a public good. The problem with the public good, of course, is precisely the assumption that someone else will take responsibility for maintaining it; without a commitment by every institution to the preservation of our common scholarly record, it could easy fall victim to the "tragedy of the commons," in which self-interest dictates taking more resources than one contributes. On the other hand, an equal danger to the public good of preservation is the assumption that others will be "free riders," using preserved resources without contributing to their development. Even if preservation might be compared, as in Waters's essay, to the annual task of wall-mending, responsible preservation programs cannot and should not lead to the production of walled gardens. As Lavoie and Dempsey (2004) point out, one of the chief characteristics of a public good is "the difficulty in excluding those who do not contribute toward the provision of the good from enjoying its benefits." To some extent, we must create strong preservation practices and programs as though everyone were participating proportionately in them, and share their benefits with everyone equally, regardless of participation level.

In this way, CLOCKSS might serve as a prime example, less for its data model or service structure than for its assumption that a core group of large institutions who *can* help create a permanent scholarly archive *should* do so in order to mitigate the risks posed to scholarship as a whole. The specific benefits that accrue to those participating institutions lie less in exclusive access to the resources they help create than in their ability to help shape that common good: "CLOCKSS participants have the opportunity to be deeply involved in all aspects of our industry and help to keep the community's best interests at the forefront" (CLOCKSS, "Benefits"). Providing adequate "community incentives"—incentives for institutions to act not just in their own self-interest but in the larger public interest—will be required for any preservation program to succeed (Blue Ribbon Task Force 2008, 8, 25). But the community itself must in some sense be the incentive; we must recognize that, by and large, the projects I've discussed in this chapter have not simply been produced *by* a community, but also *for* a community, and with the result, whether intended or not, of *producing* a community.

And yet there remains the problem of labor; *someone* must take responsibility not just for the production of new forms of digital scholarship but for their preservation into the future, a job that will only get bigger as time goes on. As Borgman (2007, 95) notes, "Files must be mounted, computers must be maintained, software must be updated, data must be backed up and migrated, and people must be paid—even if no new data are added to the database." Libraries, presses, and information technology centers will all be required to devote employee time and expertise to such digital preservation, but institutions must devote sufficient resources to these units in order to support the employees involved. Doing so in a sustainable fashion that draws upon the potential collaborations across academic units, and across institutions, will require the most strategic thinking yet about the future structure of the university itself—the subject of the next chapter.

5

The University

To imagine that funding infusions from ACLS, NEH, and Mellon will stem this tide is to imagine that sandbags will hold back a tsunami.

> —Jerome McGann, "Information Technology and the Troubled Humanities"

The bottom line is that scholarly publishing isn't financially feasible as a business model—never was, never was intended to be, and should not be. *If scholarship paid, we wouldn't need university presses.*

> —Cathy Davidson, in Carlos Alonso et al., *Crises and Opportunities: The Futures of Scholarly Publishing*

Recognize that publishing is an integral part of the core mission and activities of universities, and take ownership of it.

> —Laura Brown et al., "University Publishing in a Digital Age"

Everything that I've suggested up to this point—the need for a revitalized peer-to-peer mode of open, post-publication review of texts; the need for new understandings of authorship as dialogic, diffuse, and mobile; the need for new publishing structures that reflect a turn from focusing on texts as discrete products to texts as the locus of conversation; the need for new social modes of distribution and preservation for the texts produced within these new structures—all of these changes are aimed at the project of helping scholarly publishing in general, and university press publishing in particular, become viable within the digital environment that is becoming its inevitable future. None of these transformations, however, directly addresses the key problem with which this project began: the wholly unsustainable economic model under which such publishing currently operates. Unless that model is transformed, none of the recommendations that I've made thus far will have much effect. As I noted in the introduction, digital publishing will not do enough in and of itself to assuage the financial crisis that scholarly publishing finds itself in—though some new technologies could reduce costs by streamlining and automating the production process, digital publishing will nonetheless require significant investments of labor and other resources to create, preserve, and filter the new textual structures on which we will be working into the future. The bottom line here is clear: the current system of scholarly publishing is fiscally impossible, and building the new system necessary for the revitalization of the academy will require real investment. Where will this investment come from, and why should we be driven to make it?

This chapter is the most speculative, and the least argumentative or predictive, of this volume. I am not an economist, nor have I done time in the higher reaches of university administration. Anything I might argue could be subject to rebuttal or easy dismissal by administrators who are far more painfully aware than I am of the fiscal realities of higher education in the era of the Great Recession. Moreover, as prediction, this chapter would run the risk of becoming an exercise in futurology—the problem being, of course, that the future always eventually arrives, though without the jetpacks and the hovercars. In the main, then, this chapter is neither working to prescribe a new business model for scholarly publishing, nor to predict the future place of scholarly communication within the university structure. Instead, I want to make a few suggestions, primarily as thought experiments, about possible means of emerging from the current morass. These suggestions neither preclude nor require one another. This is not a program. It is, if anything, a reminder that thinking creatively about the future of publishing will require thinking creatively about the future of the academy as a whole. I therefore do not claim that my suggestions are the only fruitful directions in which the academy might proceed, but I believe that together they point toward what Jonathan Zittrain (2008) might refer to as a more "generative" environment for experimentation in the future form of scholarly publishing. Furthermore, the suggestions I make here are backed up, in large part, by similar recommendations contained in reports by groups including the Association of American Universities (AAU), the Association of College and Research Libraries (ACRL), the Scholarly Publishing and Academic Resources Coalition (SPARC), and numerous others. While these reports differ in many of their details, and in the pathways they propose toward the desired outcome of revitalizing scholarly publishing, the convergence of opinions in them reveals one certainty: There is no going back; the only way forward is through.

Publishing, Not for Profit

So let us begin the process of reimagining the funding of scholarly publishing by taking a hard look at the current situation, as well as several recent studies thereof. As John Thompson explores in *Books in the Digital Age*, the contemporary university press exists in a somewhat nebulous position with respect to its institution:

> Many of the American university presses have traditionally received financial assistance from their host institutions in various forms, ranging from annual operating grants to cover deficits to rent-free accommodation, free employee benefits and interest-free overdraft facilities. . . . However, not all American university presses receive direct financial assistance from their host institutions. Some are expected to break even, and in recent decades many of the university presses have experienced growing pressure to reduce their dependence on their host institutions. (Thompson 2005, 88–89)

University presses are thus both part of and distinct from their institutions, bearing the university's name and yet merely "hosted" by it; the press's employees, while receiving benefits from the university, are somehow imagined not to be university employees. The press in this model becomes an independent company run on the university campus, operating on a not-for-profit basis and yet, by and large, structured as a revenue center, required to recover its costs via sales. And, in fact, the universities that are still able to subsidize the presses they host do so in a fairly minuscule fashion; as of 2004 the average subsidy received by a university press from its host institution represented less than 8 percent of its annual budget (Givler 2004).[1] For this reason, it's likely that many university administrators and press directors are thinking about the financial future of scholarly publishing as a problem of income, asking how we can make publishing pay, rather than how we can pay for publishing. Thompson (2005, 184) suggests that "in relation to the revenue generated in current market conditions, the American university presses are overproducing and underpricing their scholarly monographs. They are able to do this provided that their host institutions are willing to subsidize the press and/or provided that they are able to generate surpluses in their other publishing activities, which they can use to create an internal subsidy for their monograph programme." Lurking behind this understanding of the production and pricing of scholarly texts, however, is the assumption that the function of the university press is and should be marketplace-driven. If this is the case, Thompson is correct: the business model of scholarly publishing is entirely wrong.

There are certainly reasons to focus on sales in scholarly publishing. The enterprise of book publishing, even scholarly publishing, can be financially lucrative, as suggested by the examples of commercial publishers like Pearson, Wiley, and so forth, or even the models presented by Oxford and Cambridge University Presses. Pearson, the largest international publishing conglomerate, reported overall sales for 2007 of £4.218 billion (approximately $8.394 billion) and higher education sales of £793 million (approximately $1.578 billion), resulting in net profits of £634 million ($1.262 billion) overall, and £161 million ($320 million) in its higher education division; for 2008, sales were £4.811 billion with a reported profit of £762 million, and even during *annus horribilus* 2009, sales were £5.624 billion with an operating profit of £858 million (see Pearson 2007, 2008, 2009). Wiley likewise reported revenue of $1.674 billion during the fiscal year ending April 2008, with a net income of $128.8 million, and revenue of $1.611 billion during the fiscal year ending April 2009, with a net income of $128.2 million (see John Wiley & Sons 2008, 2009). Even university presses can be profitable: Oxford University Press reported sales of £492.3 million during the fiscal year ending March 2008, producing a net profit of £77.2 million, and sales of £578.7 million during the following fiscal year, producing a net profit of £84 million. Cambridge University Press's more modest sales of £179.5 million from the fiscal year ending April 2008 nonetheless resulted in a net surplus of £3.0 million, while sales of £205.1 million from the following fiscal year resulted in a net surplus of £3.4 million (see Oxford University Press 2008, 2009; Cambridge University Press 2008, 2009). Of course, Pearson's revenues come overwhelmingly from trade publishing and other aspects of their media holdings, and their higher-education sales are primarily textbook-derived, and Wiley's book division is heavily subsidized by its journal-publishing program. Even Cambridge and Oxford's more traditional scholarly publishing divisions are made possible by their more profitable trade and textbook divisions. In other words, the lucrative results realized by these publishers are largely attributable to a far more diversified, market-oriented corporate structure than that of the average university press.[2]

Most university presses in the United States, however, have as the cornerstone of their missions the publication of the products of scholarly research, for use by scholars in further research, bringing intellectual distinction to their institutions through their contributions to the advancement of knowledge in key academic fields. Were the university press to follow Thompson's advice and both reduce the quantity of texts it produces and raise the prices of the resulting texts, two consequences would likely follow. First, the press would have a more difficult time fulfilling the scholarly end of its mission, as greater selectivity in publishing would require increasingly difficult decisions about which few texts to publish, running the risk of such decisions increasingly being based on the potential for sales. Almost inevitably, such choices would exercise a conservative influence over scholarship, as genuinely new ideas would present concrete financial risks; it's equally certain that more junior faculty members in book-based fields would have difficulty meeting the requirements for tenure and promotion, as publishing a scholar's first book is always something of a gamble. Second, higher prices would require the press to become increasingly reliant on university and research libraries as their primary customers. In fact, the largest market for the products of university presses is *already* university libraries (Thompson 2005, 107), which operate under budgets that are not only finite but are granted by many of the same institutions that house the presses.[3] Thus, for the university press to remain oriented toward the dissemination of scholarship in its current form and yet create a truly functional revenue model that might parallel that of the commercial scholarly presses, would in effect result in one branch of the academy holding another branch hostage, producing content that libraries must have and then charging extortive rates for it.[4]

In fact, the degree to which the largest commercial scholarly publishers have put the bite on universities (by obtaining the products of scholarship, most of which were produced through university, foundation, and government funding, without compensation to authors or their institutions—indeed, at times even demanding payment *from* them—and then selling those products back to universities via obscenely expensive journal subscriptions) might encourage us to rethink the profit-model of scholarly publishing altogether, to consider whether there's another option through which universities can reclaim the core of the publishing endeavor from the commercial presses. The commercial presses can't be beaten at their own game, as the large commercial publishing conglomerates will always be able to conduct such business more efficiently, and more ruthlessly, than the university should want to do. But nor can we simply abandon the business of scholarly publishing to them; as Thompson notes, in times of economic slowdown "commercial logic would tend to override any obligation they might feel to the scholarly community" (Thompson 2005, 98), leaving nothing to stop them from eliminating monograph publishing entirely. We can't beat them, and we can't join them; what we can do is change the game entirely.

One clear way of changing the game, dramatically and unequivocally, is a move toward the full embrace of open-access modes of digital publishing. While the notion of open access has generated a great deal of controversy among presses—who, given current financial realities, declare its proponents naive and its ideals untenable—a number of presses, including Athabasca University Press in Canada, have embraced open access as part of their commitment to operating within "a knowledge-based economy, to which we contribute by providing peer-reviewed publications unfettered by the desire to commodify thought or to restrict access to ideas" ("About the Press"). Even so, as John Willinsky (2006, p. xii) has argued, "open access is not free access . . . the open access movement is not operating in denial of economic realities. Rather, it is concerned with increasing access to more of the research literature for more people, with that increase measured over what is currently available in print and electronic formats." In fact, Willinsky, in his work with the Public Knowledge Project (PKP), has sought to make open-access publishing more affordable by producing Open Journal Systems (OJS), a software package that streamlines and automates the editorial and production mechanisms for online journals, vastly reducing their production costs. PKP is currently working to extend this model for open publishing to book production, via Open Monograph Press (OMP), a free and open modular system designed to support the production and publication of book-length scholarly texts, whether in print, online, or both (see Public Knowledge Project, "Open Monograph Press"; Willinsky 2009). Through projects such as these, open-access publishing is in fact being made *more* affordable than traditional market-based models.

However, the real call for open-access publishing models has its roots not in the subversion of market forces in the distribution of scholarship, but in the ethical desire to break down the barrier between the information "haves" and "have-nots" of the twenty-first-century university structure. Proponents of open access hope to enable institutions without substantive endowments, and those in less-wealthy states and developing nations, to have access to the most important new developments in scholarly research. Such access is arguably most crucial in medical and other scientific fields, but we must resist the suggestion that the humanities, and particularly fields such as literary and media studies, are relative luxuries that do not demand similar openness of distribution; fields such as these continue to represent the central interpretive and analytical skills of our, and our students', being in the world, and it is therefore no less important for the products of research in these fields to be made as widely available as possible. If part of the core mission of the university—particularly state-funded institutions, but including those private institutions that, as New York University's motto would have it, consider themselves to serve the public interest—is the production and dissemination of new forms of knowledge, then open-access modes of distribution would seem to be far more in keeping with that mission than would the closed, cost-recovery model.[5] Moreover, in troubled economic and political times, as lawmakers and governmental bodies take an increasingly skeptical look at higher education, raising demands for accountability and "results," open-access publishing presents an increased potential for bringing institutional accomplishments to public attention, making clear both what it is we in the academy do and why it's important that we do it. Open-access publishing is thus not merely an altruistic gift to the general public, but is in fact a means of making clear the extent to which the academy's interests *are* the public interest.[6]

Of course, even with the significant cost reductions that automated systems make possible, decreasing if not eliminating university press sales revenues through open-access distribution is hardly likely to solve the budgetary crisis the press faces. In attempting to circumvent the profit motives of publishers such as Elsevier and Wiley, some open-access publishing ventures in the sciences—most notably, the Public Library of Science projects—have managed their costs by passing them back to scholars who, via an "author-pays" model of publishing, are charged as much as $2,850 to have an article included in the journal. For better or worse, this system mostly works in the sciences, in which nearly all research is grant-supported, and in which scholars have long written publishing costs into the budgets for their grants. In the humanities, however, the vast majority of research is *not* grant-supported, but rather self-funded, and where there are grants available, they are generally too minuscule to allow for the inclusion of publishing costs. Some commentators have suggested that, in the humanities, universities should establish "a publication subvention attached to every junior professor's line, much like—but requiring far less funding than—the start-up capital that faculty positions in the sciences are endowed with as a matter of course" (Alonso 2003, 8). Such a subvention would do much to ensure that a press would be financially able to publish the junior scholar's manuscript, as $5,000 would cover the first-copy costs for a digital monograph (subsequent copies being, effectively, free). However, a university-subvention model of funding scholarly publishing would present significant risks, not least that only the wealthiest institutions would be able to provide these funds. Moreover, despite their best intentions, presses would inevitably be lured into accepting only those manuscripts that came with subventions, sacrificing potentially exciting projects in favor of those that cushion the bottom line. In the end, the costs involved in publishing, whether in the current print-based model or in the digital publishing ventures of the future, cannot be managed by passing them back to authors, whether they are covered through grants or subventions, without further restricting publishing prospects, especially in the humanities.

Aside from shifting to open access, another means of changing the game might include thinking about new revenue models under which scholarly presses charge not for the products they produce, but rather for the services they provide. These services might include the print-on-demand production of hard copies of texts made available for free in digital form. In the National Academies Press (NAP) model, for example, a free version of every text is made available online, with downloadable or print versions of the text available for a fee ("About PDFs"). The evidence is somewhat contradictory about the impact of making free, full-text digital copies of books available online on the sales rate of hard-copy texts, but most indicators suggest that this arrangement drives sales in the long term, rather than wholly cannibalizing them; the availability of the text via the Internet draws in readers via Google searches, but most of those readers still prefer reading offline (see Doctorow 2006a; Jensen 2005). However, much has also been made of NAP director of strategic web communications Michael Jensen's comments at the 2009 meeting of the American Association of University Presses, in which he appeared to suggest that NAP was losing sales, and thus losing money, in this open-access/print-on-demand model. In a conversation with me in February 2010, however, Jensen argued that he was merely trying to indicate that openness itself was not the answer to publishers' concerns about their business models, and that some deeper reformulation of publisher thinking was required. According to Jensen, NAP's mission requires it to provide as much openness as possible while still remaining self-sustaining; while this balance is becoming increasingly difficult in the current economic climate, it's nonetheless working. Almost certainly NAP has lost some sales due to its open-access model; according to Jensen, the press knows that it's giving away more than would be optimal if the question of profit were paramount—but instead, the press is seeking a way to squeak by, automating as much as possible, and producing texts as cheaply as possible, in order to remain as open as possible. Assuming that most university presses have the same mission as NAP, this open-access/print-on-demand model might be extensible.

Other services for which university presses might charge could focus on the structures through which digital texts are made available, and the modes of engagement that they might provide for readers and researchers. Those modes of engagement would ask publishers to emphasize not the individual text, but rather the interconnection of texts across their lists and across the web; as Thompson (2005, 369) suggests, "The best way to maximize the added value of delivering scholarly book content online is *to treat individual books as part of a scholarly corpus or database which has scale, selectivity and focus*" (emphasis in original). A corpus model such as Thompson describes rests at the heart of the Mellon-funded collaboration led by New York University Press (with the University of Pennsylvania, Temple University, and Rutgers University Presses), which is exploring the development of a shared platform through which to deliver a large number of electronic texts to libraries; the goal of this program would be to launch with 10,000 titles for use in research collections as well as for potential classroom adoptions (see New York University Press 2009). The value in making such a large number of titles available at once would transcend the additive value of any of the individual texts. In addition, the more that such a corpus-oriented platform provides users with tools such as the ability to tag and bookmark texts, to digitally process their contents, to discuss and respond to them, to link both forward and backward across them, and to engage with colleagues through them, the more important the corpus will become. Such tools and services will be key elements of the "value added" of the university press of the future. Developing these technologies, however, and rethinking the location of value in scholarly publishing, will require investments in experimentation, the time to allow those experiments to take root, and the flexibility to learn from their outcomes.

In other words, I am not suggesting that the answer to the financial crisis faced by scholarly presses can be found solely in the cost reductions produced by moving from print to digital distribution, or even by shifting some of the labor in the publication process from the press to its users. Both of these things will help, as will the kinds of automation that NAP uses in the production of its texts. Digital publishing, however, will always require significant investments of paid labor, in the form of programmers, designers, and other technical personnel necessary to keep the network running, as well as in the more traditional forms of publishing labor, including editing, typesetting, markup, proofreading, book design, and distribution. As noted in earlier chapters, the majority of the expense incurred in contemporary print-based university press publishing is derived not from the costs of print itself or the distribution and storage of the printed texts, but rather from the labor costs involved in editing, producing, and marketing those texts. The all-digital press might be able to reduce or even eliminate certain lines in its budget, but others—such as the costs of technology, support for that technology, design, programming, and maintenance for new digital textual forms—will of necessity increase. Although putting things on the Internet may be free, publishing, in the ways that universities should want to do it, cannot be.

One might well ask, if digital publishing isn't going to save us enough money, why we should move into it in the first place. I hope that by now I've managed to make the argument on behalf of the conversational structures that digital publishing broadly conceived can support, as well as in favor of the openness that online distribution can produce. I should also note, however, that there are certain fields—data-driven fields that rely heavily on visualization, and others, such as media studies, in which scholarly work increasingly takes mediated form—in which this mode of digital experimentation is absolutely necessary, and is paving the way for broader experimentation across the academy. But such experimentation often fails to find adequate, sustainable financial support. An example of the difficulties facing innovative scholarly publishing projects can be found in *Vectors*, which describes itself as a multimodal journal working to build a new "digital vernacular" for the scholarship of the future (see fig. 5.1). *Vectors* has received a great deal of positive attention from scholarly commentators[7] and is doing work that directly supports the mission of the institution that houses it, the Institute for Multimedia Literacy at the University of Southern California.[8] And yet, like so many other such experimental ventures and digital humanities centers across the country, *Vectors* has been funded almost exclusively with soft money, such that its editors have been required to focus much of their energy on a near-constant cycle of grant applications and other modes of fundraising to keep the journal moving forward. Moreover, this same battle is being fought by digital publishing projects across the country, which wind up getting funded as one-offs rather than being given the resources to create stable, replicable, ongoing models for the production of new scholarly texts.

Admittedly, *Vectors* has to this point been an expensive project, heavily reliant on the labor of programmers and designers who work in a team with more traditional humanities-based scholars to produce highly individuated, interactive projects. If, however, *Vectors* were considered to be fully part of the core research mission of the Institute for Multimedia Literacy—in the same way that an experimental laboratory is considered part of the core research mission in the sciences, employing both graduate students and

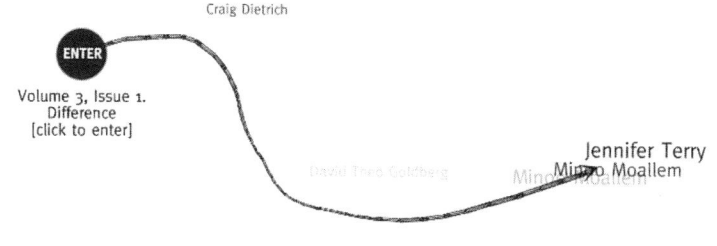

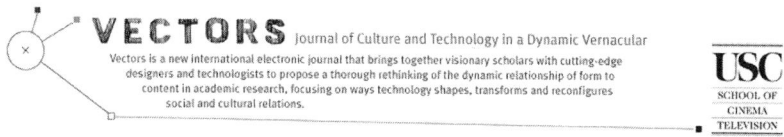

Fig. 5.1. Opening screen, *Vectors* (vectorsjournal.org)

technical professionals working on an ongoing program of research—would it be funded differently? Would we begin to understand publishing ventures not as revenue centers or idiosyncratic one-off experiments, but rather as part of the infrastructure of the institution, as key an element in its research mission as is, for instance, the library?

Raising the example of the scientific lab in the previous paragraph returns us squarely to the question of grant-based funding, as most such labs are primarily supported by grants from funding bodies such as the National Science Foundation (NSF) and the National Institutes of Health (NIH). The primary problem in transferring this model of funding to the digital humanities, however, is that there simply aren't comparable federal funds available outside the sciences. Christine Borgman (2007, 47) has argued persuasively that because in the humanities, "[p]ublication, as the public report of research, is part of a continuous cycle of reading, writing, discussing, searching, investigating, presenting, submitting, and reviewing," we must develop an "information infrastructure to support scholarship" in which we recognize that the technologies of publication are as necessary to the work of the scholar as are the technologies of research (contained within the library) and of other modes of communication (such as email). In the humanities, however, "the view still prevails that technology is not a necessary tool for research" (pp. 222–23), and thus there are all too few programs on the national level that fund technological development and experimentation in the humanities to the degree that NSF and NIH programs do for the social and natural sciences.

The Office of Digital Humanities (ODH) within the National Endowment for the Humanities (NEH) is attempting to fill that gap, but as one section of an already underfunded agency, there's only so much that ODH can accomplish. The result is that digital humanities publishing projects must look to private funding bodies, such as the Mellon and MacArthur Foundations, for support. These foundations have been generous supporters of projects such as *Vectors*, of course, but private foundation funds are of limited duration and often come with the requirement that the project become self-sustaining within a fixed period of time, in ways that are often antithetical to the projects themselves. We can all understand the oddity involved in asking a neuroscience lab to become self-supporting—the NSF and the NIH fully expect such a lab's directors to apply for further funding, which is routinely available—but asking that of digital publishing projects reveals the continued vision of publishing as a revenue-producing venture. Until we really internalize and communicate the need for ongoing support for digital humanities laboratories and digital publishing experiments, understanding them as a key element of the infrastructure of the university of the future, we're unlikely to be able to conduct the kinds of long-term publishing experiments that might help university presses find a new, workable model of production.

This shift in understanding will be crucial for the survival of scholarly publishing into the future, whether that publishing takes place in digital or print-based environments: universities must recognize that their mission extends to include not just the production of new knowledge through the research done by its faculty, but the communication of that knowledge via university-based publishing systems, which must be supported as part of the institution's infrastructure in order to relieve them of the untenable burden of cost recovery.

New Collaborations

If such publishing ventures are understood as part of the core mission of the university, and thus become funded as part of the university's infrastructure, however, there are some potentially fruitful avenues through which we can think about streamlining the labor that must take place, finding ways to avoid the reduplication of efforts and bring together work already being done in disparate administrative units in order to expand their potential. For instance, new scholarly publishing initiatives will require significant new resources for programming, design, and distribution, but will presses or libraries need their own teams of programmers, or can a fruitful partnership be developed with programmers located elsewhere in the institution? Do university publishers need metadata specialists, when this is one of the key aspects of contemporary library and information science programs? While the library, the press, and the information technology center all currently serve different aspects of the university's communication needs, and while all are often stretched to their limits in meeting the full range of those needs, joint experimentation among them might enable fruitful reimaginations of the university as a center of communication, with a reduced need for perpetual reinvention of the wheel.

An increasing number of universities are experimenting with such partnerships, particularly between their presses and libraries, recognizing that these units often serve overlapping functions within the institution. Among such collaborations, one might note the March 2009 announcement that the University of Michigan Press had been restructured as an academic unit housed under the University of Michigan Library:

> Michigan's new press-library hierarchy is not a revolution in itself. Many university presses now report to their campus libraries. But Philip Pochoda, the press's director, said in an interview that he believes this arrangement is notable because it relieves the press of pressure to be financially self-sustaining.
>
> "It removes the bottom line on a book-by-book basis," he said. "Basically we will be judged for staying within a budget," just as academic departments are. "In a sense, it will allow us to do more things that are consistent with university objectives, as opposed to commercial objectives." (Howard 2009)

The University of Michigan's publishing program has for some time included a number of experimental partnerships between the press and the library's Scholarly Publishing Office, including digitalculturebooks, a joint imprint whose titles are available free online or for sale in hard copy ("About digitalculturebooks"; see fig. 5.2). The change in the press's reporting relationship with the library now promises to free the press to undertake more such explorations of the possibilities for new publishing models, including open-access publishing.

Fig. 5.2. Digitalculturebooks website (digitalculture.org)

As the *Chronicle* points out, numerous campuses are experimenting with such relationships between their libraries and presses. The University of California Press and the California Digital Library, for instance, have partnered on a number of projects, including the UC Press E-Books Collection (formerly known as the eScholarship program), which has made approximately 500 titles publicly available via the Internet (and nearly 2,000 available to members of the UC community; see "About Us," *UC Press E-Books Collection*). Several institutions are also experimenting with the administrative structure of these units as a means of fostering increased dialogue between them; NYU Press, for instance, falls under the library's reporting structure, and the library and press share a program officer for digital scholarly publishing. Pennsylvania State University has a similar reporting structure, and has developed an Office of Digital Scholarly Publishing as one point of collaboration, supported by staff members from the press, the library, and the information technology center.[9] A January 2009 report by the Scholarly Publishing & Academic Resources Coalition (SPARC) notes that a study undertaken during the winter of 2007–8 found ongoing collaborations at twenty-six institutions; about two-thirds of these partnerships were limited to the university's press and library, while the other third included participation from other campus units, including the information technology center and academic departments (Crow 2009, 5). And more such collaborations are being developed each year.

Such new partnerships, however, present challenges for institutions, and even those institutions that are working to build such strategic relationships encounter difficulties in the process. These difficulties are less due to any dearth of administrative imagination than to the real, material differences between the various units involved. Laura Brown, Rebecca Griffiths, and Matthew Rascoff (2007) suggest, for instance, that libraries (as well as, I'd argue, information technology centers) often have resources for experimentation available, but their focus is often within the institution rather than on the broader disciplines, which restricts their view of the fields in which such experiments might operate (what audiences, for instance, the experiments might address, and how those audiences might best be reached).[10] Presses, on the other hand, have a clear sense of their markets, but often lack the resources with which to experiment, as well as the mandate for that experimentation.[11] Beneath these differences among information technology centers, libraries, and presses lies the primary challenge in bringing these units together: a radically different sense of the location of each unit's primary stakeholders. Information technology centers, for instance, have traditionally focused inward, serving the computing needs of the university's own administration, faculty, and students, while presses have, at least recently, had an outward orientation, primarily serving authors and readers from outside the institution. Libraries exist somewhere in-between, providing a key point of contact between inside and outside as they collect material from around the world for use by the university's faculty and students, and as they balance the needs of the university's users with those of the broader community. This pivot point between inside and outside, between the individual institution and the broader network of institutions within which it exists, may be the key position in the scholarly publishing program of the future.

Another key collaboration to be explored by university publishers in the future will be that with academic authors themselves, as increasing numbers of scholars take a do-it-yourself approach to publishing. More and more journals are being founded in platforms such as Open Journal Systems (OJS), which allow their scholarly editors to do the same kinds of work they have long done, while reaching around the press to make the results of that work freely and openly available to the academic community and the broader world beyond. Increasingly, scholars are developing online presences via platforms like blogs that allow them to interact with an audience more quickly, more openly, and more directly, without the intermediary of the press. Such DIY publishing is made possible by the rise of the read/write web, a technological transformation that presents a potential not unlike that which the word processor brought to scholarship. As I noted in chapter 2, prior to the word processor, typing was largely an outsourced form of labor; scholars very often passed on their typing, sometimes to the secretarial pool, sometimes to their wives. With the advent of the word processor, typing became part of the process of writing itself, such that the vast majority of scholars now manage their own typing. Similarly, the read/write web and the platforms it has enabled are making it increasingly easy for authors to integrate publishing into the process of scholarly work, and many scholars are taking advantage of these abilities.

If scholars can simply do it themselves, what need do they have of the press? Traditionally, the claim for the press's importance in the publication process has focused on authorization, on the imprimatur that the processes of review, editing, and approval lend to the texts that it publishes. I hope that chapter 1 argues persuasively enough that the role of the press in the future of online publishing will have less to do with authorizing scholarship through conventional peer review, as the forms of online peer-to-peer review that are currently in development will move toward placing that responsibility in scholars' hands. Scholars are increasingly posting their work online for comment, and though at this point very few scholars have been hired, granted tenure, or promoted primarily based on this kind of open online work, there are a few, and there will be more in the years ahead. More and more scholars are rejecting publication venues that don't provide open access, opting instead to create community-organized, disciplinarily-focused online publishing networks, including networks such as NINES and Romantic Circles in literary studies and my own MediaCommons in media studies, as well as more traditionally press-like organizations, including Open Humanities Press in critical and cultural theory. These networks are working not just toward new, speedier, and more open publishing platforms, but also in many cases toward new means of post-publication review and assessment for openly published forms of scholarship, and, perhaps most importantly, toward fostering more ongoing conversation and engagement among the scholars involved, inspiring exciting new kinds of work.

This is not to say that a university press has nothing to add to such a DIY publishing environment. One of the key roles of the press in its engagement with scholarship has traditionally been helping to improve that work, exercising an editorial function that is less about separating the wheat from the chaff (the mode of authorization) than about refining that wheat into flour. New kinds of collaborations between presses and scholars might permit this developmental editing to begin much sooner in the process, allowing a press's editors to find authors who have published shorter texts online and work with them in the process of shaping their ideas into book form, tailoring it for the press's particular audience. Such a process would recognize that not all scholarly arguments come in the shape of a book—that some texts might be strengthened by network- rather than print-based publication—and that the production of a marketable book is only one potential outcome for an argument. The university press would also be able, through its collaboration with the library, to help authors ensure that the work they're publishing online adheres to appropriate data standards that will keep those projects sustainable and preservable. And the press's longstanding excellence in marketing and dissemination could be brought to bear in gathering a readership for DIY-published scholarly work, helping to facilitate the discussion and review of new kinds of online texts.

Publishing and the University Mission

Forging new partnerships with libraries and scholars, however, will require changing the orientation of the press with relationship to the institution and its faculty, and that won't happen easily. Libraries have a clear sense of their mandate in relationship to their institutions' core functions, while presses have existed for some time in a more abstracted relationship to those functions, instead creating through the success of their lists a sense of "prestige" for the institution, without necessarily bearing any relationship to the work being done at the institution. This is not to say that *no* connections exist between the press and the university; many presses do work to maintain lists in fields in which the university is strong, and most presses have members of the faculty who serve on their editorial boards. But if the assumption is that the press should function as a revenue center, it would seem that these connections have the potential to become liabilities; as Thompson (2005, 98) argues, university presses hoping to streamline their lists "may feel some pressure to continue publishing in those disciplines which have a strong and vocal constituency within their own universities." Such tensions indicate that shifting the relationship between the press and the rest of the institution, making strategic partnerships with units such as the library possible, is not simply a matter of the redistribution of resources, but rather of a broad reconsideration of the press's relationship to the institution's core mission.

That reconsideration, however, needs to take place not solely at the level of the press directorship, but at that of the higher university administration. A number of the provosts and other administrators who participated in the study by Brown, Griffiths, and Rascoff (2007, 17) expressed strong feelings in favor of the press's outward-facing orientation: as one provost put it, "I would hate to think [that the press is] peculiarly for your own faculty." At the same time, however, those provosts' actions indicate that unless the press is intimately connected with the work of the faculty, it won't receive adequate support: "provosts put limited resources and attention towards what they perceive to be a service to the broader community" (ibid.). Moreover, if in reimagining the funding model of the university press, we need to rethink the relationship between the press and the various administrative units within the university, including the library, the information technology center, and the academic departments, then such rethinking will further require a deeper consideration of the mission of the university. As the Ithaka Report points out, "[U]niversities do not treat the publishing function as an important, mission-centric endeavor. Publishing generally receives little attention from senior leadership at universities and the result has been a scholarly publishing industry that many in the university community find to be increasingly out of step with the important values of the academy" (Brown, Griffiths, and Rascoff 2007, 3). This may be attributable to the sense, diagnosed by Bill Readings (1996), that the overall mission of the university itself became increasingly abstracted over the course of the twentieth century, shifting from that of an institution charged with the admittedly problematic task of creating and preserving a national culture and inculcating citizens into that culture, to a postmodern institution charged only with "excellence," an organization far more corporate than cultural, with no goal higher than its own advancement. It's little wonder that in such an environment scholarly publishing would be imagined as an "industry" and would receive little attention from university administrations beyond quantifiably measured success as represented on the bottom line. The function of the press simply wouldn't matter; in the university of excellence, one has a press in order to have an excellent press.

Readings argues that the university must, in order to develop a new relevance in the contemporary era, become a center of thought, a community founded on conversation, in which we focus more on listening than on speaking. In the process of listening, we agree to disagree, striving not for consensus but a form of *dissensus*, which has as its goal not concluding discussions but rather their ethical, open-ended continuation. This process of "thinking together," Readings (1996, 192) argues, "belongs to dialogism rather than dialogue," and thus the contradictions presented by a multiplicity of perspectives are not uncovered in order to be resolved, but are rather themselves the point. Dwelling in those contradictions is a desired outcome Readings mostly ties to the pedagogical process, but it presents clear implications for scholarship as well. As I argued in earlier chapters, the purpose of scholarship is conversation among scholars, if a protractedly slow one, and scholarly publishing is the form the conversation takes, the means of allowing a multiplicity of voices to be heard, and of creating the possibility for others to listen. If for no other reason than that, the channels through which these scholarly conversations take place—those modes of communication managed by the information technology center, the library and, most crucially, the press—should be included at the very core of the university's structure, the center of its research mission.

To say it more plainly: Publishing the work of its faculty must be reconceived as a central element of the university's mission. As David Parry (2009b) commented on this book's open draft, "Knowledge which is not public is not knowledge"; without making faculty research public, the university has not completed its job. That such publishing endeavors could serve as publicity for the university's programs might provide an added incentive; publicity of this kind need not have the hollow ring of what has passed for "public relations" in the past, but might instead create a means of establishing a more authentic relationship with the public based in the discussion of common areas of concern.[12] But I do want to be clear: I am not arguing that centralizing publishing within the institution will make the production and dissemination of knowledge more *efficient*; in fact, as Readings (1996, 163) points out, the current crisis faced by the university "cannot be answered by a program of reform that either produces knowledge more efficiently or produces more efficient knowledge. Rather, the analogy of production itself must be brought into question: the analogy that makes the University into a bureaucratic apparatus for the production, distribution, and consumption of knowledge." Instead, if we understand the mission of the university to be thought manifested in conversation, we must acknowledge that thought requires a mode of expression, and that conversation requires a channel to facilitate it; university-based publishing has the potential to provide both.

Where Readings's argument falls short, however, is in his conviction that thought cannot be economic and must be conceived of as part of an "economy of waste" (1996, 175); I resist this characterization not because I think that scholarly production can or should hew to the bottom line, but instead because waste—however empowering and transgressive the term may be for academics—will never sell to recalcitrant state legislatures or boards of trustees in an economic and political climate such as we now face. Donald Hall (2007, 106) similarly points out the inevitability that "intellectual growth, expansive knowledge seeking, and experimentation with the arts and humanities will be perceived as wastes of time and money when students are accumulating huge amounts of debt in a cost-driven rush to what must be very high-paying employment." The challenge, as Hall understands it, is not embracing this sense of waste, but rather reclaiming the intellectual growth created by the conversation fostered in the university as a public good rather than a private responsibility. As we build the university of the future, we must find ways to demonstrate our service to that public good, to model the open dialogic community through our scholarly networks, and to show plainly why the conversations we engage in matter. For all of these reasons, access to the work that we produce must be opened up as a site of conversation not just among scholars but also between scholars and the broader culture. Only in this way can we ensure continued support for the university not simply as a credentialing center, but rather as a center of thought.

For publishing to become central to the university's mission, the position of the press with respect to its institution will need to change in ways that may not sit well at first with university administrations or press directorships. As a thought experiment of sorts, we might ask ourselves: What would become possible if publishing were to be funded as infrastructure, rather than as a revenue center? Just as no institution would ask the library or the information technology center to focus on cost recovery, it makes sense not to ask this of the publishing function, at least insofar as that function is similarly serving the university mission. The idea that the dissemination of scholarship should be seen as "a core responsibility of the university" (Association of American Universities et al. 2008, 1) suggests that if publishing were responsibly funded, the scholarship done by the faculty would be much more likely to come to public attention.

This funding scenario raises a second question: What if the university publishing center of the future, instead of being outwardly focused as is today's university press, were instead to imagine itself in service first and foremost to the needs of its home institution? How would it help shape the work it publishes? How would it foster interactions among scholars, and between scholars and the surrounding public? What kinds of new work, and new conversations, would such a reimagined publishing center make possible? As one "press leader" quoted by Brown, Griffiths, and Rascoff (2007, 22) puts it, "[U]niversity presses have a broad mission—to be stewards of scholarship [and serve the] public good. They used to have a specific mission—to act as the showcase for the research of their particular university [and serve the] institutional good. University presses have drifted away from this second mission and we need to get back to it" (brackets in original). A properly funded university publishing center, focused on bringing the work done at that institution to the world, may well be vital to scholarly publishing's survival, much less its development, into the future. As this "press leader" indicates, such a relationship between the press and the university has deep historical roots; a brief glance backward at one example of that older model might be useful in thinking through its implications for the future.

The History of the University Press

While the Cambridge and Oxford University Presses were originally founded under royal charters permitting them to print "all manner of books," in particular religious texts (Black 1992, 7),[13] university presses in the United States were by and large founded specifically for the publication of scholarship; in this sense, as Thompson (2005, 108) points out, "they were generally seen as an integral part of the function of the university." In fact, Daniel Coit Gilman, the first president of Johns Hopkins University, established what is now the oldest continuously operating university press in the United States there in 1878, as a result of his sense that "publishing, along with teaching and research, was a primary obligation of a great university" ("About the Press").[14] Albert Muto (1992), in his history of the University of California Press, notes the importance of Johns Hopkins in leading the way toward the contemporary university's functions of knowledge production and dissemination, rather than simply focusing on instruction. Publishing was a crucial mode for that dissemination of knowledge, and thus had to be the responsibility of the institution itself: "To leave the publication of scholarly, highly specialized research to the workings of a commercial marketplace would be, in effect, to condemn it to languish unseen. If the aspiration of the university was to create new knowledge, the university would also have to assume the responsibility for disseminating it" (Givler 2002).

The history of the University of California Press reveals a similar impetus for its founding, and its history serves as a useful case study for the changes in university press publishing over the course of the last century. Like Johns Hopkins, the University of California was charged with the production and dissemination of new knowledge, and as such, "[f]aculty members were often required to publish, and graduate students encouraged to do so. Since there were few publishers in this country who welcomed specialized writings, it was soon seen to be the responsibility of the parent universities to publish—or at least to print—what these scholars produced" (Muto 1992, 1). These early U.S. university presses were founded not only as a means of disseminating knowledge produced by the academy, but as a means of showcasing the work done *at their own institutions*; only later in their development did they turn to a list-based model of publication. Thus the report presented in 1893 to the University of California Board of Regents, requesting funds for the establishment of a university press, did so "believing that it is often desirable to publish papers prepared by members of the Faculty" (Muto 1992, 18–19). The desirability of such publication stemmed from the belief that the university's mission included not just the production of knowledge but its dissemination, and not just dissemination within the bounds of the institution, but also broadly throughout the culture.

The emphasis on "papers" in the report presented to the Regents, however, is not incidental. For the first forty years of the press's life, its products were by and large monograph pamphlets; books were a rare, and in some cases "accidental" (Muto 1992, 72), form of publication. There was, in fact, little systematization of the press's methods or products. In the press's early days, the university president had the most significant role in setting editorial policy. Benjamin Ide Wheeler, president of the University of California from 1899 until 1919, was particularly powerful in this regard; it was he who "decided whether authors were eligible to submit to the Press, pressured Editorial Committee members to approve manuscripts, and even submitted manuscripts on behalf of authors" (p. 47). After his retirement, the faculty demanded a far greater degree of self-governance throughout the university, including control, via the Editorial Committee, of the press. During this period the committee established a set of rules for its operation, including rules for author eligibility and a number of subject-area boards to oversee editorial decisions that required "more expertise than any one person could provide" (p. 52). However, during this same period, the press also hired its first professional manager, Albert Allen, who in his 1915–16 report on the press's activities castigated the university committee for adhering to such a limited and internally focused publishing program:

> The University of California Press is therefore not in the general publishing business. Except for a few instances it has not issued books. It is not, in fact, a "Press" in the meaning which the activities of other institutions have given the term "University Press." Through it the University of California has served only its own purposes; it has not yet been put at the service of scholars outside of the membership of this University. . . . But the question will surely soon be raised whether . . . the University of California shall not, if and as it is able, extend the privilege of publication through its University Press to the work of others than its own members. (Muto 1992, 83)

Book publishing was not made a part of the press's mandate for several years thereafter, however, and only in April 1929 did the Editorial Committee authorize the publication of books written by scholars other than members of the UC faculty.

Finally, in 1933, the press was reorganized as "a publisher of scholarly books distributed through ordinary trade channels" (Muto 1992, 93). This reorganization required not only separating the press and the university printing office and hiring a professional managerial, editorial, and printing staff, but also restructuring the press's financial model. Prior to this point, scholarly monographs had been published on a wholly noncommercial basis, being given away to educational institutions or otherwise exchanged for the products of other similar presses, and what revenues the press's publications did produce were returned to the university's general fund; in 1933, for the first time, the press director requested that all revenues produced by the press "be retained by the Press and used for book publishing" (p. 109). The result was a shift in the press's function from a "service agency" to "a mixed organization, part service agency and part business" (ibid.). The Editorial Committee retained oversight only over series papers; the press took over control of the publication of books. This transformation of the press into a business was seen as necessary, given the heft and import of the object it was producing: "The book publishing program needed coordination and planning. It also needed more and better books to publish. Manuscript selection had always been largely passive—consideration of faculty works that came in with the University series and occasional offers from the outside"

(p. 182). Once August Frugé took over as press director in 1949, rescued the publishing program from its prior domination by the printing and business offices, and unified the functions of the Editorial Committee and the press, the modern press was finally established.

In the case of the University of California, a direct relationship can be traced between the shift toward an emphasis on book (rather than paper) publishing, the transformation of the press in part into a business, and the distancing of the press from the work of its own faculty. The University of California provides only one example of the gradual movement of the university press from an early relationship with its institution's academic mission toward a more independent, trade-oriented model. A more extreme version of this shift might be seen in the histories of university presses that are today for all intents and purposes fully trade publishers, such as Yale University Press, which despite being formally a department of the university is "financially and operationally autonomous" (Pranzatelli, "Brief History"). Yale University Press's financial success has given it rather extraordinary freedom to experiment, but arguably such freedom has required it to be oriented primarily toward the market rather than the academy, and has come at the cost of a dynamic relationship with the institution's own faculty. While transforming the press into a business would seem to support institutional aims (by promoting excellence and keeping an eye on the bottom line), such a transformation can only come at the institution's expense; what the university gains in the press's financial autonomy, it loses in the press's service to the university community. Reconnecting university publishing with the broader university community will require undoing some of the twentieth century's business-oriented transformations and returning to the fundamentals: if the dissemination of scholarship is a valuable part of the university's mission, the university must take responsibility for that process and transform the press into a publishing center whose function is intimately tied to the work of its own institution.

The Press as University Publisher

The leap from the insistence that publishing must be understood as a core aspect of the university mission to the suggestion that fully reintegrating the press into the mission of the institution will require a focus on publishing the work of the institution's faculty isn't as broad as it may seem. Most university presses have moved away from that connection to their own faculty's work, a shift that the Ithaka Report hints may be in part responsible for the rupture between many presses and their host institutions:

> Over time, and in pursuit of the largest public service to the global academic community, presses have tended to grow disconnected from the administrations at their host institutions. This is due in part to the fact that they publish works from scholars mostly off their own campuses. The highest percentage of local authors published by a university press that we came across was 25–30 percent, but most were below 10 percent. (Brown, Griffiths, and Rascoff 2007, 17)

In large part, the shift away from publishing local authors arises from the list-model of university press publication, in which the primary point of service is not to the institution but rather to "the global academic community" on a field-by-field basis. Even more, however, faculty have internalized this focus on the global rather than the local as an intellectual good, seeking under the current system "to publish their books with the most prestigious press in their field, regardless of affiliation. They actually often prefer to publish their books at presses other than their own, because institutional distance avoids any suggestion of favoritism and provides external validation" (ibid.). This concern with externality in university press publishing, from the perspective of both press and faculty, has to do with "excellence"—with ensuring the ostensible impartiality of the publishing process, and with publishing the best possible authors through the best possible presses. Without this distance, the fear on both sides seems to be, the university press will devolve into a vanity publishing outfit, required to publish anything that comes its way, thus conferring no particular prestige on its titles—in fact, quite the opposite—and bringing no prestige to its institution.

All of this obtains, however, only if the purpose of the press is to be *excellent*, rather than to facilitate the conversations that take place among the university's scholars and between those scholars and their colleagues around the world. Such a role need not cause the press to fall into the trap of becoming an echo chamber, with the university community only speaking to itself. In the conversational process, listeners are just as important as the speakers, if not more so, requiring the press as a facilitating body to become a nexus of dialogue that crosses institutional boundaries. Let us, for a moment, think about the university library's role in such a process, as it serves the institution by collecting, cataloging, preserving, and otherwise providing access for its users to the many forms through which such scholarly conversations take place. Although nearly all research libraries have some mechanism for community use of its facilities, even if only in a limited fashion, primary access to the university library's materials and services is almost always reserved to the members of the institution. The materials the library collects and the services it provides are directly driven by the needs of its user base; though all libraries aspire toward a model of completeness, any individual library is far less likely to provide access to materials in areas unrepresented within the broader institutional structure. Given the combination of idiosyncratic institutional needs, a slowly shifting user base, and budgetary limitations, libraries have developed cooperative systems, including consortial collection-sharing and interlibrary loan, that allow them to compensate for a lack of completeness by drawing upon the resources of other institutions.

What if the press were reimagined as part of a university publishing center that, parallel to and in collaboration with the library, served as another pivot point between the institution and the broader scholarly community—if, just as the library brings the world to the university, the press brought the university to the world? What if, rather than serving particular scholarly fields through the current list-based press model, the publishing center instead focused on the need to publish the work produced within the university, making it available for dissemination around the world? How would the press's function in the scholarly communication process shift? Certain parts of its current mission would remain key: the university press has developed over the course of decades expertise in the assessment of fields and of current movements in research, a deep awareness of marketing issues and familiarity with distribution channels, and, of course, a set of core editorial production talents, none of which are replicated in other areas of the campus, and all of which will remain essential to fostering ongoing scholarly conversations. But certain aspects of past editorial practice that have fallen somewhat by the wayside may again become important in the future; rather than focusing on the acquisition of completed projects, as I noted earlier, the press's editors may take on a greater development function, working with authors throughout the many stages of a project's coming into being, helping them find ways to move from a relatively amorphous idea to a fully realized project, and to shape an emerging text in concert with the technologies it might employ and the field with which it will interact. Moreover, the publishing center would be key in facilitating the feedback mechanisms of peer-to-peer review that help authors revise and improve texts, and that will help bring authors' work to the attention of the field. None of these functions would matter if the press were simply to be turned into a vanity publishing outfit; instead, the commitment of the publishing center to working with its scholars in developing their projects will, if anything, bring more "prestige" to the institution, as universities that are actively engaged in such work will increasingly draw and retain the best scholars.

We lose a few things in moving the university press from business to service agency, of course. One of these is of negligible concern for all but a select few scholarly authors: royalties. As it stands, few authors of scholarly monographs today earn more than a nominal sum on the sales of their writing; the real remuneration in most cases comes indirectly, in the form of appointments, promotions, raises, speaking engagements, and so forth.[15] A radical shift in the business model of the university press such as I'm suggesting would likely require eliminating royalties; if the press isn't profiting from the sale of its texts, there's no income to share with the author. Scholarly authors with genuinely commercially viable texts may thus be inclined to publish with commercial presses, which may still be able to afford to pay authors directly for their work. For most academics, however, the primary benefit of publishing is in getting their ideas into circulation within their fields; many would be happy to trade any financial consideration for the kinds of active promotion and distribution that a publishing agency combining the strengths of the university press and the university library would be able to provide.

There is another loss, however, that's absolutely crucial to the vast majority of academics, who are employed by institutions that do not have presses of their own; these faculty have long relied on the work done at (and thus the subsidy provided by) universities that *do* have presses in order to publish. The potential changes I'm exploring here thus have broad implications for every academic institution, and not just for those relatively few institutions that currently house university presses. Shifting the focus of the publishing center's efforts from the list model to publishing the work of its own faculty would require *every* institution to take on this publishing mission and invest in bringing the work of its faculty into public discourse. As the Ithaka Report points out, this need not mean that every institution will have to found a "press," per se, but it does mean that every institution must develop a scholarly publishing strategy to determine what it will be able to do on its own and "if and when it should combine forces with other institutions" (Brown, Griffiths, and Rascoff 2007, 5). The process of developing such a strategy will no doubt be a bumpy one for many institutions and their scholars, as existing presses may turn their attention to their own faculties' work before other institutions are fully ready to take on the task of publishing theirs. One possibility for facilitating this transition might be for extant university presses to charge press-less institutions for the service of publishing the work of their faculties. Such an arrangement would enable faculty at some institutions without presses to continue getting their work into circulation, though it would undoubtedly create difficulties for scholars at poorly funded institutions. A more sustainable possibility might be for universities to build consortial publishing centers, on the model of library collection-sharing services, allowing smaller, regional, and teaching-oriented institutions to support one another's publishing efforts. It is clear, however, that every institution that expects its faculty to publish will have to find ways to take on responsibility for ensuring that publishing options are available.

Some precursors to a transition like the one I am suggesting are already beginning at a number of schools through the implementation of institutional repositories, usually under the auspices of the library. Being a library project, such repositories demonstrate clear thinking about access, but the lack of involvement of the press in their development has resulted in some significant drawbacks, preventing the repository from becoming a form of publishing in its own right. These repositories are too often clunky, database-driven, atomistic endeavors, focusing far more on storage than on use; as the Ithaka Report notes, "institutional repositories so far tend to look like 'attics' (and often fairly empty ones), with random assortments of content of questionable importance" (Brown, Griffiths, and Rascoff 2007, 16). Involvement of the university press in the design, implementation, and promotion of the institutional repository—reimagined and rebranded as an institutional publishing system—might help transform it from an attic into which random items are shoved (and promptly forgotten) to an active, developing form of publication. The University of California has begun developing such a model, under the leadership of Catherine Mitchell, director of the eScholarship group at the California Digital Library (CDL), who notes that the word "repository" has been "erased . . . from our conversation," replaced with the notion of "services." The alliance that has developed between the CDL and the University of California Press, under the auspices of UCPubS (or UC Publishing Services), has enabled the institution to provide its faculty with a range of digital and print-based publishing options, both open-access and market-oriented, in formats both traditional and innovative (see Open Access Videos 2009; Mitchell and Cerruti 2008–9).

As the Ithaka Report indicates, presses as they currently function have a much stronger sense of audience and of the emerging directions of scholarship in particular disciplines than do libraries, and shifting away from the list model of publishing runs the risk of eroding the press's current strengths: its channels of distribution and its role in facilitating the advancement of work in particular fields. Some of those tasks must remain within the press, which can work with the library to strategize its relationship to particular fields within the institution. But other parts of it might best be managed in collaboration with the membership-driven disciplinary and interdisciplinary organizations that already set the agenda for various fields through their ongoing conferences and other initiatives. Similarly, some of the weight of bringing together the work being done at the many institutions across the country and around the world will fall on scholarly societies, who might, under such a system, invest less in their own independent publishing ventures than in aggregating and indexing the texts published by university publishing centers across the web, making those texts available to their memberships through virtual collections. In this sense, we might find an increasing hybridization of the functions of journals and the bibliographies that index them; journals may increasingly become focused venues for the republication of texts in particular areas, and databases such as the *MLA International Bibliography* may serve large-scale versions of the same function, fulfilling a key aspect of the publication process by gathering not just bibliographic data produced by journals, but also links to a much wider assortment of publishing venues across the web.

One hopes, of course, that such indexes might be made independent of the commercial scholarly publishers, with funding and access granted through membership fees. There is cause for caution here, as the example of AnthroSource demonstrates. Developed through collaboration between the American Anthropological Association (AAA) and the University of California Press, AnthroSource was the disciplinary society's vision of a portal that would provide its membership access to all of the relevant work in the field, including the society's many journals, but also archival materials, museums, researcher field notes, and so forth. The portal did come to include access to all of AAA's journals, but when the publishing contract between the organizations expired, "in a controversial, quick, and not entirely transparent process, the AAA chose, to the surprise of many in and beyond the association (especially libraries), not to renew its print-publication contract with the University of California Press, and, instead, awarded the new contract to Wiley-Blackwell" (Kelty et al. 2008, 561). The digital version was tied to the print publication contract, so that a project designed to increase the open circulation of work in anthropology was suddenly cached behind a pay wall; even more, Wiley-Blackwell proceeded to *double* the subscription cost of *American Anthropologist*. While this transfer of AnthroSource's ownership to a commercial publisher no doubt brought the AAA some necessary revenue, it would be worth asking whether the benefits of that revenue outweigh the costs of restricted access, not to mention the increased costs to our libraries. As Chris Kelty has suggested in a discussion of this move,

[P]ublishers and scholarly societies have become large, bureaucratic organizations sedimented in their modes of doing things, sometimes for good reasons (stability, reliability), sometimes for bad (tradition, fear, self-interest). Free Software is a reminder of why these organizations were started in the first place and I think they (and the Open Access movements as well) force us to ask once more, and in detailed ways, what are scholarly societies for? Why did we create them? What do they do for us as scholars and as citizens, and what reasons do they have for existing? (Kelty et al. 2008, 563)

Scholarly organizations, no less than university presses, need to be held responsible by their memberships for increasing the visibility of scholarship, both within and outside the academy.

Sustainability

It is, of course, quite possible that the university will not be able to provide universal access to the products of its scholarly publishing endeavors for free—or will not be able to do so for long, in any event. In one way or another, university press publishing must be made financially sustainable. The stakes of sustainability are greatly heightened in the digital age, of course; as Kevin Guthrie, Rebecca Griffiths, and Nancy Maron point out,

> In the print world, if a publisher failed or its books went out of print, some number of those books would still be available on library shelves. And sometimes events would revitalise the academic value of those materials and they would come back into circulation. When an online resource fails, its content may become completely unavailable, resulting in a real loss to teaching, learning, and research, not to mention the loss of the initial investment required to create it. It is important therefore for the developers of these resources to think carefully and strategically about sustainability and long-term access to the materials they generate as they build these resources. (Guthrie, Griffiths, and Maron 2008, 9)

While the Guthrie report's focus is more market-oriented than I argue that the products or functions of the university should be, the question of sustainability remains an important one: unless adequate means of support are developed for the scholarly publishing ventures of the future, whatever form they take, we'll wind up right back in the same boat, with the added danger that the projects we've created in the interim may simply disappear. As

Guthrie and his colleagues argue, however, ensuring financial sustainability for scholarly publishing ventures is not simply a matter of charging enough for their use so that funds are available to maintain the projects; rather, it requires, first, properly assessing where the value lies in the project, and second, ensuring that adequate plans have been made for the project's future development.

The question of the location of value in future scholarly publishing ventures is more complicated than it may at first appear. The university press, like most "content provider" industries, has long been in the business of selling the content that it produces—books, journals, and so forth. As Lawrence Lessig (2008) argues, however, the most successful potential business model of the digital age is not necessarily the sale of closed, proprietary content, but a "hybrid" model in which some content may be made available for free. The creation of value in a hybrid economy may lie in services or tools rather than products; the value in a system such as Flickr, for instance, comes not from providing a wealth of photographic content—users do that, and are able to do so through a basic level of service available for free—but in providing access to a suite of tools that allow users to share, tag, search, connect, and so forth. The value in the system, which users are willing to pay for, is the means of interacting with the content, rather than the content itself. Scholarly publishing would appear to be in a similar circumstance; its content is primarily "user generated" and is made precisely to be shared, creating the most substantive benefits for its authors when its distribution is as broad and as open as possible. Given that, the greatest value added by the scholarly publishing process of the future likely will lie not in the content itself, but in the tools that enable authors to produce and readers to interact with that content, and with one another via that content.

If there is something to be monetized in scholarly publishing, it's thus less likely to be the products than the process; the audience for the products of university presses is too small to be commercially viable, as Daniel Coit Gilman acknowledged more than a century ago. Even more, the audience is composed of *the same people* who are producing the content in the first place, and as attempts to monetize other forms of user-created content on the Internet suggest, users are more likely to pay for services than for the stuff created through those services. How to create those services—which might include editorial advising and support, networks for peer review, marketing and promotion, and so forth—and how best to interlink the services of university publishing groups and disciplinary organizations, presents the greatest challenge as we work toward the creation of a sustainable future for scholarly publishing. One potential future might include university presses coming together—whether through a professional organization such as the Association of American University Presses, a publishing-oriented non-profit organization such as Ithaka, or a more ad-hoc consortium such as that being led by NYU Press with support from the Mellon Foundation—to develop a common network and suite of tools to which each university's publishing initiative would contribute, developing its imprint within the larger community. Such an interlinked network of networks would enable presses to create individual identities while sharing their strengths, to experiment with new cross-institutional collaborations, and to minimize certain costs of tool development and maintenance. An example of such a cross-institutional platform can be found in Giant Chair, a U.S.-based company that has worked with all of the French university publishers to create a single portal for the promotion and distribution of their texts, and which is in the process of bringing together a suite of tools that will allow university presses both to maintain their own brand identities and to collaborate on new publishing projects (see *GiantChair*; *Le Comptoir des presses d'universités*).

In the end, however, responsibility for the success of such a publishing initiative must rest within the university, whether that university is contributing to the development of a pan-academic network or producing its own publishing system. It will be difficult to make scholarly publishing self-sustaining as an enterprise, but that doesn't mean that we can simply allow it to die; if scholars are to publish, their institutions must accept responsibility for—and fully support—the platforms that make such publishing possible. While corporate partners may be required for the development of the systems and tools that publishing will use into the future, we cannot simply wait for those companies to innovate on our behalf. Corporate priorities will never be the same as those of the university, and for the university to wait for corporate-produced publishing tools and processes to be presented to us threatens scholarly publishing with strangulation; imagine how different the landscape of instructional technology might look today if universities had taken the lead on creating learning management systems, rather than allowing corporate providers to mire them in ever-increasing cruft and licensing fees.

All of what I'm proposing requires a radical reexamination of the funding model under which scholarly publishing operates, moving the press from being a revenue center within the university toward being part of a broader service unit within the institution. None of this is meant to suggest that there isn't a need for accountability in university press publishing, but rather that, as Readings argues, accountability must be about something that exceeds accounting; we must learn to evaluate—and thus to value—the function of scholarly publishing in ways other than simply examining the bottom line. Just as the library serves an indispensable role in the university's mission, so will the scholarly publishing unit of the future; these endeavors must not fall prey to the administrative requirement, now hobbling university presses, that they focus on cost recovery. Instead, scholarly publishing units must be treated as part of the institution's infrastructure, as necessary as the information technology center, as indispensable as the library, organizations increasingly central to the mission of the twenty-first century university.

Conclusion

In late August 2009, after completing this manuscript and submitting it to NYU Press, which sent it out to readers as part of a conventional peer-review process, I began another process that would put my money where my mouth was, so to speak: with the press's blessing, I posted the entire manuscript (save, of course, for this conclusion) online, using CommentPress, in order to facilitate an open review. As the chapter on peer review notes, I'm hardly the first author—or even the first in my field—to have opened a draft manuscript for comment in this way; the Institute for the Future of the Book posted McKenzie Wark's draft of *Gamer Theory* online in a CommentPress prototype (Wark 2006), and Noah Wardrip-Fruin posted the manuscript of *Expressive Processing* on his group blog, seeking the feedback of the community with whom he'd been writing and discussing his work for some time.

My experiment, however, was somewhat different from those previous ones: the Institute published *GAM3R 7H30RY* as an experiment in developing conversation in the margins of a text, rather than understanding that discussion as related to the processes of peer review. And while Wardrip-Fruin was seeking peer review of a sort for *Expressive Processing*, in that he wanted critical feedback from the text's best readers, he explicitly did not position the blog-based review of the manuscript as being in any sense in competition with the traditional blind reviews that MIT Press commissioned. By contrast, I hoped to be able to use this process as a means of getting some information about the differences between open and closed review, as a test of some of my ideas about open review, and as a way of thinking about the kinds of systems that might produce the best possible forms of open review.

So I set up a WordPress instance on the MediaCommons server and installed the CommentPress plugin; I tinkered with the site's configuration and design a bit, and then I loaded in the text. Perhaps that's not the best phrase for it; "loading in the text" sounds like a breezily automated mode of working in the network era, and this was far from automated. It was instead a clunky process of copying, pasting, and hand-coding things like italics and footnotes. That said, after several days of very tedious work, the book was, arguably, "published."

The next issue, however, was making it public. On September 15, 2009, I emailed nine colleagues with whom I'd discussed the project in earlier stages, asking them to stop by, take a look, and leave some comments before I began announcing the project's availability widely. Over the next week or so, two of those colleagues read and commented on the entire manuscript and three others read a chapter or two and left a few comments, and I responded to those comments where it seemed appropriate for me to do so. Finally, on September 28, we announced the open-review experiment widely, inviting comment and response from any interested reader.

This open review wasn't a perfect process, but it was illuminating. Forty-four unique commenters left a total of 295 comments, producing a much wider range of opinion and critique than any traditional review process could. I was also able to respond to the comments, allowing me to discuss the text with key colleagues at a much earlier stage than I would have otherwise; reviewers likewise discussed the text with one another, sometimes disagreeing on points of assessment. Beyond the comments themselves, however, I gained other information about how the text had been received that I would never have gotten otherwise. For instance: I know that in the nine months following the project's launch, it received over 31,000 pageloads, with over 12,000 unique visitors coming by for the first time, more than 3,300 of whom made multiple return visits. The project was taught during the spring 2010 semester in at least three graduate seminars and one undergraduate course and was written about and linked to in more than twenty venues, all of which came to my attention through the traces their inbound links left on the text. There's even a review of the project in a scholarly journal—a review that appeared months before the book's print edition.

My first impulse is to place those figures alongside the fact that the average scholarly press monograph in the humanities sells fewer than 400 copies over its lifetime. If the purpose of publication is getting one's work into circulation, my still-in-process manuscript arguably succeeded far better than most finished academic books ever will.

On the other hand, these numbers reveal some potential issues in web-based publishing and open-review processes that we need to take note of as well. First, take the case of those 3,300 repeat visitors to the project: a repeat visit is defined by my statistics service as a return to the site an hour or more later by a visitor who has had a cookie set by the site, and thus previously visited the site using the same computer and browser. It's likely that this figure is a bit inflated, since it fails to account for readers who visited the site both at home and at work, or with both a computer and a mobile device. It probably also includes some curious individuals who wanted to look at the site in multiple browsers, but might leave out others who routinely clear their cookies. Moreover, we don't really know much about who those readers are, and insofar as some would argue that the real purpose of publication is not simply getting one's work into circulation, but rather getting it in front of the right audience, simple site statistics don't provide the information necessary to know how well we've succeeded. We do know, however, who the vast majority of the commenters on the manuscript are, and we can assess their comments in light of the other work that we know them to have done.

Alongside the comments produced in the open-review process, I received two thoughtful, thorough traditional peer reviews that had been commissioned by NYU Press. Because both reviewers agreed to share their identities with me, I have a context within which to understand their comments, but this openness is not the usual situation. In my case, however, both reviewers approached the manuscript sympathetically but critically, evaluating the text both in its entirety—commenting on its overall argument and organization—as well as chapter by chapter. Each review prodded me to press a bit harder on issues I raised but didn't fully develop, and each pointed to problematic passages that distracted from the argument's flow. Each was enthusiastically positive about the manuscript but gave me fruitful directions in which to think about my revisions.

Each set of reviews—the online comments and the traditional evaluations—demonstrates the best of what peer review has to offer: sharp, thoughtful criticism intended to help make a project better. Comparing them reveals a few clear benefits produced by open, online review, and a few issues that the peer-to-peer review systems of the future, and those who participate in them, will have to take into consideration. The benefits are perhaps obvious: a wider range of intelligible perspectives and voices, able to uncover a larger number of problems; a venue for elaborating on or complicating the responses through discussion. The challenges may be less clear, but digging into the two sets of reviews reveals some key differences that might call our attention to aspects of traditional review that we don't want to leave behind.

CommentPress allows us to track the portions of the online manuscript that received the most comments, thus revealing which aspects of the project either hold the greatest interest or present the greatest difficulty for readers (see fig. c.1). Looking at the distribution of comments, it's readily apparent

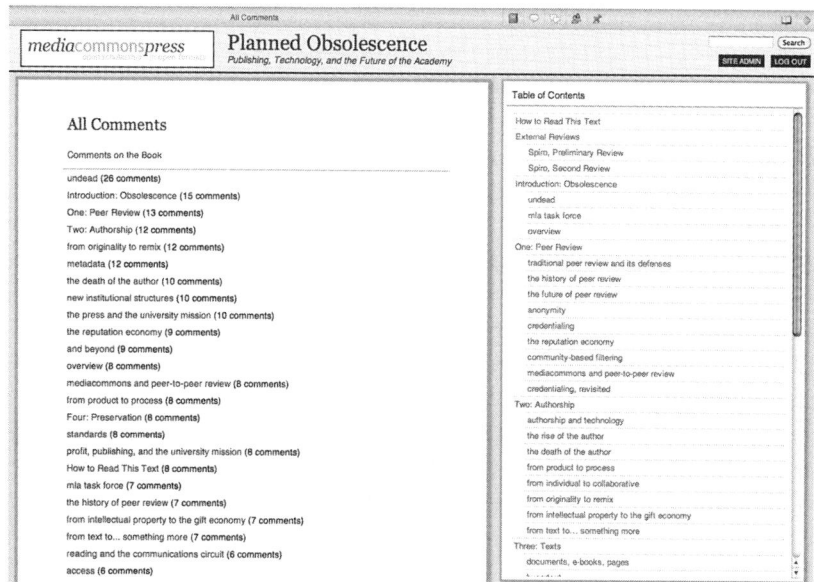

Fig. C.1. Kathleen Fitzpatrick, *Planned Obsolescence* (screenshot from the author's collection)

that the early sections of the text received more reviewer attention than did later chapters. This may be due to the daunting nature of sitting down to read an entire book manuscript in a browser window, and it's equally possible that, had we released the manuscript serially (as Wardrip-Fruin did with *Expressive Processing*), discussion might not only have been sustained but have developed and grown over time. This raises a key question about whether the online long-form text will need to be serialized in order to develop its audience over time.

Moreover, there is an equally serious question to be raised about how to read the absence of comment: does reviewer silence within a particular section of the text indicate a lack of interest, or rather that everything's okay? The inscrutability of such silence presents difficulties not just for the author's process of revision but also for evaluators' assessment of the review process; the mere existence of comments does not necessarily correlate with a project's quality, but does it say something about the engagement of its readers, and thus the impact the project will have within the scholarly community?

While an open, online review process produces a greater number of reviewers, it's hard to ensure that those reviewers take on a project in its entirety, or even to know whether they have done so. By contrast, in a traditional review process, two or three reviewers agree to read and comment on a manuscript as a whole, and generally speaking, their reviews will comment on both sections of the text where there are problems and those that work well. Moreover, given that they're largely written after the reviewer has read the whole project, traditional reviews lend themselves to a more holistic perspective on a manuscript, focusing on its overall argument and structure, while the paragraph-by-paragraph orientation of CommentPress lends itself to more locally oriented responses. On the one hand, these differences point toward the need for technical solutions: we must design a peer-to-peer review system that both allows for fine-grained paragraph-level commenting and encourages larger-scale overview discussions.

On the other hand, the issues raised in comparing the online review process to the traditional reviews indicate that the system that needs the most careful engineering is less technical than it is social: for peer-to-peer review to succeed, we must find ways to build the commitment to a scholarly community that such a system will require. As with most of the challenges facing academic publishing that I've discussed in the course of this book, these social challenges are far more significant than are the technical difficulties we face. After all, scholars have only so much time and energy to contribute to the peer-review process, and publishers of new forms of scholarship similarly have a limited amount of time to devote to reviewer-wrangling. As more texts are posted for this kind of open review, participation in the review process for any single text will inevitably decline, unless we find ways to reward the effort that goes into commenting on one another's work.

It's possible from this perspective to find oneself a bit dismayed by some of the figures that I quoted earlier. While it's great that more than 3,300 readers made multiple return visits to the project, we don't know how much of the text any of them actually read; what we do know is that somewhere in the vicinity of 8,700 visitors wandered into the site, whether from a post on Twitter or on someone's blog or from a Google search, and then wandered away again, never to return (unless such returns were hidden by the use of another computer or a cookie-less browser). And while 44 commenters had something to say about the manuscript, the vast majority of those who stayed and read never commented—though this was also true of 4 of the 9 people from whom I specifically requested feedback. Participation rates in online review processes are perhaps a bit lower than we might like, and reading online is perhaps a bit more partial and broken-up than we might prefer—but we also know at least anecdotally that most readers of scholarly texts do not in any literal sense actually sit down and read them start to finish. A very large percentage of such readers begin with either the table of contents or the index, seeking out the portions of the text that they need and leaving the rest unread. This begins to suggest that whatever notion we may have of a "pure" reading process being fragmented and adulterated by our web-browsing techniques is likely greatly exaggerated.

Raw metrics will never be enough to tell us about the success or failure of a piece of scholarship. That we now have access to those metrics in the age of digital publishing is useful, of course, for figuring out how texts get used in networked discourse—for tracing the links through which readers come to a text, for instance, or where the particular points of interest in an argument lie. But the numbers themselves, without analysis or context, cannot tell us much.

That context, however, is readily available. The online review of this text has left behind a record of the text's coming into being, via the discussions that the draft provoked and the questions that readers raised, both in the margins of the text and on a range of other websites that linked to the project. Moreover, the impact of those discussions and questions is visible here, in this text, as the print edition can be compared with the online draft, and as I've taken pains to cite the points at which readers' responses have influenced my thinking. Assessing the value of those discussions and responses requires careful reading, and it's arguable that advocating such reading is fighting an uphill battle. One of the reasons that we like the binary result of the conventional peer-review process, in which the text in question has either been published or not, is that we've all already got too much to read; the gatekeeping function of peer review keeps us from having to read dreck, while the binary result of peer review gives us an assessment of quality without the time investment that reading requires.

Finding ways to foster productive online discussions of texts, assess those discussions, and use those assessments in the evaluation of a text all present challenges for the future of scholarly publishing. These processes raise a host of further questions as well: When an online draft of a text is so easily posted and disseminated, and when reviews of that text—not just peer reviews, but post-publication book reviews—can appear even faster than a print edition can, what does the specific function of the printed book become? Where does the print edition stand with respect to the online version? Is it a second edition? Which is the version of record? Which should be cited? How should the online version be preserved? Answering these questions with a shrug and a "we'll see" in the portion of this text that's supposed to be the most conclusive is uncomfortable, to say the least, but for the moment, that's the most honest response. The answers to these questions are dependent upon the "practice" in the phrase "community of practice"; conventions for that community's interactions cannot be designed without a lot of experimentation, some of which will no doubt produce unexpected outcomes and result in future practices that would be unintelligible to us today. It's obvious that "best practices" cannot develop in advance of the practices themselves, and that conventions must go through the process of becoming conventional. And yet this is a frightening prospect, as we begin the process of letting go of established ways of working and step into the unknown. We must remind ourselves why we're setting out down this path: our established ways of working are becoming increasingly untenable, and the culture that surrounds us—that *funds* us—demands that we rethink our approach to communication, both among ourselves and with the rest of the world.

Given the extraordinary challenge that change presents for the academy—the degree to which "We Have Never Done It That Way Before" has become our motto—we might do well to ask how much of what I propose in this volume is really feasible. It's much more likely, of course, that simple inertia will keep us rolling in the direction we're already headed. I do believe, however, that change is coming, and coming more quickly than we imagine.

During the question-and-answer period following a talk I gave recently, I was quite surprised to be asked where my optimism comes from. And then I was surprised by my own surprise, and got so caught up in thinking about why the question caught me off-guard that I wasn't able to answer it in any satisfying way. It took me a few days to process the thought. My surprise came in part because I hadn't thought of myself or my argument as all that optimistic. *Utopian*, perhaps, but not optimistic. And in parsing out the distinctions between those two modifiers I came to realize that if I am at all optimistic about the course of scholarly publishing over the next decades, it's in a sense similar to that in which Karl Marx was optimistic about the fate of capitalism in the mid-nineteenth century. The contradictions in our current systems are simply too great to be sustained; if I am optimistic, it's because I am certain that a revolution in scholarly publishing is unavoidable.

However, I want to recognize the points at which Marx's analysis fell short: the spots where he veered from diagnostics into prescriptions, the degree to which he took for granted the ability and desire of those oppressed by a system to take the risks necessary to create a new one, the failure to account for the power of an established system to incorporate and defuse resistance, the ways his followers created new corruptions in adapting his theories into practice. It's not at all unthinkable that my own utopianism could fall victim to these same problems, and so I've tried to avoid the prescriptive, focusing less on what the future of scholarly publishing will look like than on how we'll need to think differently about our relationships—as scholars, publishers, librarians, and administrators—to the process of publishing. Only in coming to such a new understanding of the systems through which we publish, and of our roles within those systems, can we hope to create a new mode that might free us from the current crisis. Without a sufficient collective will to change, we could easily find ourselves in an increasingly profit-driven, corporate-controlled publishing environment in which the gap between the publishing "haves" and "have nots" (and thus between research faculty and teaching faculty, and between top research institutions and the rest of us) continues to widen.

As I write this conclusion, it's just been announced that Rice University Press, reopened in 2006 as an all-digital press after the 1996 closure of its print-based predecessor, will be shuttered for fiscal reasons. Highly public declarations of "failure" in key publishing experiments such as this one, and such as the *Nature* open-review experiment discussed in chapter 1, too often allow us to dismiss the prospects for change, generalizing one situation to a blanket sense that some new way of doing things simply cannot work. As Clay Shirky (2009) argues, this is what revolutions look like: "The old stuff gets broken faster than the new stuff is put in place." This is true in no small part because we spend an awful lot of time trying to make the new stuff work exactly like the old stuff did, rather than working with the new on its own terms.

Change is coming to scholarly publishing, one way or another—but what form that change will take, and whether it will work for or against us, remains to be seen. The result, of course, is that this book is haunted by several looming unanswered questions: What would a viable economic model for non-profit scholarly publishing look like? How should presses, libraries, and information technology centers negotiate their relationships? How can we get scholars to accept and participate in these new publishing and review processes? These questions remain unanswered in part because of their enormity, but also because of the very nature of networked technologies. These technologies are emergent, not just in the sense of coming-into-being, but also in the sense of being spontaneously self-organizing. The technologies on which the future of scholarly publishing depends are built of flux, such that any answers about systems to manage those technologies' futures can only ever be provisional.

What we need, not just in our texts but in our publishing systems and in our institutions as well, is the kind of agility that will allow us to avoid calcifying some particular moment of the system's structure in a misguided attempt to achieve the stability that we've long assumed in the print universe. Jonathan Zittrain (2008, 99) explores what he calls the "generative pattern" of new technological development, a gradual but seemingly inexorable move from the rich, fertile openness of new systems to the increasingly closed, patrolled state of established systems. The shift that Zittrain describes, from the generativity of the early open Internet to the world of locked-down, "appliancized," tethered devices that we now run the risk of inhabiting, operates in other cultural registers as well, including scholarly discourse: fields are repeatedly born in revolutionary insight; come to maturity through a rich period of contentious debate; achieve a kind of institutional recognition; and then ossify into the established, canonical mode of discourse against which new revolutionary insights will rebel.

It would be all too easy for such ossification to take over in digital scholarly publishing; the path from revolution to the ways things have always been done is well-trod. But if the new communication systems that we develop for networked environments are to remain generative—if they are to continue to inspire not just new work but new *possibilities* for our work—we must actively fight on behalf of instability, of the frighteningly uncertain, of the wide-open and new. We need to be rigorous in our experimentation, of course; we need to produce work of the highest quality and integrity, and ensure that our work is as carefully preserved as possible. But all of the players in the production of future scholarship, including students, librarians, editors and publishers, and administrators, must not simply embrace change, but create the change that will keep scholarship generative. Change is here: we can watch our current publishing system suffocate, leaving the academy not just obsolete but irrelevant, or we can work to create a communication environment that will defy such obsolescence, generating rich scholarly discussions well into the future.

Notes

NOTES TO THE INTRODUCTION

1. The January 2009 followup report, *Reading on the Rise: A New Chapter in American Literacy* (NEA 2009) has gotten virtually no media attention. While the NEA is, unsurprisingly, quick to take the increase it finds in adult literary reading as evidence of the impact of the previous reports and the success of programs created in their wake—suggestions that the cultural wildlife preserve created for the book is fostering the regeneration of the species—this followup also explicitly includes "online" literary reading in its assessment, which neither earlier report had done, indicating an acceptance of diversification in the ecosystem.

2. This was well prior to the budget slashing produced by the 2008–9 collapse of the California economy.

3. The irony here being that the book went on to exceed the threshold sales requirement for that original, larger press as well.

4. See, for instance, Sarah Juliet Lauro and Karen Embry's "A Zombie Manifesto" (2008), Meghan Sutherland's "Rigor/Mortis" (2007), and Peter Dendle's "The Zombie as Barometer of Cultural Anxiety" (2007), to cite only a few recent titles.

5. As further evidence of the zeitgeist, if you need it, see also David Sirota's "What's with All the Zombies?" (2009).

6. Natalia Cecire, in a comment on the online version of this project, noted: "Part of the argument of this book is that scholarship per se cannot and should not be thought of apart from scholarly communication. So while the relationship between zombie publishing and a zombie profession isn't, I agree, strictly causal, it's also more than just 'no[t] . . . unrelated.' The zombie university consumes braaaains at an amazing rate, yet lacks autonomy. It's thus unable to make any use of brains as such: brains that think, make decisions, write Ph.D. dissertations, and try to get a first monograph published are turned into braaaains, an undifferentiated mass of intellectual labor ready to be consumed. That's the anxiety incited by the zombie university, which is not only undead (like the undead but urbane vampire) but also inarticulate, unable to speak except to cry out for more braaaains. To rehabilitate the university would first of all entail restoring its ability to speak" (Cecire 2010).

7. On the afterlives of media, see Lisa Gitelman (2008, 2000); Paul Levinson (1997); and Jeffrey Sconce (2000).

8. Calls for moving away from the scholarly monograph, given its apparent status as an artifact no one reads anymore, have been on the rise of late; see, for instance, Mark Bauerlein's report for the American Enterprise Institute, "Professors on the Production Line, Students on Their Own" (Bauerlein 2009), as well as *Inside Higher Ed*'s story about the report (Redden 2009).

1. Perhaps unsurprisingly, this issue has been taken on by librarians, if not by faculty; see, for example, Regalado (2007).

2. See Cohen (2007). Many pro-Wikipedia commentators responded to the Middlebury ban by noting, quite sensibly, that college students shouldn't be citing encyclopedias in the first place. The locus of most of the concern about Wikipedia in this case, however, was the fact that "anyone" can edit its entries.

3. The creators of Citizendium claim that they hope to create "an enormous, free, and *reliable* encyclopedia" that "aims to improve on the Wikipedia model by adding 'gentle expert oversight' and requiring contributors to use their real names." The suggestion, of course, is that authority demands such expert guidance, and expert status is conferred through traditional modes of authorization. See Citizendium, "CZ:About."

4. See also Harnad (1998, 291), who presents many of the same concerns: "Every editor of a learned journal, commentary journal or not, is in a position to sample what the literature would have looked like if everything had appeared without review. Not only would a vanity press of raw manuscripts be unnavigable, but the brave souls who had nothing better to do than to sift through all that chaff and post their commentaries to guide us would be the last ones to trust for calibrating one's finite reading time." The implication, of course, is that without the power to determine whether a manuscript can be published or not, the prestige will drain out of the reviewing process, leaving scholars with only the opinions expressed by the *hoi polloi*.

5. See especially Roy and Ashburn (2001), who indicate that it was not in spite of but rather *due to* the peer-review process that published studies of the anti-inflammatory drugs Celebra and Vioxx excluded data about those drugs' potential for causing heart damage. See also the revelation on *The Scientist* that Elsevier published six fake journals (Grant 2009b), and that Merck paid the publisher "to produce several volumes of a publication that had the look of a peer-reviewed medical journal, but contained only reprinted or summarized articles— most of which presented data favorable to Merck products" (Grant 2009a). Perhaps more famously, in what has been referred to as "Climategate," claims that peer review may have been manipulated in promoting work in climate science resulted in calls among scientists for reform of the review process (Pearce 2010); I thank Nick Mirzoeff (2010) for that reference.

6. See, for instance, Fabiato (1994), Meyers (2004), Rennie (2003), and Spier (2002), all of whom draw heavily from Kronick (1990).

7. Given the overwhelming focus in the sciences on the institution of peer review, we might ask about the degree to which its adoption by the humanities is further evidence of the desire to transform our fields into "human sciences" as a defense against claims—put forward with the greatest impact in university budgets—that our work is insufficiently rigorous and serious to be considered "research."

8. Prior to the establishment of this committee, the selection of manuscripts was in the sole hands of the society's secretary; this transition was important both in the history of the society and of academic publishing, as this was the first time that the society made a public claim of its affiliation with and responsibility for the journal.

9. However, Kronick (2004, 181) reports that more than 20 percent of the attributed papers published in the journal while Alexander Monro was editor (1731 forward) were in fact written by Monro himself.

10. Spier (2002) argues that the first known description of a peer-review process may be found in a late ninth-century medical text.

11. Kronick (2004, 268) suggests that the letter "represented a form in which a scientific article could be disseminated for comment and may be considered equivalent to reading a paper at a scientific meeting before submitting it to a publisher or editor for peer review."

12. See also Weller (2001, 3–6), for a suggestive list of scientific journals and the moments and modes in which they adopted editorial peer review.

13. Worth noting is the challenge posed to this already quite open system by a new preprint server named viXra; according to a recent story on *Physicsworld.com* (Cartwright 2009), viXra removes any restrictions on the kinds of papers that can be uploaded. Scholars associated with viXra allege that some researchers have been blocked from uploading papers based on the moderators' sense that their work is too speculative; others report that their papers have been "dumped" in the generic "physics" category, where they're unlikely to be found and read. See also viXra, "Why viXra?"

14. See also Pöschl (2004).

15. See Godlee (2000, 66–67) for an account of one instance of reviewer fraud. See also Campanario (1998).

16. Scholarly book publishing generally presents an exception to this state of affairs, though only if the editor has decided based upon the reviews to take the manuscript to the press's editorial board for approval. In that case, the author's response to the reviews is requested; however, this response is generally directed not to the readers, but to the board, further complicating the flow of conversation.

17. Peters and Ceci (1982/2004) specifically rule out the possibility that reviewers felt the work to be redundant with the existing literature, even if they couldn't recall the exact source, as no such indication appears in the reviewers' reports.

18. Godlee (2000, 72) suggests that science has, since the time of Peters and Ceci's experiment, become "less clubby and more competitive," while nonetheless indicating that reviewer bias with respect to the institutional prestige of an author remains operative.

19. See also Godlee (2000, 74–75) and Zuckerman and Merton (1971, 86).

20. See Blair, Brown, and Baxter (1994) for an exploration of one remarkable instance of such intellectual or ideological bias among blind reviewers.

21. This qualifier points to the need for further exploration of the requirements with respect to peer review in different disciplines: A study conducted by Zuckerman and Merton (1971) investigated the differing outcomes of peer review across disciplines, noting that the rejection rate in the humanities was far higher than that in the social or natural sciences. A more recent report (National Humanities Alliance 2009) points to two compelling findings: first, that the per-article cost of journal publishing in the humanities and social sciences is more than three times that of the science, technical, and medical (STM) fields, and second, that this increased cost is due in no small part to the increased selectivity of those journals. Where the STM journals under study (which seem to be primarily the official journals of learned societies) have an acceptance rate of around 42 percent, the humanities and social science journals publish about 11 percent of submissions.

22. This concern about the shift in responsibility for reviewing the work of younger scholars is echoed in the final report of the MLA Task Force on Evaluating Scholarship for Tenure and Promotion (Modern Language Association of American 2006), which, while at pains to dissociate the reliance on press judgments from peer review itself, nonethe-

less acknowledges that "this apparatus of external peer review also created the conditions whereby individual departments can practically abdicate their responsibility to review the scholarly work of the very colleagues they have appointed to tenure-track positions" (p. 56).

23. Thanks to David Parry (2009a) for guiding me to this point.

24. Recent controversies between the so-called "deletionist" and "inclusionist" Wikipedians, as well as the brief brouhaha around the introduction of flagged and patrolled edits, complicate Anderson's model a bit, of course, but the focus remains on the evaluation of content rather than contributors. See "The Battle for Wikipedia's Soul" (2008) and Wales (2009).

25. Perhaps needless to say, this is far from an uncontroversial stance. One crucial bit of debate arose around the figure of Essjay, a high-ranking editor who presented himself as "a tenured professor of religion at a private university," though in actuality he held no advanced degrees. When asked whether a figure like Essjay posed a problem for Wikipedia's credibility, founder Jimmy Wales initially said, "I regard it as a pseudonym and I don't really have a problem with it" (Schiff 2006)—but later "proposed a rule whereby the credentials of those Wikipedia administrators who chose to assert them would be verified" (Zittrain 2008, 141). The key distinctions here are that this policy applies to administrators only, who have a significantly higher degree of authority within the site than do editors, and that it applies only to those who *assert* their credentials in support of their arguments.

26. Schwartz should certainly understand the value of trust in the digital world, given the need to rebuild its reputation that Sun faced after the dot-com bust; see Falkow. Schwartz's phrase has become the tagline for the Open Media Commons service operated by Sun; see Open Media Commons.

27. Notably, John Holbo (2005) appropriated the term in a blog post speculating on a cooperative electronic publishing model.

28. See Lanham (2006) on the rhetorical implications of this new scarcity.

29. See, for instance, discussions of Google's PageRank algorithm, which arguably measures popularity of pages through an analysis of inbound links (Regalado 2007), but which others interpret as "inherently conservative," granting further authority to the already popular (Vaidhyanathan 2007).

30. The comparison to eBay is perhaps a bit unfortunate, resulting in faintly crass images of intellectual commerce, but there's something apt in the relationship as well, suggesting that electronic scholarly publishing might function as a locus for the exchange of ideas in which producers and consumers can find one another without the need for an intermediary. Lindsay Waters (2004, 9) argues, however, that the marketplace "is not a concept that should be considered the ultimate framework for the free play of ideas." See also Shatz (2004) for a more elaborated argument against the marketplace metaphor.

31. See, for instance, "Dr Ian Walker's Philica details."

32. Numerous pundits insisted that opening Facebook to any user might, in the end, prove to be the service's undoing, though many were primarily lamenting their loss of exclusivity. danah boyd (2007a, 2007b), however, has argued that the success of social-networking systems has largely hinged on the ability to control the social context in which one's profile appears.

33. As I discuss in chapter 2, however, one of the most exciting aspects of a digital publishing environment such as the one in which the electronic version of this text was published is that the text could be updated to reflect MediaCommons's actual state, and

yet versioned, to preserve for the historical record what I'd thought it would look like at a particular point in time.

34. Beyond this, of course, lies user frustration with the sudden overflow of Facebook applications that resulted when the site's developers opened up the system's API. In very short order, Facebook went from being a focused and contained, if limited, platform to a wild mishmash of annoying and seemingly pointless content. Perhaps a peer-to-peer reviewing system for Facebook apps—a community-based filtering system—might have helped stem the overflow; see Iskold (2007).

35. See, as only two among many possible citations, Seglen (1997) and Richard Smith (2006). Don Brenneis (email to the author, April 17, 2008) has likewise drawn my attention to the grave concern in the United Kingdom about chancellor Gordon Brown's decision to replace the Research Assessment Exercise, which previously determined funding for British universities, with a very narrow set of metrics including citation indexes; see Alexandra Smith (2006).

NOTES TO CHAPTER 2

1. If you are one of the lucky few who feels no anxieties about writing, I envy you—and, on some level, disbelieve you: anxieties about writing are usually unspoken and yet nearly universal among academics, right up there with imposter syndrome. And even if you honestly feel you have no worries about your writing life, consider this: when was the last time you had to write a document in committee? If there were no jaw-clenching moments in that process, or if you've never become irate about the way your writing has been edited, then I *really* envy you.

2. If anything, questioning those frameworks seems to have added to our anxieties about our own writing; Ede and Lunsford (2001, 355) point out that "however we theorize the subject and author, problems of writing and of scholarly (and pedagogical) practice decidedly remain. Amid such intense questioning, a kind of paralysis seems possible." Indeed, I would say it seems likely. Little wonder, then, that we prefer to leave such notions in theory: "We scholars in English studies, it appears, are often more comfortable theorizing about subjectivity, agency, and authorship than we are attempting to enact alternatives to conventional assumptions and practices" (ibid., p. 356).

3. Lessig (2006, 32) goes on to argue that because these codes are programmable, and thus plastic, they can be reprogrammed to better serve our needs: "We should expect—and demand—that [technology] can be made to reflect any set of values that we think important." For the time being, I ignore this quite obviously correct point and instead think about what the academy can learn from network technologies, rather than vice versa. In the next chapter, I turn my attention to network design and new scholarly publishing structures.

4. See Heim (1999, 1): "[T]he practice of writing on a computer is becoming the standard operation for information workers; word processing is no longer restricted to the narrow domain of office automation. It would seem that not only the speed of intellectual work is being affected, but the quality of the work itself"; Bolter (1991, 5): "Change is the rule in the computer, stability the exception, and it is the rule of change that makes the word processor so useful"; and Poster (1990, 111): "Compared to the pen, the typewriter, or the printing press, the computer dematerializes the written trace. . . . Writers who begin to work with

computers report their astonishment at how much easier many aspects of the process of writing have become or that writing is now very much like speaking."

5. I return to this sense of conversation in the following chapter, as I turn to think about textual structures.

6. Hesse (1996, 24) notes that this mode of textual circulation "looks a lot like a mechanical version of the Internet"; it certainly bears resemblances to the mode of Internet communication that utopian thinkers like John Perry Barlow applaud, and that more pessimistic respondents such as Andrew Keen (2007) and Jaron Lanier (2006) deplore, if not to the Internet as it actually functions.

7. What the "words" have done with their words has been far more participatory than Jackson's original project description suggests. "Words" were required to submit photographs of the tattoos to confirm their participation, and were invited to add "footnotes" to the project's website, annotating their words; many of these participants have constructed their own narratives around those words, making at least this small part of Jackson's narrative—and, not incidentally, her website—their own; see "Skin Footnotes." Amanda French (2009a) points out another layer of "readers" for this project: those who encounter the "words" out in the world, utterly decontextualized.

8. So argued Howard Owens (2007) on his blog: "Blogs are arguably the first web-native publishing model, so it only makes sense that blogs would provide a template for how to publish online." Well before that, Michele Tepper (2003, 20) described blogs as "perhaps the first native publishing format for the Web." This point always seems to be made with "arguably" inserted, as I have done, which suggests that the idea has managed to enter the conventional wisdom without anyone ever having done an empirical study to back it up. Interestingly, I posed the question of support for such a statement on my own blog, and thus provoked a compelling discussion about what the true value of blogging's "firstness" would be and about the erasure of Usenet from histories of the digital in the wake of the web. See Fitzpatrick (2007b).

9. See Walker (2003) for a good basic definition of the blog.

10. See "About Us," *Technorati*. In a recent interview, blogger Matthew Baldwin claimed, only somewhat hyperbolically, that "blogs are so ubiquitous these days that announcing you write one is like announcing you have a liver" (Stallings 2008).

11. George Carr (2010) reminded me that textbook publishing introduces a particular complication to the ideas about versioning I discuss here; textbook versioning is often implemented in support of a baldly commercial form of planned obsolescence that ruthlessly replaces each previous edition with what is ostensibly the most up-to-date information, but is often in reality only slightly updated and repaginated, with the explicit goal of eliminating the resale of used books. Although I am here focused on scholarly rather than textbook publishing, it's worth bearing in mind the ways that commercial versioning practices in print publishing are affecting our students; this is *not* the goal I have in mind for our work.

12. "Another bald, bitter point about Fordist demands on scholarly productivity: the university itself has become a degree factory, and in the case of humanities Ph.D.s is of course churning out a much greater supply than the (job) market will bear. Right now the gorfed-up system of academic publishing means that that oversupply goes quietly away, having demonstrably failed to meet an objective standard of excellence, and the universities are therefore free to continue taking tuition money from fresh-faced innocents" (French 2009b).

13. On this tension in digital scholarship, see Kirschenbaum (2009a); Brown et al. (2009).

14. This bears enormous consequences for the preservation of digital texts into the future; I discuss these issues in chapter 4.

15. Not coincidentally, all three of us also blogged the panel: see Fitzpatrick (2008a); Burke (2008); Blankenship (2008).

16. Dozens of other academic bloggers have written about the relationship between the public mode of blogging and the more traditionally private, formal mode of producing scholarship. For example, John Holbo (2006), in the course of discussing a draft of a paper he was preparing for the 2006 Modern Language Association convention about the relationship between blogs and scholarly publishing, indicated the usefulness, for him, of finding "some draft, penultimate, suitably developed—that needed a good knocking about. And the best place to get that these days, for me, is on the web. Post a draft. Get responses. Make improvements. The fact that then there is generally some artifactual record of the knocking-about is a plus, not a minus." He went on to argue: "One thing that electronic publication could conceivably end is the finality of the book. This is a delicate point, because you have to preserve an inviolable archival record of what was written. But it ought to be possible to create version 2.0 of your book, in response to criticism, if version 2.0 would really be a lot, a lot better."

17. These assumptions about singular authorship have given rise not only to the devaluation of coauthored texts, to which I now turn my attention, but also to concerns about plagiarism and appropriation, and to the scholarly citation practices intended to mitigate them. I turn to those issues in the next section.

18. As Joseph Harris noted: "[A]lmost all the routine forms of marking an academic career—CVs, annual faculty activity reports, tenure and promotion reviews—militate against [collaboration] by singling out for merit only those moments of individual 'productivity,' the next article or grant or graduate course" (quoted in Ede and Lunsford 2001, 356).

19. See, for instance, Fox and Faver (1984, 348): "[T]he separation of tasks and the joining of specializations may enable collaborators to increase their efficiency." See also Austin and Baldwin (1991); Gelman and Gibelman (1999); Neubauer and Brewer (2004); Hart (2000).

20. All of these scholars point as well to the costs involved in collaboration, which can include slower production (through delays incurred in waiting for collaborators' responses), higher research expenses (incurred in travel and communication), and emotional requirements (incurred in the need to maintain good working relationships in circumstances that can be trying). New digital technologies can potentially, at least, reduce the financial costs of collaboration.

21. The irony is that while electronic publishing creates anxieties about our ideas being appropriated, it in fact presents a kind of protection against such thefts; when I publish a blog post containing part of an argument I'm working on, that blog post is time-stamped, thus creating material evidence that I wrote those words then. If anything, that evidence should powerfully mitigate our fears that our ideas will be stolen.

22. EMI, holder of copyright on *The Beatles*, ordered the album to be withdrawn from retail distribution, which in fact may have created the notoriety that spurred its widespread success on the Internet.

23. On the historical development, cultural significance, and legal implications of remix/mashup culture, see Lessig (2008); Jenkins (2006),

24. See, for instance, Lessig (2001); Vaidhyanathan (2001, 2004); Saint-Amour (2003); Willinsky (2006).

25. Ede and Lunsford (2001, 359) note that "the old cloak of the originary author-genius has been spruced up and donned first by the law and then by corporate entrepreneurial interests," suggesting that, far from disrupting the figure of the author, the corporation has instead appropriated it, becoming perversely more individual than the individual.

26. *Fortune* included *In Rainbows* as number 59 in its list of the "101 Dumbest Moments in Business," saying: "Can't wait for the followup album, *In Debt*" ("101 Dumbest Moments").

27. This claim focuses on the publication of scholarship, leaving out the comparatively lucrative textbook market; textbooks and their relationship to digital publishing are another can of worms entirely.

28. I focus in greater detail on the potential business models for the scholarly press of the future in chapter 5.

29. On the history and development of Creative Commons, see Kelty (2008, 258–63); Lessig (2001, 2005).

30. U.S. Constitution, Article 1, Section 8, Clause 8.

31. Technically, of course, this isn't true; striking the keys triggers a switch that completes a circuit that sends an electrical signal to a microcontroller, which then translates that signal into a code sent to the computer processor, which finally uses that code to produce certain effects (instructions to a hard drive causing voltage changes that result in magnetic inscription on its surface; instructions to a display device causing pixels to appear on a screen). But the effect for most computer users is what I describe above.

NOTES TO CHAPTER 3

1. This presentation was later published as "Little Jobs: Broadsides and the Printing Revolution" (Stallybrass 2007).

2. Stallybrass's later rhetoric is somewhat toned down, while still making the same point: "The conceptual gluttony of 'the book' consumes all printing as if all paper was destined for its voracious mouth" (2007, 340).

3. Both the commentable draft and the republished version are available at http://docs.plannedobsolescence.net. Thanks are due to Bob Stein, Ben Vershbow, Jesse Wilbur, and Eddie Tejeda for making the technology available for my experiment, and to Bob, Ben, Dan Visel, K.G. Schneider, Mark Bernstein, Richard Pinneau, and Sebastian Mary for their helpful comments on the draft. Thanks are also due to Shana Kimball and Judith Turner of the *Journal of Electronic Publishing* for their willingness to participate in this experiment.

4. For more on the history of Voyager's Expanded Books project, one might begin with the Wikipedia entry (http://en.wikipedia.org/wiki/Expanded_Books).

5. This statement was true when it was originally written, before the release of the first iPad; since that time, of course, the market has begun to shift, such that publishers now predict a fast-approaching e-book tipping point (Tappuni 2011).

6. Moreover, the attempt to imagine such alternatives often results in a profound anti-technological backlash; see, among others, Kernan (1990); Birkerts (1994).

7. That said, even famed bibliophile Nicholson Baker (2009) was able to see the potential appeal of the Kindle, if not the success of its actual execution.

8. In fact, remnants of such rear-view mirrorism still linger in automotive design, such as front-wheel steering. Thanks to Dan Visel (2007) for this insight.

9. And as Dorothea Salo (2009a) reminds me, the early book itself was rife with such rear-view mirrorism tying it to the manuscript form it replaced: "[C]onsider, for example, the history of the typeface, which started as a (rather brutish and ugly) aping of the manuscript hand, but soon developed its own design canons that were for the most part wholly divorced from handwriting."

10. See also George Landow's argument that "hypertext promises to embody and test aspects of theory, particularly those concerning textuality, narrative, and the roles or functions of reader and writer" (1997, 2), suggesting hypertext's more thorough fulfillment of earlier arguments about print-based texts.

11. Mark Bernstein (2007) of Eastgate left a comment on an early draft of the article from which this chapter developed, noting that "[a]ll Storyspace hypertexts will soon be available today for Mac OS X. And, of course, they run fine on Windows XP and Vista." This is excellent news, though it does raise an additional conundrum for electronic textuality more generally: it's rare that one is required to pay for an upgrade in the codex realm; a new edition might have corrections or features that a reader might prefer, but the old edition rarely stops working. Moreover, the codex is platform-independent; it's all but impossible to imagine a circumstance in which readers of the hardcover are left behind while the paperback remains up-to-date. I explore the problems presented by the preservation of digital texts in chapter 4.

12. The proprietary publisher Eastgate bears most of the responsibility for the stuckness of such early hypertexts, indicating that one of the dangers in translating traditional publishing industry models to the digital realm is precisely that of remaindered texts; while a book that has gone out of print, released by a publisher that has gone out of business, remains readable, a digital title that loses currency runs the risk of becoming technologically illegible. As Robert Coover (1992) pointed out, "[E]ven though the basic technology of hypertext may be with us for centuries to come, perhaps even as long as the technology of the book, its hardware and software seem to be fragile and short-lived." A second point arises in no small part in response to that first: the Electronic Literature Organization, through its committee for Preservation, Archiving, and Dissemination, has of late put significant energy into the preservation and protection of texts such as these. See Montfort and Wardrip-Fruin (2004); Liu et al. (2005). See also chapter 4, in which I further explore these issues.

13. As Dorothea Salo (2009b) notes, this atomization has profound effects not just on scholars' ability to find and use the objects in these databases, but on libraries' ability to preserve and protect the databases. I take this issue up in chapter 4.

14. Several excellent resources now exist designed to help scholars find the right tools for conducting new forms of digital scholarship; most notable among these may be the Digital Research Tools Wiki, which organizes a number of such tools by their potential use. See also the Transliteracies project (*Transliteracies*), which houses a number of extensive reviews of such tools.

15. See Anderson (1991) and Habermas (1989). Certain obvious criticisms can be leveled at both theorists, most notably that the public sphere they describe somewhat overstates its universality, given that only those admitted to the coffee houses—white men of a certain economic standing—were able to become part of that public. It is nonetheless key that the technologies of reading played a crucial role in developing that public's sense, however faulty, of itself.

16. See Esposito (2003); see also Price (2004); and Darnton (1982, 78), who writes: "Reading itself has changed over time. It was often done aloud and in groups, or in secret and with an intensity we may not be able to imagine today."

17. Hesse (1996) ties the individualism associated with the book and its author not to the technologies of print or the codex, but rather to the philosophical and political debates of the Enlightenment, which were staked upon understanding the individual thinker as the origin of knowledge.

18. And, as Natalia Cecire (2009) reminded me, what is "[h]idden, in this model, is the labor of research assistants, of course, who are often co-reading with and/or predigesting for the author."

19. As we saw in the previous chapter, even within such a dynamic networked environment a place remains for the individual author, and therefore for the individual text; as Sebastian Mary (2007) commented on the draft of the article that later developed into this chapter, "I'd argue that the net makes visible the activity that takes place prior to a text being enshrined in a form evoking the tradition of the book. Hence, dynamic community-based net activity doesn't replace in-depth, fixed, authoritative scholarly work but rather facilitates those aspects of scholarship that are plainly more fluid and mutable, speeding up conversation and removing the shackles of Authority from kinds of print that chafe under its yoke. Or, to put it another way, I think there always comes a point where you want to write a book—but not everything works best when published that way."

20. "Doing the comments this way (next to, not below, the parent posts) came out of a desire to break out of the usual top-down hierarchy of blog-based discussion" (Vershbow 2006a).

21. Thanks to Ben Vershbow and Bob Stein for their additions to my thinking about the issues revolving around discussion of these two projects.

22. And, of course, this text as a whole has been through a CommentPress-based open review, the results of which remain available; see *Planned Obsolescence*.

23. See Bogost's tendentiously titled post, "Reading Online Sucks" (2008), in which he suggests the need for deeper consideration of the material differences between print and screen in digital publishing formats.

24. Thanks to Shana Kimball for sharing this observation with me.

NOTES TO CHAPTER 4

1. As Baker addresses, and as I discuss later in this section, the primary way in which the assumed permanence of print is being challenged today is through the deaccessioning practices of libraries.

2. Thanks to Dorothea Salo (2009c) for this point.

3. See, however, Terry Harpold (2009, 5) on the shortcomings of emulators, as well as the difficulties faced in their production: "Writing software that duplicates the myriad interactions of hardware and software is an exceedingly difficult task, and emulators are often buggy and incomplete in their support of the systems they reproduce. Many are hobbyist projects created by enthusiasts of programs designed for an obsolete system, most often, games; they may be less interested in reproducing the complete behavior of the OS than in supporting those features needed by their favorite programs. Emulation projects usually lack the support of—or are actively opposed by—the publishers of emulated systems, who wish to maintain control over their intellectual property even when it is no longer in use."

4. Thanks to Lisa Spiro, whose most generous peer review of this manuscript guided me to this point.

5. Although the scandal over Amazon's removal of legally purchased copies of two of George Orwell's novels from users' Kindles has recently brought the issue to widespread attention, Clifford Lynch (2001) raised questions about this very concern with respect to e-books ten years ago, asking libraries to consider whether their purchases result in ownership of "*objects* or *access*." This question is even more pressing in the area of digital journals, particularly considering the bundling practices and astronomically inflated subscription costs of many commercial journal publishers. In the era of print journals, when a library canceled a subscription (or when a journal ceased publishing), the library maintained ownership of the issues released during the subscription period. Whether that will continue to be true in the digital era—whether, for instance, libraries have the right to create backup archives of digital journals to which they subscribe—is still being negotiated. I return to this question later in the chapter.

6. See "About W3C" (2008). The W3C's management of HTML and the standards that it focuses on are far from uncontroversial, however; see Baron (2006).

7. That HTML also provides the <i> tag, which specifies italics, points to the fact that the separation between structure and presentation became increasingly difficult to manage in the early days of HTML, resulting in the development, in 1996, of Cascading Style Sheets (CSS), which allow web designers to specify how particular HTML tags should *look* when rendered in a browser.

8. That there could conceivably be a thing referred to as an "Internet community" only indicates how early in the Internet's spread these developments took place; 1994 seems recent in many ways, but in Internet time, it's positively paleolithic.

9. Problems with HTML as a coding language include, as Steven DeRose (1999) notes, a fixed, non-customizable tagset that prevents users from creating many of the kinds of documents they need; also, despite being theoretically focused on structure, as a descendant of SGML, HTML was in its first decade subject to a kind of format-creep, becoming treated as more akin to word-processing software than true document markup. Worst, perhaps, is that despite the interventions of the W3C in its attempts to establish valid HTML markup, most browsers will attempt to interpret any code a document contains, meaning that "[i]n effect, there is almost no erroneous HTML," and therefore no impetus for users to conform to the standards meant to provide document longevity (pp. 12–13).

10. Thus, before the header of most HTML pages, you will find a tag something like <!DOCTYPE html PUBLIC "-//W3C//DTD XHTML 1.0 Transitional//EN" "http://www.w3.org/TR/xhtml1/DTD/xhtml1-transitional.dtd">, which indicates the specific DTD to which the page claims adherence.

11. XML is often referred to as a subset of SGML, developed in order to streamline and simplify the unwieldiness of SGML's specification.

12. Bob Sutor ("Open Source vs. Open Standards") draws an important distinction between de facto standards and community standards; Microsoft Word's "doc" filetype is an example of the former, and the struggles of many users to find alternate means of working with such filetypes is evidence of the ways one standard's lock on a particular market might not reflect the best interests or practices of a community.

13. Of course, not all electronic texts are produced for the web; the discussion in this chapter is admittedly limited in that regard, but as the example of Storyspace-created hypertexts might indicate, the basic issues with respect to the openness of standards are nonetheless applicable to non-web texts.

14. See Sutor ("Open Source vs. Open Standards"). This set of standards was only forcibly opened as a result of the breakup of the AT&T monopoly, which likewise opened the telephone lines to the transmission of non-voice data.

15. Ironically, perhaps, in June 2009 Blackboard issued a promise to its customers to adhere more closely to open standards; see Young (2009).

16. Thanks to Lisa Spiro for guiding me to this point.

17. See Matt Kirschenbaum's comment (2009b) on the draft of this book, and particularly on the fact that the Variable Media Network's preservation project has moved forward, while the Electronic Literature Organization's has not, because the former was funded and the latter was not.

18. Thanks to Barbara Hui and George Williams for this observation, which they shared with me via Twitter on July 22, 2009. That I don't have an appropriate framework for citing their contributions represents a failure of metadata that's much to the point; Twitter appears to be ephemeral, and so hasn't yet provided means of preservation via persistent archiving or linking, or means of citation. (Which is to say that I could have included URLs for the individual posts involved had I grabbed them right away, but those URLs very quickly become unrecoverable, as Twitter's API places a limit on the number of posts into the past one can retrieve.) This difficulty in recovering the location of a post becomes a problem as the service trends away from ephemeral status updates and toward the more substantive conversations that are taking place within it, which suggests the ways that metadata requirements change over time. Coincidentally, as I am revising this endnote, the Library of Congress has announced that it will be receiving the entirety of Twitter's archive of public tweets; how this material will be archived and made available for research is as yet unclear. See Raymond (2010).

19. See Doctorow (2001) for a discussion of the reasons metadata usage often breaks down online, including that "People lie."

20. See *Dublin Core Metadata Initiative* and Open Archives Initiative ("Open Archives Initiative Protocol").

21. For more on the ways Google works and some of the problems it poses for the organization of knowledge, see Grimmelmann (2009).

22. Thanks to Amanda French for this observation, which was provided via Twitter on July 22, 2009, as well as the observation about disambiguation in the previous sentence; see French (2009c).

23. Thanks to Kari Kraus (2009) for reminding me of this point. See also Zotero ("Make Your Site Zotero Ready").

24. It's shocking to remember that, not so long ago, our library cataloging systems didn't provide us with this crucial bit of information. Not knowing whether a text is actually available in my library *before* I walk there is unthinkable to me today, suggesting the extent to which the kinds of information we consider crucial in our metadata change over time.

25. See also Koehler (2004) for a longitudinal study that suggests both that link degradation stabilizes after an initial, precipitous drop, and that links to different kinds of web objects degrade at different rates.

26. See the seventh edition of the *MLA Handbook*: "Inclusion of URLs has proved to have limited value, however, for they often change, can be specific to a subscriber or a session of use, and can be so long and complex that typing them into a browser is cumbersome and prone to transcription errors. Readers are now more likely to find resources on the Web by searching for titles and authors' names than by typing URLs" (Modern Language Association of America 2009, 182). Note, of course, that the assumption is that a reader wanting to find a cited resource would need to transcribe that URL rather than simply clicking on a link; the default assumption in this handbook is still that the *citation itself* will appear in print.

27. Sean Gillies (2010) pointed out in a comment on the online version of this project that "[t]he problem with URLs isn't inherent fragility but that we often don't get the identifier space of our information architecture straight before we begin to publish resources on the web. Major web 'properties' like Wikipedia can and do maintain their URLs as their infrastructures change. 9 years ago http://www.wikipedia.org/wiki/Computing was served by a Perl CGI script on a single server. Now it's served by 200 application servers, 20 database servers and 70 cache servers. Wikipedia's data has moved many times, yet the original URL still exists, now redirecting to a language-specific variant (http://en.wikipedia.org/wiki/Computing in my case). Maintaining the original URL is Wikipedia's policy. Nine years might not seem very long to a librarian, but there's no technical reason why (given funding) that policy can't continue indefinitely, even if Wikipedia grew tenfold, physically relocated their data center, switched to app servers written in Erlang, or switched from Squid to Varnish."

28. Other forms of identifying digital objects by name rather than location exist, including Uniform Resource Names (URNs); URLs and URNs are both subsets of the larger category of Uniform Resource Identifiers (URIs). Technically, the W3C has deprecated the term URL in favor of URI, but popularly, the location-based term remains the norm, as it is location through which web browsers address the object.

29. The International DOI Foundation has announced its plans to move toward an economic model based on fees paid by registration agencies, who may in turn charge publishers wishing to register DOIs (International DOI Foundation 2006, 78).

30. That said, the most common reason most people need backups does not originate with hard disk failure but rather with human intervention: the accidental deletion of the wrong file, the theft of a laptop, and so on.

31. The continued viability of service providers also presents a potential crisis for the locator issue discussed in the last section; a range of URL-shortening services have come into vogue recently, and the failure of one such service, tr.im, at least temporarily meant that links using such shortened URLs would not resolve.

32. See, for instance, Manoff (2009, 2): "Access and preservation, two key historical functions of academic and research libraries, are more difficult to reconcile in a digital environment."

33. See Thibodeau (2002): "In addition to identifying and retrieving the digital components, it is necessary to process them correctly. To access any digital document, stored bit sequences must be interpreted as logical objects and presented as conceptual objects. So digital preservation is not a simple process of preserving physical objects but one of preserving the ability to reproduce the objects. The process of digital preservation, then, is inseparable from accessing the object. You cannot prove that you have preserved the

object until you have re-created it in some form that is appropriate for human use or for computer system applications." See also Waters (2002, 87): "User access in some form is needed in any case for an archive to certify that its content is viable."

34. See Fitzpatrick (2010) for more on the ethical issues and the misinformation surrounding open access.

35. Questions have been raised, for the obvious reasons, about the sustainability of a system that does not require participation in order to receive its benefits (see, for instance, Morrow et al. 2008, 17). CLOCKSS, however, believes that it will be able to reduce fees at the end of five years, once an endowment has been raised (see CLOCKSS, "FAQ").

36. The JISC report referred to below describes the benefits and drawbacks of each of these philosophies as follows: "The advantages of source file preservation [as used by Portico] is that it is very complete (and likely to include more content than appears in the journal); is received directly from the publisher and is frequently delivered or converted to a few normalized formats facilitating long-term preservation. The disadvantages are that it requires a large upfront investment; there is no assurance that the archive will actually be needed; and the presentation will almost certainly differ from that of the publisher. The advantages of harvesting presentation files (rendition archiving) [the LOCKSS approach] are that it is possible to retain the look and feel of the publication and initial costs are likely to be lower. The disadvantages of this technique are that it may be more difficult to preserve the content over time (for example, a strategy for the large scale migration of presentation files from one format to another is still untested)" (Morrow et al. 2008, 9).

37. Portico is moving toward the preservation of e-book holdings, with hundreds of titles (primarily published by Elsevier and Walter de Gruyter) listed as "queued" on their website.

NOTES TO CHAPTER 5

1. In fact, as Brown, Griffiths, and Rascoff (2007, 19) indicate, press directors feel that "they are held to a different standard than all the cost centers on campus, that they are essentially penalized for pursuing a cost recovery model, which then becomes the basis for evaluating their performance. When they perform well (in financial terms) they are 'rewarded' by having subsidies cut. When they run too large a deficit they are threatened with closure." And in fact many are threatened with closure right now regardless of the size of their deficits: The year 2009 saw the potential shuttering of presses at institutions including Louisiana State University and Utah State University; 2010 saw the closure of Southern Methodist University's press.

2. Note that profits rose for three out of four of these presses, and declined only slightly for the fourth, despite the major financial reversals during 2008–9, when news of layoffs across the publishing industry was rampant, leading to speculation about the uncertain future of book publishing more broadly (see Rich 2008).

3. This situation will, Thompson (2005, 368) suggests, intensify in the digital future: "[T]he principal market for scholarly book content in electronic form is likely to be institutional rather than individual."

4. The rub, of course, is that while every institution has a library, not every institution has a press, and thus a select few universities are producing the scholarly material consumed by all. I address this issue later in the chapter.

5. I acknowledge the troubling implications of this Fordist mode of describing the work of the academy; the problematic notion of intellectual "production" is discussed below.

6. See Willinsky (2006, xi): "[O]pen access to research archives and journals has the potential to change the public presence of science and scholarship and increase the circulation of this particular form of knowledge." See also Borgman (2007, 103): "Research funding agencies, both public and private, have yet another set of incentives for open access to publications. Repositories offer a mechanism to ensure that the research they fund is disseminated and accessible."

7. See, for instance, Pressman ("Vectors"), who notes that Vectors "makes evident how innovations in publishing use digital technologies to promote connections between the various vectors shaping intellectual intersections across disciplines and geographies."

8. The University of Southern California (USC), a major research university, does not house a university press. One might ask whether Vectors provides USC with the beginnings of a nexus around which a university publishing center could be formed. What possibilities for digital publishing should institutions without presses explore? I return to this question later.

9. See Brown, Griffiths, and Rascoff (2007, 26); see also Penn State University Libraries, "Office of Digital Scholarly Publishing."

10. See Brown, Griffiths, and Rascoff (2007, 16): "[L]ibrarians have limited skills and experience in marketing content to build awareness and usage. . . . And no library publishing alternative can begin to compete with the prestige that a university press imprint confers on scholarship, nor replace the credentialing power that presses have developed over decades." The same is arguably true of information technology centers, which generally keep abreast of technological developments but are at times resistant to experimentation that might appear to expose the campus network to malicious intrusion, and (with the very notable exception of instructional technologists) are often focused on issues of enterprise computing, with little freedom to explore the role that computing might play in pedagogy and research. Dorothea Salo (2009d) notes, however, in the online discussion of the draft of this book, that the problems in library experimentation may stem more from the fact that "faculty don't think of the library as a potential collaborator in this realm," and that "libraries feel as beleaguered as presses when it comes to resources for experimentation and room for the sort of failure one learns from."

11. Brown, Griffiths, and Rascoff (2007, 19) note that presses "are caught in a 'catch 22,' where they lack room for experimentation because their budgets are so tight, and thus cannot inspire interest in their administrators to fund anything new."

12. Thanks to Amanda French (2009d) for helping me find my way to this point.

13. Note that the first press at Harvard, Cambridge Press (founded 1636; closed 1692) was similarly focused on the publication of religious and legal texts (Givler 2002).

14. Givler (2002) notes that "Gilman's famous dictum, 'It is one of the noblest duties of a university to advance knowledge, and to diffuse it not merely among those who can attend the daily lectures—but far and wide,' articulated a clear, specific role for university presses."

15. As Willinsky (2006, 6) points out, "[S]cholarly publishing runs on a different economic basis than the rest of the publishing world. Researchers and scholars are not paid a penny by journal publishers for original manuscripts presenting the results of perhaps thousands of dollars' worth of research. Rather, in publishing their work, the authors are banking on a longer-term investment in what might be cast as human rights and vanities." Similarly, Gary Hall (2008, 46) notes that "academics tend not to be too concerned about getting paid a fee for, or receiving royalties from their research publications . . . the main priority of most academics is to have their research read by as many people as possible, in the hope, not only of receiving greater levels of feedback and recognition for their work, and thus an enhanced reputation, but also of having the biggest possible impact on future research, and perhaps even society. So they are perfectly willing to in effect give their work away for free to anyone who can bring this about."

Bibliography

"About CommentPress." 2007. *CommentPress*, July 25. <http://www.futureofthebook.org/commentpress/about/>.

"About digitalculturebooks." *digitalculturebooks*. <http://www.digitalculture.org/about.html>.

"About PDFs." *The National Academies Press*. <http://www.nap.edu/about/about_pdf.html>.

"About the Press." *Athabasca University Press*. <http://www.aupress.ca/index.php/about/>.

"About the Press." *Johns Hopkins University Press*. <http://www.press.jhu.edu/about/index.html>.

"About Us." *Technorati*. <http://technorati.com/about/>.

"About Us." *UC Press E-Books Collection*. <http://publishing.cdlib.org/ucpressebooks/about.html>.

"About W3C." 2008. *World Wide Web Consortium*, April 29. <http://www.w3.org/Consortium/>.

Alonso, Carlos J., et al. 2003. *Crises and Opportunities: The Futures of Scholarly Publishing*. New York: American Council of Learned Societies.

Anderson, Benedict. 1991. *Imagined Communities: Reflections on the Origin and Spread of Nationalism*. New York: Verso.

Anderson, Chris. 2006a. *The Long Tail: Why the Future of Business Is Selling Less of More*. New York: Hyperion.

———. 2006b. "Wisdom of the Crowds." *Nature Online*. <http://www.nature.com/nature/peerreview/debate/nature04992.html>.

Apps, Ann, and Ross MacIntyre. 2006. "Why OpenURL?." *D-Lib Magazine* 12 (5) <http://www.dlib.org/dlib/may06/apps/05apps.html>.

Association of American Universities, Association of Research Libraries, The Coalition for Networked Information and National Association of State Universities and Land Grant Colleges. 2008. "The University's Role in the Dissemination of Research and Scholarship—A Call to Action." <http://www.aau.edu/WorkArea/DownloadAsset.aspx?id=9478>.

Austin, Ann E., and Roger G. Baldwin. 1991. *Faculty Collaboration: Enhancing the Quality of Scholarship and Teaching*. ASHE-ERIC Higher Education Report no. 7. ERIC Clearinghouse on Higher Education, George Washington University, 1991. <http://www.eric.ed.gov/ERICWebPortal/contentdelivery/servlet/ERICServlet?accno=ED346805>.

Bady, Aaron, et al. *Cliopatria: A Group Blog*. <http://hnn.us/blogs/2.html>.

Baker, Nicholson. 2009. "A New Page." *The New Yorker*, August 3. <http://www.newyorker.com/reporting/2009/08/03/090803fa_fact_baker>.

———. 2001. *Double Fold: Libraries and the Assault on Paper*. New York: Random House.

Baron, David. 2006. "More W3C Controversy." *David Baron's Weblog*. August 18. <http://dbaron.org/log/2006-08#e20060818a>.

Barthes, Roland. 1967/86. "The Death of the Author." Reprinted in *The Rustle of Language*, 49–55. New York: Hill and Wang.

"The Battle for Wikipedia's Soul." 2008. *The Economist*. March 6. <http://www.economist.com/search/displaystory.cfm?story_id=10789354>.

Bauerlein, Mark. 2009. *Professors on the Production Line, Students on Their Own*. AEI Working Paper 2009-01. American Enterprise Institute. <http://www.aei.org/docLib/Bauerlein.pdf>.

Bazin, Patrick. 1996. "Toward Metareading." In *The Future of the Book*, ed. Geoffrey Nunberg, 153–68. Berkeley: University of California Press.

Benkler, Yochai. 2006. *The Wealth of Networks: How Social Production Transforms Markets and Freedom*. New Haven, CT: Yale University Press.

Bernstein, Mark. 2007. Comment on "CommentPress: New (Social) Structures for New (Networked) Texts." July 25. < http://docs.plannedobsolescence.net/cpdraft/anti-hypertext/#comment-98>.

Bertram, Chris, et al. *Crooked Timber*. <http://www.crookedtimber.org>.

Biagioli, Mario. 2002. "From Book Censorship to Academic Peer Review." *Emergences* 12 (1): 11–45.

Birkerts, Sven. 1994. *The Gutenberg Elegies: The Fate of Reading in an Electronic Age*. New York: Random House.

Black, Michael H. 1992. *A Short History of Cambridge University Press*. Cambridge: Cambridge University Press.

Blair, Carole, Julie R. Brown, and Leslie A. Baxter. 1994. "Disciplining the Feminine." *Quarterly Journal of Speech* 80 (4): 383–409.

Blankenship, Laura. 2008. "Scholarly Collaboration in the Digital Age." *Geeky Mom*. January 11. <http://geekymom.blogspot.com/2008/01/scholarly-collaboration-in-digital-age.html>.

Bloch, R. Howard, and Carla Hesse. 1993. "Introduction." *Representations* 42: 1–12.

Blue Ribbon Task Force on Sustainable Digital Preservation and Access. 2008. *Sustaining the Digital Investment: Issues and Challenges of Economically Sustainable Digital Preservation*. December.

Bogost, Ian. 2008. "Reading Online Sucks." *Ian Bogost*. March 7. <http://www.bogost.com/blog/reading_online_sucks.shtml>.

Boice, Robert. 1990. *Professors as Writers: A Self-Help Guide to Productive Writing*. Stillwater, OK: New Forums Press.

Bolker, Joan. 1998. *Writing Your Dissertation in Fifteen Minutes a Day: A Guide to Starting, Revising, and Finishing Your Doctoral Thesis*. New York: Holt.

Bolter, J. David. 1996. "Ekphrasis, Virtual Reality, and the Future of Writing." In *The Future of the Book*, ed. Geoffrey Nunberg, 253–72. Berkeley: University of California Press.

———. 1991. *Writing Space: The Computer, Hypertext, and the History of Writing*. Hillsdale, NJ: Lawrence Erlbaum Associates.

Borgman, Christine L. 2007. *Scholarship in the Digital Age: Information, Infrastructure, and the Internet*. Cambridge, MA: MIT Press.

Bosak, Jon. 1999. "XML Ubiquity and the Scholarly Community." *Computers and the Humanities* 33 (1): 199–206.

boyd, danah. 2007a. "Loss of Context for Me on Facebook." *Apophenia*, August 10. <http://www.zephoria.org/thoughts/archives/2007/08/10/loss_of_context.html>.

———. 2007b. "Viewing American Class Divisions through Facebook and MySpace." *Apophenia*, June 24. <http://www.danah.org/papers/essays/ClassDivisions.html>.

"Breaking Gender Cliques at Work?" 2006. *Slashdot*, August 31. <http://ask.slashdot.org/article.pl?sid=06/08/31/1755259>.

Brown, John Seely, and Paul Duguid. 2000. *The Social Life of Information*. Boston: Harvard Business School Press.

Brown, Laura, Rebecca Griffiths, and Matthew Rascoff. 2007. "Ithaka Report: University Publishing in a Digital Age." <http://www.ithaka.org/strategic-services/university-publishing>.

Brown, Susan, et al. 2009. "Published Yet Never Done: The Tension between Projection and Completion in Digital Humanities Research." *Digital Humanities Quarterly* 3 (2). <http://digitalhumanities.org/dhq/vol/3/2/000040.html>.

Brownlee, Christen. 2006. "Peer Review under the Microscope." *Science News* 170 (25): 392–93.

Burke, Timothy. 2008. "Liveblogging NITLE, 'Scholarly Collaboration and Small Colleges in a Digital Age.'" *Easily Distracted*, January 11. <http://weblogs.swarthmore.edu/burke/?p=488>.

Burnard, Lou. 2000. "Text Encoding for Interchange: A New Consortium." *Ariadne* 24. <http://www.ariadne.ac.uk/issue24/tei/>.

Burnham, John C. 1990. "The Evolution of Editorial Peer Review." *Journal of the American Medical Association* 263 (10): 1323–29.

Bush, Vannevar. 1945. "As We May Think." *Atlantic Monthly*, July, 101–8.

Cambridge University Press. 2009. *Annual Report & Accounts for the year ending 30 April 2009*. <http://www.cambridge.org/about/annualreport/downloads/annual_report_2009.pdf>.

———. 2008. *Annual Report & Accounts for the year ending 30 April 2008*. <http://www.cambridge.org/about/annualreport/downloads/annual_report_2008.pdf>.

Campanario, Juan Miguel. 1998. "Peer Review for Journals as It Stands Today, Part 2." *Science Communication* 19 (4): 277–306.

Campbell, Philip. 2006. "Nature's Peer Review Trial." *Nature*. <http://www.nature.com/nature/peerreview/>.

Carr, George. 2010. Comment on *Planned Obsolescence*. February 17. <http://mediacommons.futureofthebook.org/mcpress/plannedobsolescence/two-authorship/from-product-to-process/#comment-989>.

Cartwright, Jon. 2009. "Fledgling Site Challenges arXiv Server." *Physicsworld.com*. July 15. <http://physicsworld.com/cws/article/news/39845>.

Cecire, Natalia. 2010. Comment on *Planned Obsolescence*. January 4. <http://mediacommons.futureofthebook.org/mcpress/plannedobsolescence/2010/01/04/zombies/#comment-705>.

———. 2009. Comment on *Planned Obsolescence*. October 24. <http://mediacommons.futureofthebook.org/mcpress/plannedobsolescence/three-texts/reading-and-the-communications-circuit/#comment-220>.

Chartier, Roger. 1993. "Libraries without Walls." *Representations* 42: 38–52.

Citizendium. "CZ:About." <http://en.citizendium.org/wiki/CZ:About>.

CLOCKSS. "Benefits." <http://www.clockss.org/clockss/Benefits>

———. "FAQ." <http://www.clockss.org/clockss/FAQ>.

Cohen, Dan. 2008. "Introducing Omeka." *Dan Cohen's Digital Humanities Blog*, February 20. <http://www.dancohen.org/2008/02/20/introducing-omeka/>.

Cohen, Dan, et al. 2009. "Final Report." *Tools for Data-Driven Scholarship*, March 25. <http://mith.umd.edu/tools/?page_id=60>.

Cohen, Noam. 2007. "A History Department Bans Citing Wikipedia as a Research Source." *New York Times*, February 21. <http://www.nytimes.com/2007/02/21/education/21wikipedia.html?_r=1>.

Coover, Robert. 1992. "The End of Books." *New York Times Book Review*, June 21, 1, 23–25.

Cornell University Library. "The arXiv endorsement system." *arXiv*. <http://arxiv.org/help/endorsement>.

Crewe, Jennifer. 2004. "Scholarly Publishing: Why Our Business Is Your Business Too." *Profession*: 25–31.

CrossRef.org. "Fast Facts." <http://www.crossref.org/01company/16fastfacts.html>.

Crow, Raym. 2009. *Campus-Based Publishing Partnerships: A Guide to Critical Issues*. Scholarly Publishing and Academic Resources Coalition and Association of Research Libraries, January. <http://www.arl.org/sparc/partnering/guide/>.

Damrosch, David. 1995. *We Scholars: Changing the Culture of the University*. Cambridge, MA: Harvard University Press.

Darnell, Rick. 1998. "SGML and HTML DTD: A Brief History of SGML." *HTML 4 Unleashed*. Sams.net Publishing. <http://www.webreference.com/dlab/books/html/3-2.html>.

Darnton, Robert. 1982. "What Is the History of Books?" *Daedalus* 111 (3): 65–83.

Davidson, Cathy. 2009. " 'Research': How Peer Review Counts and Doesn't." *Cat in the Stack*, April 20. <http://www.hastac.org/node/2105>.

Davidson, Cathy, and David Theo Goldberg. 2007. "The Future of Learning Institutions in a Digital Age." *Institute for the Future of the Book*. January. <http://www.futureofthebook.org/HASTAC/learningreport/>.

Dendle, Peter. 2007. "The Zombie as a Barometer of Cultural Anxiety." In *Monsters and the Monstrous: Myths and Metaphors of Enduring Evil*, ed. Scott Niall, 45–57. Amsterdam: Rodopi.

DeRose, Steven. 1999. "XML and the TEI." *Computers and the Humanities* 33 (1): 11–30.

"Development Roadmap." 2010. *Zotero*. September 29. <http://www.zotero.org/support/development_roadmap>.

Digital Research Tools Wiki. <http://digitalresearchtools.pbworks.com/>.

"digress.it." <http://digress.it/>.

Doctorow, Cory. 2006a. "Giving It Away." *Forbes*, December 1. <http://www.forbes.com/2006/11/30/cory-doctorow-copyright-tech-media_cz_cd_books06_1201doctorow.html>.

———. 2006b. "Science Fiction Is the Only Literature People Care Enough About to Steal on the Internet." *Locus*, July. <http://www.locusmag.com/2006/Issues/07DoctorowCommentary.html>.

———. 2003. *Down and Out in the Magic Kingdom*. New York: T. Doherty Associates.

———. 2001. "Metacrap." August 26. <http://www.well.com/~doctorow/metacrap.htm>.

Donaldson, Ian. 1998. "The Destruction of the Book." *Book History* 1 1–10.

"Dr Ian Walker's Philica details." *Philica.* <http://philica.com/user_details.php?user_code=1>.

Drucker, Johanna. 2008. "The Virtual Codex from Page Space to E-space." In *A Companion to Digital Literary Studies*, ed. Susan Schreibman and Ray Siemens, 216–32. Oxford: Blackwell.

Dublin Core Metadata Initiative. <http://dublincore.org/>.

Ede, Lisa, and Andrea A. Lunsford. 2001. "Collaboration and Concepts of Authorship." *PMLA* 116 (2): 354–69.

———. 1990. *Singular Texts/Plural Authors: Perspectives on Collaborative Writing.* Carbondale: Southern Illinois University Press.

Eisenstein, Elizabeth L. 1979. *The Printing Press as an Agent of Change: Communications and Cultural Transformations in Early Modern Europe.* Cambridge: Cambridge University Press.

Elish, Madeleine Clare, and Whitney Trettien. 2009. "Acts of Translation: Digital Humanities and the Archive Interface." In *Media in Transition 6.* April. <http://web.mit.edu/comm-forum/mit6/papers/Elish.pdf>.

Esposito, Joseph J. 2003. "The Processed Book." *First Monday* 8 (3). <http://firstmonday.org/htbin/cgiwrap/bin/ojs/index.php/fm/article/viewArticle/1038/959>.

"Exclusive: Warner Chappell Reveals Radiohead's 'In Rainbows' Pot of Gold." 2008. *Music Ally.* October 15. <http://musically.com/blog/2008/10/15/exclusive-warner-chappell-reveals-radioheads-in-rainbows-pot-of-gold/>.

Fabiato, Alexandre. 1994. "Anonymity of Reviewers." *Cardiovascular Research* 28: 1134–39.

Falkow, Sally. "The Flip Side of Corporate Blogging." *The Navigator.* <http://navigator.bacons.com/CURRENT/flip_side_of_blogging.asp>.

Fish, Stanley. 1980. *Is There a Text in This Class? The Authority of Interpretive Communities.* Cambridge, MA: Harvard University Press.

Fitzpatrick, Kathleen. 2010. "On Open Access Publishing." *Society for Critical Exchange,* January 15. <http://societyforcriticalexchange.org/blog/blog3.php/2010/01/15/on-open-access-publishing>.

———. 2009. *Planned Obsolescence: Publishing, Technology, and the Future of the Academy* (online review project). September 26. <http://mediacommons.futureofthebook.org/mcpress/plannedobsolescence>.

———. 2008a. "Scholarly Collaboration in the Digital Age." *Planned Obsolescence.* January 11. <http://www.plannedobsolescence.net/scholarly-collaboration-in-the-digital-age/>.

———. 2008b. "The Bolter Principle." *Planned Obsolescence.* June 29. <http://www.plannedobsolescence.net/the-bolter-principle/>.

———. 2008c. "Future Writing, Take Two." *Planned Obsolescence.* July 2. <http://www.plannedobsolescence.net/future-writing-take-two/>.

———. 2007a. "MediaCommons: Scholarly Publishing in the Age of the Internet." *MediaCommons.* March 29. <http://mediacommons.futureofthebook.org/mcpress/mediacommons>.

———. 2007b. "Again with the Blegging." *Planned Obsolescence.* July 12. <http://www.plannedobsolescence.net/again-with-the-blegging/>.

———. 2007c. "Blogging: Firstborn or Second Coming?." *Planned Obsolescence.* July 13. <http://www.plannedobsolescence.net/blogging-firstborn-or-second-coming/>.

———. 2007d. "CommentPress: New (Social) Structures for New (Networked) Texts." *MediaCommons.* <http://mediacommons.futureofthebook.org/mcpress/cpfinal/>.

———. 2007e. "CommentPress: New (Social) Structures for New (Networked) Texts." *Journal of Electronic Publishing* 10 (3). < http://hdl.handle.net/2027/spo.3336451.0010.305>.

———. 2006. *The Anxiety of Obsolescence: The American Novel in the Age of Television*. Nashville: Vanderbilt University Press.

———. 2002–present. *Planned Obsolescence* (blog). <http://www.plannedobsolescence.net>.

Foucault, Michel. 1969/77. "What Is an Author?" In *Language, Counter-Memory, Practice: Selected Essays and Interviews*, ed. Donald F Bouchard, 113–138. Ithaca, NY: Cornell University Press.

Fox, Mary Frank, and Catherine A. Faver. 1984. "Independence and Cooperation in Research: The Motivations and Costs of Collaboration." *Journal of Higher Education* 55 (3): 347–59.

French, Amanda. 2009a. Comment on *Planned Obsolescence*. September 22. <http://mediacommons.futureofthebook.org/mcpress/plannedobsolescence/two-authorship/the-death-of-the-author/#comment-25>.

———. 2009b. Comment on *Planned Obsolescence*. September 23. <http://media-commons.futureofthebook.org/mcpress/plannedobsolescence/four-preservation/metadata/#comment-41>.

———. 2009c. Comment on *Planned Obsolescence*. September 30. <http://media-commons.futureofthebook.org/mcpress/plannedobsolescence/two-authorship/from-product-to-process/#comment-125>.

———. 2009d. Comment on *Planned Obsolescence*. September 30. <http://mediacom-mons.futureofthebook.org/mcpress/plannedobsolescence/five-the-university/new-institutional-structures/#comment-124>.

Gelman, Sheldon R., and Margaret Gibelman. 1999. "A Quest for Citation? An Analysis of and Commentary on the Trend toward Multiple Authorship." *Journal of Social Work Education* 35 (2): 203–13.

Germano, William P. 2005. *From Dissertation to Book*. Chicago: University of Chicago Press.

———. 2001. *Getting It Published: A Guide for Scholars and Anyone Else Serious about Serious Books*. Chicago: University of Chicago Press.

GiantChair. <http://giantchair.com/>.

Gillies, Sean. 2010. Comment on *Planned Obsolescence*. January 11. <http://media-commons.futureofthebook.org/mcpress/plannedobsolescence/four-preservation/locators/#comment-783>.

Ginsparg, Paul. 2002. "Can Peer Review Be Better Focused?" *Science and Technology Libraries* 22 (3–4): 5–17.

Gitelman, Lisa. 2008. *Always Already New: Media, History, and the Data of Culture*. Cambridge, MA: MIT Press.

———. 2000. *Scripts, Grooves, and Writing Machines: Representing Technology in the Edison Era*. Palo Alto, CA: Stanford University Press.

Givler, Peter. 2004. "Universities and Their Presses in Hard Economic Times." *Association of American University Presses*. <http://www.aaupnet.org/aboutup/hardtimes.html>.

———. 2002. "University Press Publishing in the United States." *Association of American University Presses*. <http://www.aaupnet.org/resources/upusa.html>.

Godlee, Fiona. 2000. "The Ethics of Peer Review." In *Ethical Issues in Biomedical Publication*, ed. Anne Hudson Jones and Faith McLellan, 59–84. Baltimore: Johns Hopkins University Press.

Grant, Bob. 2009a. "Merck Published Fake Journal." *TheScientist.com*, April 30. <http://www.the-scientist.com/blog/display/55671/>.

———. 2009b. "Elsevier Published 6 Fake Journals." *TheScientist.com*, May 7. <http://www.the-scientist.com/blog/display/55679/>.

Greenblatt, Stephen. 2002. "A Special Letter from Stephen Greenblatt." *Modern Language Association*, May 28. <http://www.mla.org/scholarly_pub>.

Grimmelmann, James. 2009. "The Google Dilemma." *New York Law School Law Review* 53 (4): 939–50.

Grossman, Lev. 2006. "Time's Person of the Year: You." *Time*, December 13. <http://www.time.com/time/magazine/article/0,9171,1569514,00.html>.

Guédon, Jean-Claude, and Raymond Siemens. 2002. "The Credibility of Electronic Publishing: Peer Review and Imprint." *TEXT Technology* 11 (1): 17–35.

Guthrie, Kevin, Rebecca Griffiths, and Nancy Maron. 2008. *Sustainability and Revenue Models for Online Academic Resources: An Ithaka Report*. Ithaka, May. <http://www.ithaka.org/publications/sustainability>.

Habermas, Jürgen. 1989. *The Structural Transformation of the Public Sphere: An Inquiry into a Category of Bourgeois Society*. Cambridge, MA: MIT Press.

Hall, Donald. 2007. *The Academic Community: A Manual for Change*. Columbus: Ohio State University Press.

———. 2002. *The Academic Self: An Owner's Manual*. Columbus: Ohio State University Press.

Hall, Gary. 2008. *Digitize This Book! The Politics of New Media, or Why We Need Open Access Now*. Minneapolis: University of Minnesota Press.

Handle System. 2009. "Quick Facts." April 29. <http://handle.net/factsheet.html>.

Harnad, Stevan. 1998. "Learned Inquiry and the Net: The Role of Peer Review, Peer Commentary and Copyright." *Learned Publishing* 11 (4): 283–92.

Harpold, Terry. 2009. *Ex-Foliations: Reading Machines and the Upgrade Path*. Minneapolis: University of Minnesota Press.

Hart, Michael. 1992. "Gutenberg: The History and Philosophy of Project Gutenberg." *Project Gutenberg*, August. <http://www.gutenberg.org/wiki/Gutenberg:The_History_and_Philosophy_of_Project_Gutenberg_by_Michael_Hart>.

Hart, Richard L. 2000. "Co-Authorship in the Academic Library Literature: A Survey of Attitudes and Behaviors." *Journal of Academic Librarianship* 26 (5): 339–45.

Heim, Michael. 1999. *Electric Language: A Philosophical Study of Word Processing*. New Haven, CT: Yale University Press.

Hesse, Carla. 1996. "Books in Time." In *The Future of the Book*, ed. Geoffrey Nunberg, 21–36. Berkeley: University of California Press.

Hillesund, Terje. 2007. Comment on "CommentPress: New (Social) Structures for New (Networked) Texts." October 23. <http://docs.plannedobsolescence.net/cpfinal/toward-the-future/#comment-151>.

Holbo, John. 2006. Comment on "Vanity Publishing." *The Valve*, December 23. <http://www.thevalve.org/go/valve/article/vanity_publishing/#13435>.

———. 2005. "Will Work for Whuffie – or – Anything You Can Do, I Can Do Meta." *The Valve*, November 19. <http://www.thevalve.org/go/valve/article/will_work_for_whuffie_or_anything_you_can_do_i_can_do_meta/>.

Holbo, John, et al. *The Valve*. <http://www.thevalve.org/go>.

"How Did the Moderation System Develop?" *Slashdot*. <http://slashdot.org/faq/com-mod.shtml#cm520>.

Howard, Jennifer. 2009. "U. of Michigan Press Reorganizes as a Unit of the Library." *Chronicle of Higher Education*, March 23. <http://chronicle.com/daily/2009/03/14210n.htm?utm_source=at&utm_medium=en>.

"In Media Res." 2006–. *MediaCommons*. <http://mediacommons.futureofthebook.org/imr/>.

International DOI Foundation. 2006. *The DOI Handbook*. <http://www.doi.org/handbook_2000/DOIHandbook-v4-4.pdf>.

Iskold, Alex. 2007. "Facebook: What If More Is Less?" *ReadWriteWeb*, September 27. <http://www.readwriteweb.com/archives/facebook_what_if_more_is_less.php>.

Jackson, Shelley. 2003. "Skin." *Shelley Jackson's Ineradicable Stain*, August. <http://www.ineradicablestain.com/skin.html>.

Jenkins, Henry. 2006. *Convergence Culture: Where Old and New Media Collide*. New York: New York University Press.

Jensen, Michael. 2007a. "Authority 3.0: Friend or Foe to Scholars?" *Journal of Scholarly Publishing* 39(1): 297–307.

———. 2007b. "The New Metrics of Scholarly Authority." *Chronicle of Higher Education*, June 15. <http://chronicle.com/article/The-New-Metrics-of-Scholarly/5449>.

———. 2005. "Presses Have Little to Fear from Google." *Chronicle of Higher Education*, July 8. <http://chronicle.com/article/Presses-Have-Little-to-Fear/25775/>.

Jerz, Dennis. 2009. Comment on *Planned Obsolescence*, December 21. <http://mediacommons.futureofthebook.org/mcpress/plannedobsolescence/three-texts/hypertext/#comment-499>.

John Wiley & Sons, Inc. 2009. *Annual Report*. <http://www.wiley.com/legacy/annual_reports/ar_2009/>.

———. 2008. *Annual Report*. <http://www.wiley.com/legacy/annual_reports/ar_2008>.

Johns, Adrian. 1998. *The Nature of the Book: Print and Knowledge in the Making*. Chicago: University of Chicago Press.

Joyce, Michael. 2000. *Othermindedness: The Emergence of Network Culture*. Ann Arbor: University of Michigan Press.

———. 1987/90. *Afternoon, a story*. Watertown, MA: Eastgate Systems.

Keen, Andrew. 2007. *The Cult of the Amateur: How Today's Internet Is Killing Our Culture*. Boston: Nicholas Brealey.

Keep, Christopher. 1999. "The Disturbing Liveliness of Machines: Rethinking the Body in Hypertext Theory and Fiction." In *Cyberspace Textuality: Computer Technology and Literary Theory*, ed. Marie-Laure Ryan, 164–181. Bloomington: Indiana University Press.

Kelty, Christopher M. 2008. *Two Bits: The Cultural Significance of Free Software*. Durham, NC: Duke University Press.

Kelty, Christopher M., et al. 2008. "Anthropology of/in Circulation: The Future of Open Access and Scholarly Societies." *Cultural Anthropology* 23 (3): 559–88.

Kenney, Anne R., et al. 2006. *E-Journal Archiving Metes and Bounds: A Survey of the Landscape*. CLIR Reports. Council on Library and Information Resources, September. http://www.clir.org/pubs/abstract/pub138abst.html.

Kernan, Alvin B. 1990. *The Death of Literature*. New Haven, CT: Yale University Press.

Kirschenbaum, Matthew. 2009a. "Done: Finishing Projects in the Digital Humanities." *Digital Humanities Quarterly* 3 (2) <http://digitalhumanities.org/dhq/vol/3/2/000037.html>.

———. 2009b. Comment on *Planned Obsolescence*. October 18. <http://mediacommons.futureofthebook.org/mcpress/plannedobsolescence/four-preservation/standards/#comment-186>.

———. 2008. *Mechanisms: New Media and the Forensic Imagination*. Cambridge, MA: MIT Press.

———. 2003. Blog comment. *Planned Obsolescence*, December 16. <http://www.plannedobsolescence.net/in-the-interim/#comment-1835>.

Knight, Kim. 2006. "Collex." *Transliteracies Project: Research in the Technological, Social, and Cultural Practices of Online Reading*. <http://transliteracies.english.ucsb.edu/post/research-project/research-clearinghouse-individual/research-reports/collex>.

Koehler, Wallace. 2004. "A Longitudinal Study of Web Pages Continued: A Consideration of Document Persistence." *Information Research* 9 (2). <http://informationr.net/ir/9-2/paper174.html>.

Koop, Thomas, and Ulrich Pöschl. 2006. "Systems: An Open, Two-Stage Peer-Review Journal." *Nature*. <http://www.nature.com/nature/peerreview/debate/nature04988.html>.

Kraus, Kari. 2009. Comment on *Planned Obsolescence*. September 26. <http://mediacommons.futureofthebook.org/mcpress/plannedobsolescence/four-preservation/metadata/#comment-66>.

Kristeva, Julia. 1986. "Word, Dialogue and Novel." In *The Kristeva Reader,* ed. Toril Moi, 34–61. New York: Columbia University Press.

Kronick, David A. 2004. *"Devant le deluge" and Other Essays on Early Modern Scientific Communication*. Lanham, MD: Scarecrow.

———. 1990. "Peer Review in 18th-Century Scientific Journalism." *Journal of the American Medical Association* 263 (10): 1321–22.

Kroski, Ellyssa. 2006. "Authority in the Age of the Amateur." *InfoTangle*, February 20. <http://infotangle.blogsome.com/2006/02/20/authority-in-the-age-of-the-amateur/>.

Landow, George P. 1997. *Hypertext 2.0*. Baltimore: Johns Hopkins University Press.

Lanham, Richard A. 2006. *The Economics of Attention: Style and Substance in the Age of Information*. Chicago: University of Chicago Press.

———. 1992. "From Book to Screen: Four Recent Studies." *College English* 54 (2): 199–206.

Lanier, Jaron. 2006. "Digital Maoism: The Hazards of the New Online Collectivism." *Edge*. <http://www.edge.org/3rd_culture/lanier06/lanier06_index.html>.

Lapham, Lewis, ed. 2007. *The President's Address to the Nation*. Institute for the Future of the Book. <http://www.futureofthebook.org/iraqspeech/>.

———. 2006. *Iraq Study Group Report*. Institute for the Future of the Book. <http://www.futureofthebook.org/iraqreport/>.

Lauro, Sarah Juliet, and Karen Embry. 2008. "A Zombie Manifesto: The Nonhuman Condition in the Era of Advanced Capitalism." *Boundary 2: An International Journal of Literature and Culture* 35 (2): 85–108.

Lavoie, Brian, and Lorcan Dempsey. 2004. "Thirteen Ways of Looking at . . . Digital Preservation." *D-Lib Magazine* 10 (7/8). <http://www.dlib.org/dlib/july04/lavoie/07lavoie.html>.

Lazinger, Susan S. 2001. *Digital Preservation and Metadata: History, Theory, Practice.* Englewood, CO: Libraries Unlimited.

Le Comptoir des presses d'universités. <http://www.lcdpu.fr/>.

Lessig, Lawrence. 2008. *Remix: Making Art and Commerce Thrive in the Hybrid Economy.* New York: Penguin.

———. 2006. *Code: Version 2.0.* New York: Basic Books.

———. 2005. *Free Culture: The Nature and Future of Creativity.* New York: Penguin.

———. 2001. *The Future of Ideas: The Fate of the Commons in a Connected World.* New York: Random House.

Lessing, Doris. 2008. *The Golden Notebook.* New York: Institute for the Future of the Book. <http://thegoldennotebook.org/>.

Levien, Raph. "Advogato's Trust Metric." *Advogato.* <http://www.advogato.org/trust-metric.html>.

Levinson, Paul. 1997. *The Soft Edge: A Natural History and Future of the Information Revolution.* New York: Routledge.

Lieberman, Mark, et al. *Language Log.* <http://itre.cis.upenn.edu/~myl/languagelog/>.

Liu, Alan, et al. 2005. *Born-Again Bits: A Framework for Migrating Electronic Literature.* Electronic Literature Organization. <http://eliterature.org/pad/bab.html>.

LOCKSS. "Home." <http://lockss.org/lockss/Home>.

———. "How It Works." <http://lockss.org/lockss/How_It_Works>.

———. "LOCKSS Alliance." <http://lockss.org/lockss/LOCKSS_Alliance>.

Long, Elizabeth. 1993. "Textual Interpretation as Collective Action." In *The Ethnography of Reading,* ed. Jonathan Boyarin, 180–211. Berkeley: University of California Press.

Love, Courtney. 2000. "Courtney Love Does the Math." *Salon.com,* June 14. <http://www.salon.com/technology/feature/2000/06/14/love>.

Luey, Beth. 2002. *Handbook for Academic Authors.* New York: Cambridge University Press.

Lynch, Clifford. 2001. "The Battle to Define the Future of the Book in a Digital World." *First Monday* 6 (6). <http://firstmonday.org/htbin/cgiwrap/bin/ojs/index.php/fm/article/viewArticle/864/773>.

Manoff, Marlene. 2009. "The Digital Record and the Future of Libraries." Paper delivered at the Media in Transition 6 conference, Cambridge, MA.

Manovich, Lev. 2001. *The Language of New Media.* Cambridge, MA: MIT Press.

marthaquest. 2008. "Comment on Doris Lessing's *The Golden Notebook* – Suggestions," November 13. <http://thegoldennotebook.org/forum/comments.php?DiscussionID=51&page=1#Item_0>.

Mary, Sebastian. 2007. Comment on "CommentPress: New (Social) Structures for New (Networked) Texts." August 1. <http://docs.plannedobsolescence.net/cpdraft/scholarly-discourse-networks/#comment-58>.

McCown, Frank, et al. 2005. "The Availability and Persistence of Web References in *D-Lib Magazine.*" *Proceedings of the 5th International Web Archiving Workshop (IWAW 2005).* Vienna, Austria, July 24 <http://www.iwaw.net/05/papers/iwaw05-mccown1.pdf>.

McGann, Jerome. 2005. "Information Technology and the Troubled Humanities." *TEXT Technology* 14 (2): 105–21.

McKenzie, D. F. 1999. *Bibliography and the Sociology of Texts*. Cambridge: Cambridge University Press.

McLuhan, Marshall. 1962. *The Gutenberg Galaxy: The Making of Typographic Man*. Toronto: University of Toronto Press.

"MediaCommons: A Digital Scholarly Network." <http://mediacommons.futureofthe-book.org/>.

Meyers, Barbara. 2004. *Peer Review Software: Has It Made a Mark on the World of Scholarly Journals?* Aries Systems Corporation. <http://www.editorialmanager.de/pdfs/peerreview.pdf>.

Mirzoeff, Nick. 2010. Comment on *Planned Obsolescence*. February 10. <http://mediacommons.futureofthebook.org/mcpress/plannedobsolescence/one/#comment-923>.

Mitchell, Catherine, and Laura Cerruti. 2008–9. "Local, Sustainable, and Organic Publishing: A Library-Press Collaboration at the University of California." *Against the Grain* 20 (6). <http://www.against-the-grain.com/TOCFiles/v20-6_Mitchell_Cerruti.pdf>.

Modern Language Association of America. 2009. *MLA Handbook for Writers of Research Papers*. 7th ed. New York: Modern Language Association of America.

———. 2006. *Report of the MLA Task Force on Evaluating Scholarship for Tenure and Promotion*. <http://www.mla.org/pdf/task_force_tenure_promo.pdf>.

Montfort, Nick, and Noah Wardrip-Fruin. 2004. *Acid-Free Bits: Recommendations for Long-Lasting Electronic Literature*. Electronic Literature Organization. <http://eliterature.org/pad/afb.html>.

Morrow, Terry, et al. 2008. "A Comparative Study of e-Journal Archiving Solutions: A JISC Funded Investigation." JISC Collections, May. < http://www.jisc-collections.ac.uk/Reports/e-journal-archiving-comparative-study/>.

Moulthrop, Stuart. 2005. "After the Last Generation: Rethinking Scholarship in the Days of Serious Play." *Proceedings of the 6th Digital Arts and Culture Conference*. <http://iat.ubalt.edu/moulthrop/essays/dac2005.pdf>.

Mullen, Carol A., and Frances K. Kochan. 2001. "Issues of Collaborative Authorship in Higher Education." *Educational Forum* 65 (2): 128–35.

Muto, Albert. 1992. *The University of California Press: The Early Years, 1893–1953*. Berkeley: University of California Press.

Mylonas, Elli, and Allen Renear. 1999. "The Text Encoding Initiative at 10: Not Just an Interchange Format Anymore—But a New Research Community." *Computers and the Humanities* 33 (1): 1–9.

National Endowment for the Arts. 2009. *Reading on the Rise: A New Chapter in American Literacy*. <http://www.nea.gov/research/ReadingonRise.pdf>.

———. 2007. *To Read or Not To Read: A Question of National Consequence*. <http://www.nea.gov/research/ToRead.pdf>.

———. 2004. *Reading at Risk: A Survey of Literary Reading in America*. <http://www.nea.gov/pub/ReadingAtRisk.pdf>.

National Humanities Alliance. 2009. "The Future of Scholarly Journals Publishing among Social Science & Humanities Associations: Report on a Study Funded by a Planning Grant from the Andrew W. Mellon Foundation." September. <http://www.nhalliance.org/research/scholarly_communication/index.shtml>.

Nelson, T. H. 1965. "Complex Information Processing: A File Structure for the Complex, the Changing, and the Indeterminate." In *Association for Computing Machinery: Proceedings of the 1965 20th National Conference*, 84–100. New York: ACM Press, 1965.

Neubauer, Bruce J., and Gene A. Brewer. 2004. "Virtual Scholarly Collaboration: A Case Study." *Journal of Computing Sciences in Colleges* 19 (4): 92–98.

New York University Press. 2009. "NYU Press Leads Group Receiving Mellon Grant for UP Electronic Book Project." *From the Square*. June 26. <http://www.fromthesquare. org/?p=563>.

NINES. "What Is NINES?" <http://www.nines.org/about/what_is.html>.

No Brief Candle: Reconceiving Research Libraries for the 21st Century. Washington, DC: Council on Library and Information Resources. <http://www.clir.org/pubs/reports/ pub142/pub142.pdf>.

Nowviskie, Bethany. 2009. "Monopolies of Invention." *Bethany Nowviskie*. December 30. <http://nowviskie.org/2009/monopolies-of-invention/>.

———. 2007. "Collex: Facets, Folksonomy, and Fashioning the Remixable Web." In *Digital Humanities 2007*. <http://www.digitalhumanities.org/dh2007/abstracts/paper_152_ nowviskie.pdf>.

Nunberg, Geoffrey. 2009. "Google Books: A Metadata Train Wreck." *Language Log*. August 29. <http://languagelog.ldc.upenn.edu/nll/?p=1701>.

———. 1993. "The Places of Books in the Age of Electronic Reproduction." *Representations* 42: 13–37.

O'Donnell, James. 1996. "The Pragmatics of the New: Trithemius, McLuhan, Cassiodorus." In *The Future of the Book*, ed. Geoffrey Nunberg, 37–62. Berkeley: University of California Press.

"101 Dumbest Moments in Business: 59. Radiohead." 2008. *Fortune*, January 16. <http:// money.cnn.com/galleries/2007/fortune/0712/gallery.101_dumbest.fortune/59.html>.

Ong, Walter J. 2002. *Orality and Literacy: The Technologizing of the Word*. London: Routledge.

Open Access Videos. 2009. "Catherine Mitchell: On Services, Users & Alliances." Vimeo. January 20. <http://vimeo.com/2900627>.

Open Archives Initiative. "Open Archives Initiative Protocol for Metadata Harvesting." <http://www.openarchives.org/pmh/>.

Open Media Commons. "Open Media Commons." <http://openmediacommons.org/>.

Owens, Howard. 2007. "What We've Learned from Blogs – How to Grow Audience." *Media Blog*. July 9. <http://www.howardowens.com/2007/ what-weve-learnd-from-blogs-how-to-grow-audience/>.

Oxford University Press. 2009. *Annual Report of the Delegates of the University Press 2008/09*. <http://www.oup.com/pdf/OUP_Annual_Report_2008-09.pdf>.

———. 2008. *Annual Report of the Delegates of the University Press 2007/08*. <http://www. oup.com/pdf/2008_annual_report.pdf>.

Parry, David. 2009a. Comment on *Planned Obsolescence*. September 22. <http:// mediacommons.futureofthebook.org/mcpress/plannedobsolescence/one/ credentialing/#comment-22>.

———. 2009b. Comment on *Planned Obsolescence*. September 27. <http://mediacom-mons.futureofthebook.org/mcpress/plannedobsolescence/five-the-university/ new-institutional-structures/#comment-85>.

Paskin, Norman. 2010. "Digital Object Identifier (DOI) System." *Encyclopedia of Library and Information Sciences*, 3d ed. London: Taylor and Francis.

Pearce, Fred. 2010. " 'Climategate' Was PR Disaster That Could Bring Healthy Reform of Peer Review." *The Guardian*, February 9. <http://www.guardian.co.uk/environment/2010/feb/09/climate-emails-pr-disaster-peer-review>.

Pearson. 2009. *Annual Report and Accounts*. <http://www.pearson.com/media/files/cosec/pearson%5FRA%2D2009.pdf>.

———. 2008. *Annual Report and Accounts*. <http://www.pearson.com/media/files/press-releases/2008/pearson%5FARA%5F2008.pdf>.

———. 2007. *Annual Report and Accounts*. <http://www.pearson.com/media/files/annual-reports/pearson%5Freport%5F2007.pdf>.

Penn State University Libraries. "Office of Digital Scholarly Publishing." <http://www.libraries.psu.edu/psul/odsp.html>.

Peters, Douglas P., and Stephen J. Ceci. 1982/2004. "Peer Review Practices of Psychological Journals: The Fate of Published Articles, Submitted Again." Reprinted in David Shatz, *Peer Review: A Critical Inquiry*, 191–214. Lanham, MD: Rowman and Littlefield.

Philica. "An Introduction to Using Philica." <http://philica.com/tutorial.php>.

———. "Philica FAQs." <http://philica.com/faq.php>.

Poe, Marshall. 2006. "The Hive." *The Atlantic*, September. <http://www.theatlantic.com/doc/print/200609/wikipedia>.

Portico. "Portico's Archival Approach." <http://portico.org/about/approach.html>.

Pöschl, Ulrich. 2004. "Interactive Journal Concept for Improved Scientific Publishing and Quality Assurance." *Learned Publishing* 17 (2): 105–13.

Poster, Mark. 2001. *What's the Matter with the Internet?* Minneapolis: University of Minnesota Press.

———. 1990. *The Mode of Information: Poststructuralism and Social Context*. Chicago: University of Chicago Press.

Pranzatelli, Robert. "A Brief History of Yale University Press." *Yale University Press*. <http://yalepress.yale.edu/yupbooks/centennial/briefhistory.asp>.

Pressman, Jessica. "Vectors: Journal of Culture and Technology in a Dynamic Vernacular." *Transliteracies Project: Research in the Technological, Social, and Cultural Practices of Online Reading*. <http://transliteracies.english.ucsb.edu/post/research-project/research-clearinghouse-individual/research-reports/vectors-journal-of-culture-and-technology-in-a-dynamic-vernacular>.

Price, Leah. 2004. "Reading: The State of the Discipline." *Book History* 7: 303–20.

Public Knowledge Project. "Open Monograph Press." <http://pkp.sfu.ca/omp>.

Quinet, Raphael. 2000. "Social Experiment on Slashdot Moderation." *Advogato*, January 24. <http://www.advogato.org/article/27.html>.

Radway, Janice. 2004. "Research Universities, Periodical Publication, and the Circulation of Professional Expertise: On the Significance of Middlebrow Authority." *Critical Inquiry* 31 (1): 203–28.

Raggett, Dave. 1998. "A History of HTML." <http://www.w3.org/People/Raggett/book4/ch02.html>.

Raymond, Matt. 2010. "How Tweet It Is! Library Acquires Entire Twitter Archive." *Library of Congress Blog*, April 14. <http://www.loc.gov/tweet/how-tweet-it-is.html>,

Readings, Bill. 1996. *The University in Ruins*. Cambridge, MA: Harvard University Press.

Redden, Elizabeth. 2009. "Unread Monographs, Uninspired Undergrads." *Inside Higher Ed*, March 18. <http://www.insidehighered.com/news/2009/03/18/production>.

Regalado, Mariana. 2007. "Research Authority in the Age of Google: Equilibrium Sought." *Library Philosophy and Practice*. <http://www.webpages.uidaho.edu/~mbolin/regalado.htm>.

Renear, Allen H. 2004. "Text Encoding." In *A Companion to Digital Humanities*, ed. Raymond Siemens, Susan Schreibman, and John Unsworth, 218–39. Oxford: Blackwell.

Rennie, Drummond. 2003. "Editorial Peer Review: Its Development and Rationale." In *Peer Review in Health Sciences*, ed. Fiona Godlee and Tom Jefferson, 1–13. London: BMJ Books.

———. 1994. "Commentary on Fabiato, A., 'Anonymity of Reviewers.'" *Cardiovascular Research* 28: 1142–43.

Rheingold, Howard. 1993. *The Virtual Community: Homesteading on the Electronic Frontier*. Reading, MA: Addison-Wesley.

Rich, Motoko. 2008. "Publishers Announce Staff Cuts." *New York Times*, December 3, B1.

Rosenblatt, Bill. 1997. "The Digital Object Identifier: Solving the Dilemma of Copyright Protection Online." *Journal of Electronic Publishing* 3 (2). <http://hdl.handle.net/2027/spo.3336451.0003.204>.

Roy, Rustum, and James R. Ashburn. 2001. "The Perils of Peer Review." *Nature* 414 (6862): 393–94.

Ruecker, Stan, and Alan Galey. 2009. "Design as a Hermeneutic Process: Thinking Through Making from Book History to Critical Design." In *Digital Humanities 2009*, 240–41. College Park, MD: Alliance of Digital Humanities Organizations.

Saint-Amour, Paul K. 2003. *The Copywrights: Intellectual Property and the Literary Imagination*. Ithaca, NY: Cornell University Press.

Salo, Dorothea. 2009a. Comment on *Planned Obsolescence*. September 28. <http://mediacommons.futureofthebook.org/mcpress/plannedobsolescence/three-texts/documents-e-books-pages/#comment-104>.

———. 2009b. Comment on *Planned Obsolescence*. September 28. <http://media-commons.futureofthebook.org/mcpress/plannedobsolescence/three-texts/database-driven-scholarship/#comment-105>.

———. 2009c. Comment on *Planned Obsolescence*. September 29. <http://mediacommons.futureofthebook.org/mcpress/plannedobsolescence/four-preservation/#comment-112>.

———. 2009d. Comment on *Planned Obsolescence*, September 29. <http://mediacommons.futureofthebook.org/mcpress/plannedobsolescence/five-the-university/new-institutional-structures/#comment-119>.

Schiff, Stacy. 2006. "Know It All." *The New Yorker*, July 31. <http://www.newyorker.com/archive/2006/07/31/060731fa_fact>.

Schneider, Karen G. 2007. "Lots of Librarians Can Keep Stuff Safe: Libraries Are Able to Safeguard Content with LOCKSS, Open Source Digital Preservation Software." *Library Journal*, August 15. <http://www.libraryjournal.com/article/CA6466645.html>.

Sconce, Jeffrey. 2000. *Haunted Media: Electronic Presence from Telegraphy to Television*. Durham, NC: Duke University Press.

SEASR. <http://seasr.org/>.

Seglen, Per O. 1997. "Why the Impact Factor of Journals Should Not Be Used for Evaluating Research." *British Journal of Medicine* 314: 497.

Shatz, David. 2004. *Peer Review: A Critical Inquiry*. Lanham, MD: Rowman and Littlefield.

Shirky, Clay. 2009. "Newspapers and Thinking the Unthinkable." *Clay Shirky*, March 13. <http://www.shirky.com/weblog/2009/03/newspapers-and-thinking-the-unthinkable/>.

———. 2008. *Here Comes Everybody: The Power of Organizing without Organizations*. New York: Penguin.

———. 2005. "Ontology Is Overrated." *Clay Shirky's Writings about the Internet*. <http://www.shirky.com/writings/ontology_overrated.html>.

Siemens, Ray, John Unsworth, and Susan Schreibman, eds. 2004. *A Companion to Digital Humanities*. Oxford: Blackwell. <http://www.digitalhumanities.org/companion/>.

Silvia, Paul J. 2007. *How to Write a Lot: A Practical Guide to Productive Academic Writing*. Washington, DC: American Psychological Association.

Simone, Raffaele. 1996. "The Body of the Text." In *The Future of the Book*, ed. Geoffrey Nunberg, 239–51. Berkeley: University of California Press.

Sirota, David. 2009. "What's with All the Zombies?" *Salon.com*, October 10. <http://www.salon.com/opinion/feature/2009/10/10/zombies/>.

"Skin Footnotes." *Shelley Jackson's Ineradicable Stain*. <http://www.ineradicablestain.com/footnotes.html>.

Smith, Alexandra. 2006. "Scientists concerned over research assessment changes." *The Guardian*, December 7. <http://www.guardian.co.uk/education/2006/dec/07/higher-education.researchassessmentexercise>.

Smith, Richard. 2006. "Commentary: The Power of the Unrelenting Impact Factor—Is It a Force for Good or Harm?" *International Journal of Epidemiology* 35 (5): 1129–30.

Sperberg-McQueen, C. M., and Lou Burnard, eds. 2009. *TEI P5: Guidelines for Electronic Text Encoding and Interchange*. The TEI Consortium.

Spier, Ray. 2002. "The History of the Peer-Review Process." *TRENDS in Biotechnology* 20 (8): 357–58.

Spiro, Lisa. Peer review of *Planned Obsolescence*. <http://mediacommons.futureofthebook.org/mcpress/plannedobsolescence/external-reviews/spiro-second-review/>.

Stallings, Ariel Meadow. 2008. "Matthew Baldwin: Writer, Blogger, Pretty Okay Guy." *Microspotting*. <http://www.microspotting.com/blog/matthew-baldwin-defective-yeti>.

Stallybrass, Peter. 2007. "Little Jobs: Broadsides and the Printing Revolution." In *Agent of Change: Print Culture Studies after Elizabeth L. Eisenstein*, ed. Sabrina A. Baron, Eric N. Lindquist, and Eleanor F. Shevlin, 315–41. Amherst: University of Massachusetts Press.

———. 2006. "Textual Studies and the Book." Paper presented at the Modern Language Association of America convention, Philadelphia, December.

———. 2002. "Books and Scrolls: Navigating the Bible." In *Books and Readers in Early Modern England*, ed. Jennifer Andersen and Elizabeth Sauer, 42–79. Philadelphia: University of Pennsylvania Press.

Stein, Bob. 2006. "Jaron Lanier's Essay on 'The Hazards of the New Online Collectivism.'" *if:book*, August 8. <http://www.futureofthebook.org/blog/archives/2006/08/jaron_laniers_essay_on_digital.html>.

Stephens, Mitchell. 2006. "Holy of Holies: On the Constituents of Emptiness." <http://www.futureofthebook.org/mitchellstephens/holyofholies/>.

Sun, Sam, Larry Lannom, and Brian Boesch. 2003. "RFC 3650 Handle System Overview," *Handle System*, November. <http://www.handle.net/rfc/rfc3650.html>.

Sunstein, Cass R. 2006. *Infotopia: How Many Minds Produce Knowledge*. New York: Oxford University Press.

Sutherland, Meghan. 2007. "Rigor/Mortis: The Industrial Life of Style in American Zombie Cinema." *Framework: The Journal of Cinema and Media* 48 (2): 64–78.

Sutor, Bob. "Open Source vs. Open Standards." *Bob Sutor*. <http://www.sutor.com/newsite/drupal/osvsos>.

Swales, John, and Christine B. Feak. 2004. *Academic Writing for Graduate Students: Essential Tasks and Skills*. Ann Arbor: University of Michigan Press.

Tappuni, Jane. 2011. "UK Trade Publishers Predict 2012 Will Be Revenue Tipping Point for E-Books." *Publishing Technology*. March 23. <http://blog.publishingtechnology.com/blogs/uk-trade-publishers-predict-2012-revenue-tipping-point-e-books/>.

Tepper, Michele. 2003. "The Rise of Social Software." *netWorker* 7 (3): 19–23.

Text Encoding Initiative. "History." <http://www.tei-c.org/About/history.xml>.

———. "The Preparation of Text Encoding Guidelines." <http://www.tei-c.org/Vault/SC/teipcp1.txt>.

———. "Projects Using the TEI." <http://www.tei-c.org/Activities/Projects/>.

Thatcher, Sanford G. 1995. "The Crisis in Scholarly Communication." *Chronicle of Higher Education*, March 3: 1.

Thibodeau, Kenneth E. 2002. "Overview of Technological Approaches to Digital Preservation and Challenges in the Coming Years." In *The State of Digital Preservation: An International Perspective*, 4–31. Washington, DC: Council on Library and Information Resources. <http://www.clir.org/pubs/reports/pub107/pub107.pdf>.

Thompson, John B. 2005. *Books in the Digital Age: The Transformation of Academic and Higher Education Publishing in Britain and the United States*. Cambridge: Polity Press.

Toschi, Luca. 1996. "Hypertext and Authorship." In *The Future of the Book*, ed. Geoffrey Nunberg, 169–207. Berkeley: University of California Press.

Transliteracies: Research in the Technological, Social, and Cultural Practices of Online Reading. <http://transliteracies.english.ucsb.edu/category/research-project>.

Tweney, Dylan. 2003. "Q&A: Cory Doctorow." *SFGate.com*, January 23. <http://www.sfgate.com/cgi-bin/article.cgi?f=/g/a/2003/01/23/cdoctorow.DTL>.

Vaidhyanathan, Siva. 2007. "Where Is This Book Going?" *The Googlization of Everything*, September 25. <http://www.googlizationofeverything.com/2007/09/where_is_this_book_going.php>.

———. 2004. *The Anarchist in the Library: How the Clash Between Freedom and Control Is Hacking the Real World and Crashing the System*. New York: Basic Books.

———. 2001. *Copyrights and Copywrongs: The Rise of Intellectual Property and How It Threatens Creativity*. New York: New York University Press.

Van de Sompel, Herbert, and Oren Beit-Arie. 2001. "Open Linking in the Scholarly Information Environment Using the OpenURL Framework." *D-Lib Magazine* 7 (3). <http://www.dlib.org/dlib/march01/vandesompel/03vandesompel.html>.

Vectors: Journal of Culture and Technology in a Dynamic Vernacular. <http://www.vectorsjournal.org/>.

Vershbow, Ben. 2006a. "GAM3R 7H30RY 1.1 is live!" *if:book*, May 22. <http://www.futureofthebook.org/blog/archives/2006/05/gam3r_7h30ry_will_go_live_toda.html>.

———. 2006b. "Small Steps Toward an N-dimensional Reading/Writing Space." *if:book*, December 6. <http://www.futureofthebook.org/blog/archives/2006/12/small_steps_toward_an_n-dimensional.html>.

Visel, Dan. 2007. "Horseless Carriages." *if:book*, July 27. <http://www.futureofthebook.org/blog/archives/2007/07/horseless_carriages.html>.

———. 2006. "Learning to Read." *if:book*, April 20. <http://www.futureofthebook.org/blog/archives/2006/04/learning_to_read_1.html>.

viXra. "Why viXra?" <http://vixra.org/why>.

Wales, Jimmy. 2009. "What the MSM Gets Wrong about Wikipedia—and Why." *Huffington Post*, September 21. <http://www.huffingtonpost.com/jimmy-wales/what-the-msm-gets-wrong-a_b_292809.html>.

Walker, Jill. 2003. "Final Version of Weblog Definition." *jill/txt*, June 28. <http://jilltxt.net/archives/blog_theorising/final_version_of_weblog_definition.html>.

Wardrip-Fruin, Noah. 2009a. "Blog-Based Peer Review: Four Surprises." *Grand Text Auto*, May 12. <http://grandtextauto.org/2009/05/12/blog-based-peer-review-four-surprises/#0>.

———. 2009b. *Expressive Processing: Digital Fictions, Computer Games, and Software Studies*. Cambridge, MA: MIT Press.

———. 2008. "EP Meta: Chapter Four." *Grand Text Auto*, February 16. <http://grandtextauto.org/2008/02/16/ep-meta-chapter-four/>.

Wark, McKenzie. 2006. *GAM3R 7H30RY*. Institute for the Future of the Book. <http://www.futureofthebook.org/gamertheory/>.

Waters, Donald J. 2005. *Urgent Action Needed to Preserve Scholarly Electronic Journals*. Association of Research Libraries. <http://www.arl.org/bm~doc/ejournalpreservation_final.pdf>.

———. 2002. "Good Archives Make Good Scholars: Reflections on Recent Steps toward the Archiving of Digital Information." In *The State of Digital Preservation: An International Perspective*, 78–95. Washington, DC: Council on Library and Information Resources. <http://www.clir.org/pubs/reports/pub107/pub107.pdf>.

Waters, Lindsay. 2004. *Enemies of Promise: Publishing, Perishing, and the Eclipse of Scholarship*. Chicago: Prickly Paradigm Press.

Weller, Ann C. 2001. *Editorial Peer Review: Its Strengths and Weaknesses*. Medford, NJ: Information Today.

Willinsky, John. 2009. "Toward the Design of an Open Monograph Press." *Journal of Electronic Publishing* 12 (1). <http://dx.doi.org/10.3998/3336451.0012.103>.

———. 2006. *The Access Principle: The Case for Open Access to Research and Scholarship*. Cambridge, MA: MIT Press.

Wittenberg, Kate. 2006. "Beyond Google: What Next for Publishing?" *Chronicle of Higher Education*, June 16: B20.

Young, Jeffrey R. 2009. "Blackboard Pledges to Follow Open Standards More Closely." *Chronicle of Higher Education*, June 24. <http://chronicle.com/wiredcampus/article/3844/blackboard-pledges-to-follow-open-standards-more-closely>.

———. 2008. "Blog Comments and Peer Review Go Head to Head to See Which Makes a Book Better." *Chronicle of Higher Education*, January 22. <http://chronicle.com/free/2008/01/1322n.htm>.

———. 2006. "Books 2.0: Scholars Turn Monographs into Digital Conversations." *Chronicle of Higher Education*, July 28: A20.

Zittrain, Jonathan. 2008. *The Future of the Internet and How to Stop It*. New Haven, CT: Yale University Press.

Zotero. "Make Your Site Zotero Ready." <http://www.zotero.org/support/make_your_site_zotero_ready>.

Zuckerman, Harriet, and Robert K. Merton. 1971. "Patterns of Evaluation in Science: Institutionalization, Structure, and Functions of the Referee System." *Minerva* 9: 66–100.

Index

academic culture: academic blogging, 107–108; authorship in, 53; conservatism of, 10, 19, 31, 84, 194; employment practices, 53; helpfulness and, 11; productivity in, 67–68, 203n18; public reinvention of, 55; publishing practices, 53; separation of criticism and creation, 86. *See also* humanities

academic publishing. *See* scholarly publishing

Academic Self, The (Hall), 18–19

Academic Writing for Graduate Students (Swales and Feak), 51–52

academics: anxieties about writing, 50–52, 59–60, 68, 88, 201n1, 201n2; resistance to changes in libraries, 127; resistance to electronic publishing, 19–20, 31, 41; resistance to non-textual forms of scholarly publishing, 86; resistance to open peer review, 19–20

Access Principle, The (Willinsky), 9–10, 145

"acid-free bits" campaign, 6

adult literary reading, 197n1

Adventure (interactive fiction), 99, 123, 126

Advogato, 36

Afternoon (Joyce): access to, 99, 122, 123; on a Mac computer, 6; opening screen, 97; students' attempts to comprehend, 98

"Agrippa" (Gibson), 122

Allen, Albert, 177

Amazon, 151, 207n5

American Anthropological Association (AAA), 183

American Anthropologist (journal), 183

American Association of University Presses, 186

American Council of Learned Societies (ACLS), 3

Anarchist in the Library, The (Vaidhyanathan), 16

Anderson, Benedict, 105, 205n15

Anderson, Chris, 32–33, 41

Anderson, Tim, 86

Andreessen, Marc, 54

AnthroSource, 183–184

Anxiety of Obsolescence, The (Fitzpatrick), 1–2, 4

Apple, Classic mode, 6, 123

arXiv, 23–25, 145–146

"As We May Think" (Bush), 98

Association for Computational Linguistics, 134

Association for Computers in the Humanities, 134

Association for Literary and Linguistic Computing, 134

Association of American Universities (AAU), 156

Association of College and Research Libraries (ACRL), 156

Association of Research Libraries (ARL), 3

Athabasca University Press, 160

Atmospheric Chemistry and Physics (journal), 27

"author-pays" model of publishing, 161–162

authority: authoritative digital archives, 101–102; of closed texts, 77; in networked scholarly publishing, 73; of print culture, 58, 69; stability as sign of, 67; of Wikipedia entries, 35

"Authority 3.0" (Jensen), 37

authorship, 50–88; academic culture, 53; academic employment practices, 53; anxieties about writing, 50–52, 59–60, 68, 88, 201n1, 201n2; association of texts and ideas with authors, 75; assumptions about, 59; authors as privileged creatures of the state, 58–59; author's rights, 59; authors separated from texts, 65, 74; being "scooped," 75; of closed texts, 77; communal framework for, 56; of compilations, miscellanies and commentaries, 78; completeness, textual, 57, 67–68, 76; computer as cowriter, 87–88; copyright, 80–81; death of the author, 60–65; digital authorship practices, 65; hypertext, 62–63; in-public work, 70–72, 75; individuality, 57, 60, 72–75, 76, 206n17; intertextuality, 78–79; language, 60–61; of multimodal content, 83–84; nature of, rethinking the, 52–53; network technologies, 52, 60; originality, 57, 76–79; origins, 59–60; "pay what you will" downloading, 81–82; plagiarism, 77; poststructuralism, 60; print culture, 57–58; from product to process, 66–72; property ownership, 57, 58–59, 77, 83; publishing practices, 53; remixing, 79–80, 83; in revolutionary France, 58–59; sharing of knowledge, 82–83; tools for, improvement of, 82–83; transdiscursivity, 62; typing, 54, 87, 170; versioning, 67, 69, 71–72; word processing, 54, 87, 170, 201n4. *See also* writing

Badke, Bill, 17
Baker, Kevin, 113
Barthes, Roland, 11, 60–62, 78
Bazin, Patrick, 89
Benkler, Yochai, 16
Berners-Lee, Tim, 54, 55, 130
Bernstein, Mark, 205n11
Biagioli, Mario, 21–22, 23, 32
Blackboard, 133
Blankenship, Laura, 71, 75
blind review, 29–30

Bloch, Howard, 56–57, 73
Blogger, 66
blogs, 66–71, 107–110; academic blogging, 107–108; blog-based review, 33–35, 116; comments on entries, 66; community-oriented structure, 110; decentralization/displacement of authority structures, 16; expectations, 66; as first Web-native publishing format, 109, 202n8; in-public work, 70–71; intellectual theft, 203n21; linking, 66–67; persistent ephemerality of, 6–7; "pingbacks," 66; present work, emphasis on, 109–110; scholarship, 71, 110; spread of, 66, 109; temporal demands on bloggers, 118–119; textual changes over time, 68–69; time-stamping of entries, 203n21; "trackbacks," 66; versioning, 67
Blue Ribbon Task Force on Sustainable Digital Preservation and Access, 121, 124–125, 127–128, 152–153
Bogost, Ian, 86, 116
Boice, Robert, 52
Bolter, Jay David, 51, 54, 62–63, 96
"Bolter Principle" (Fitzpatrick), 51
book publishing: completeness, textual, 57; credentialing, 32; individuality, 57; originality, 57; peer review in, 21–22; property ownership, 57
books: binding as source of bookishness, 91–92; circulation of, 108–109; codex form, future of, 99; codex form, platform-independent nature of, 205n11; codex form, shift to, 91–92; codex form, web-native replacements for, 92–93, 96–97 (*see also* CommentPress); codex form as model for electronic texts, 94, 95–96; ephemeral nature of, 122; from failed publishers, 184–185; marking one's place in, 92; pages, focus on, 91; preservation compared to preservation of digital data, 209n33; random access to content, 91–92
Books in the Digital Age (Thompson), 157–158
"Books in Time" (Hesse), 58–59

Borgman, Christine: access to digital documents, 137; business model for e-book publishing, 151; coauthorship and collaboration in scholarly publishing, 73; costs of preserving digital data, 154; necessity of publishing technologies to scholars, 165; new systems and practices for scholarly publishing, 9–10; *Scholarship in the Digital Age,* 9–10; user-created metadata, 138

boyd, danah, 200n32

Brown, John Seely, 100

Brown, Laura: cost recovery model for university presses, 210n1; experimentation by university libraries, 169; Ithaka Report ("University Publishing in a Digital Age") (with Griffiths and Rascoff), 115, 155, 172, 178–179, 181, 182; publishing and university's core mission, 155

BuddyPress, 45

Burke, Timothy, 71, 75

Burnard, Lou, 133, 135

Bush, Vannevar, 98

Bush administration, George W., 112, 113

California Digital Library (CDL), 168, 182

Cambridge University Press, 158, 175

Carr, George, 202n11

cars as "horseless carriages," 94

Cayley, John, 87–88

Ceci, Stephen, 28–29

Cecire, Natalia, 196n6

Celebra, 198n5

Center for History and New Media, 102–103

Cerf, Vint, 54

Chartier, Roger, 95–96

Chronicle of Higher Education (journal), 33

citation analysis, 139

citation indexes, 47

Citizendium, 17, 198n3

"Climategate," 198n5

Cliopatria (blog), 108

CLOCKSS (Controlled LOCKSS), 149, 154, 210n35

coffee-house model of public reading and debate, 106, 108

Cohen, Dan, 103

Collex, 102

Colonyiddes, Michael, 122–123

CommentPress, 109–120, 188–193; author's use of, 93, 115, 188–189, 193; chunks of text, comments on, 109, 110–111, 112, 114–115, 117–118, 190–191; database-driven scholarship, integration with, 119–120; dependence on software developer and other software, 117; *GAM3r 7H30RY* (Wark) on, 110–111, 116, 188; *Golden Notebook, The* (Lessing) on, 117–118; "Holy of Holies" (Stephens) on, 111–114; Institute for the Future of the Book, 109, 111, 116, 117; *Iraq Study Group Report* on, 112–114; Ithaka Report ("University Publishing in a Digital Age"), web-based version, 115; open peer review, 115–116; as open-source software, 115; paragraph-by-paragraph orientation, 192; release 0.9, 114–115; release 3.0, 117; users' readiness for online interaction, 113–114

completeness, textual: authorship, 67–68, 76; book publishing, 57; print culture, 76

Condorcet, Nicolas de, 58–59

Connolly, Dan, 131

Convergence Culture (Jenkins), 16

Coover, Robert, 205n12

copyright, 80–81

Corporation for National Research Initiatives, 142–143

corpus model of publishing, 163

Council on Library and Information Resources, 126, 146

Creative Commons licensing, 83

credentialing: book publishing, 32; citation indexes, 47; peer review, 30–32, 47–49; reputation separate from, 33; Wikipedia, 32–33

"Credibility of Electronic Publishing" (Guédon and Siemens), 15

Crewe, Jennifer, 3

Crises and Opportunities (Alonso et. al.), 155

"crisis in scholarly publishing," 3

Crooked Timber (blog), 108

CrossRef, 143–144

"crowdsourced" information, 140–141

D-Lib Magazine, 142–143
Damrosch, David, 75–76
Danger Mouse, 79
Darnton, Robert, 105
database-driven scholarship, 100–104, 119–120
Davidson, Cathy: financial basis of scholarly publishing, 155; HASTAC working paper, 114; on peer review, 15; tenure reviews, materials used in, 48; warnings of "crisis in scholarly publishing," 3
Dempsey, Lorcan, 153
DeRose, Steven, 207n9
"Destruction of the Book" (Donaldson), 89
Dewey Decimal System, 141
digital archives: authoritative, 101–102; "light" *vs.* "dark" archives, 148; open-access archives, 145–146, 211n6; Open Archives Initiative Protocol for Metadata Harvesting (OAI-PMH), 139; renditions archiving (harvesting presentation files) *vs.* source file preservation, 149–150, 210n36
Digital Item Declaration Language, 136
digital media: belief in ephemeral nature of, 121–123, 124; mobility of, 142–144; proneness to obsolescence, 6. *See also* preservation of digital data
Digital Object Identifier (DOI), 143–144
digital objects: accessibility of, need for, 128, 144–152; availability of, 103–104; Digital Item Declaration Language, 136; finding, 101–102; handle systems, 142–144; for humanities, 102; NINES (Networked Infrastructure for Nineteenth-century Electronic Scholarship), 101–102; translating object identifiers to URLs, 142–144
digital publishing. *See* electronic publishing
digitalculturebooks, 167–168
Digitize This Book! (Hall), 145
dissensus, 42–43, 173
Doctorow, Cory, 37–38, 82
Document Type Definition (DTD), 131–132
Domain Name System (DNS), 143

Donaldson, Ian, 89
dot-com crash, 3
Down and Out in the Magic Kingdom (Doctorow), 37–38
Drucker, Johanna, 92, 94, 95, 100
Drupal, 45
DSpace, 146
Dublin Core Metadata Initiative, 139
Duguid, Paul, 100

e-books: business model for e-book publishing, 151–152; mimicking of print books, 95; preservation of, 150–152; reflection of contemporary views of nature, 96; uptake of, 94, 204n5
"E-Journal Archiving Metes and Bounds" (Council on Library and Information Resources), 146–147
Eastgate, 6, 205n12
economics of scarcity *vs.* economics of abundance, 37
Ede, Lisa, 12, 74, 75–76, 204n25
Eisenstein, Elizabeth, 58
Electronic Literature Organization: "acid-free bits" campaign, 6; funding, 208n17; preservation and protection of electronic texts, 205n12; X-Lit Initiative, 136–137
electronic publishing, 99–120; association of texts and ideas with authors, 75; backwards compatibility with print publishing, 84; broadening our sense of texts, 93; Center for History and New Media, 102–103; codex form, future of, 99; codex form as model for electronic texts, 94, 95–96; commitment to being present to respond quickly, 119; communal discussion and debate, 107; communal engagement in discussion and debate, 106–107; community, necessity for, 41–42; conversations and interactions produced by, 119–120, 164; database-driven scholarship, 100–104, 119–120; "delivery" as provision of access rights, 146–148; development of ideas in, 95; disciplinarily-focused online

publishing networks, 170; distinguishing publishing phase from distinction phase, 15; economics of abundance, 37; exhibit-building projects, 102–103; finality of the book, ending the, 203n16; funding as one-off efforts, 164; "hybrid" model of, 185; interactive fiction, 99; Juxta, 102; Omeka, 102–103; open-access publishing, 145; peer review in, 16, 18; preexisting communities, necessity of, 116–117, 119; preservation and protection of electronic texts, 205n12; resistance to, 19–20, 31, 41; serialization of content, 190–191; technologies based on book circulation practices, 108–109; TEI (Text Encoding Initiative), 133–137; uptake of, 104, 114; user-generated metadata to expert-created data, 102; users' readiness for online interaction, 113–114; virtual machine support for preservation, 99; willingness to pay for services rather than content, 185. *See also* CommentPress; digital objects; networked scholarly publishing; preservation of digital data

electronic scholarship: Collex, 102; database-driven scholarship, 100–104, 119–120; interactivity in, 90; multimodal scholarship, 83–84, 90, 152; NINES (Networked Infrastructure for Nineteenth-century Electronic Scholarship), 101–102, *103*, 119, 170; Pliny software, 104; remixing, 12–13, 79–80, 83, 100; SEASR (Software Environment for the Advancement of Scholarly Research), 104; Zotero, 141. *See also* digital objects

electronic texts: access to, 99, 205n12; preservation of, 6; productive online discussions of, 193; readers' expectations, 69; technological illegibility, risk of, 205n12; understanding of literature, 63. *See also* preservation of digital data

Electronic Transactions on Artificial Intelligence (ETAI), 26–27

Elish, Madeleine Clare, 102

Elsevier B. V., 161, 198n5

emulation, emulators, 123–124, 125–126, 206n3

Englebart, Douglas, 96

eScholarship program, 168, 182

Esposito, Joseph, 105, 107

exhibit-building projects, 102–103

Expanded Books, 94

Expressive Processing (Wardrip-Fruin), 33, 116, 188, 191

Facebook: extension of offline social networks into digital environments, 44; opening its API, 201n34; opening to any user, 200n32; students' embrace of, 107

Faden, Eric, 86

Fish, Stanley, 105

Flanagan, Mary, 86

Flickr, 185

Foucault, Michel, 21–22, 50, 61–62, 65

Freud, Sigmund, 62

Friendster, 44

From Dissertation to Book (Germano), 52

Frugé, August, 178

Future of Ideas, The (Lessig), 55

"Future Writing, Take Two" (Fitzpatrick), 51

Galey, Alan, 92

GAM3r 7H30RY (Wark), 110–111, 116, 188

Gamer Theory (Wark), 110, 188

George Mason University Center for History and New Media, 141

Germano, Bill, 3, 52

Getting It Published (Germano), 52

Giant Chair, 186

Gibson, William, 122

Gilman, Daniel Coit, 175, 185

Ginsparg, Paul, 24, 30

Godlee, Fiona, 28, 29

Goldberg, David Theo, 114

Golden Notebook, The (Lessing), 117–118

Google, 139

Google Books, 139, 140

Google Scholar, 139

"Googlebombing," 139

Grand Text Auto (GTxA) (blog), 33–35

Greenblatt, Stephen, 3

Grey Album, The (smashup), 79

Griffiths, Rebecca: books from failed publishers, 184–185; cost recovery model for university presses, 210n1; experimentation by university libraries, 169; Ithaka report ("University Publishing in a Digital Age") (with Brown and Rascoff), 115, 155, 172, 178–179, 181, 182

Guédon, Jean-Claude, 15, 22–23, 31

Gutenberg Galaxy, The (McLuhan), 57–58

Guthrie, Kevin, 184–185

Habermas, Jürgen, 105, 205n15

Hall, Donald, 10, 18–19, 174

Hall, Gary, 145, 212n15

Handbook for Academic Authors (Luey), 52

handle systems, 142–144

Harpold, Terry, 206n3

Harris, Joseph, 203n18

Hart, Michael, 101

Harvard University Press, 3

HASTAC (Humanities, Arts, Science, and Technology Advanced Collaboratory), 114

Hesse, Carla: authorship in networked scholarly publishing, 73; authorship in revolutionary France, 58–59; death of the book, potential, 56–57; individual authorship, 60, 206n17; reinvention of intellectual community, 55; temporality in public communications, 69–70

"History of the Peer-Review Process" (Spier), 15

Holbo, John, 203n16

"Holy of Holies" (Stephens), 111–114

Horowitz, David, 10

How to Write a Lot (Silvia), 52

HTML (HyperText Markup Language), 130–132, 205n9

humanities: average lifetime sales of scholarly monographs in, 189; citation practices, 146; coauthorship and collaboration in, 73, 75–76; "data-driven scholarship" in, 104; digital objects for, 102; digital publishing projects, 166;

obsolescence, 13–14; Ph.D.s, production of, 202n12; ridiculous articles in, 68; self-funded nature, 161; technological development and experimentation in, 166; TEI (Text Encoding Initiative), 133–137; valuation within universities, 13

hypertext, 6, 95–100; authorship, 62–63; disorientation, sense of, 97–98; establishing relationships among texts, 79; invention of, 96; negative reactions to, students', 97–98, 107; reader participation in producing text's meaning, 97, 98; reading, 63

imagined communities, 105

In Media Res, 9, 114

In Rainbows (album), 81–82

In Syndication, 9

individuality: authorship, 60, 72–75, 76, 206n17; in book publishing, 57; in marking academic careers, 203n18; originality, 76

Infocom, 99

"Information Technology and the Troubled Humanities" (McGann), 155

Infotopia (Sunstein), 1, 42

Inside Higher Ed (journal), 7

Institute for Multimedia Literacy, 164–165

Institute for the Future of the Book: author's involvement with, 8–9, 15, 110; building communities from scratch, 116; CommentPress, 109, 111, 116, 117; MediaCommons, 8–9, 110

intellectual property, 81–82

interactive fiction, 99

intertextuality, 78–79

Iraq Study Group Report, 112–114

Ithaka, 149

Ithaka Report (Brown, Griffiths and Rascoff), 115, 155, 172, 178–179, 181, 182

J-STOR, 149

Jackson, Shelley, 63–65, 202n7

Jenkins, Henry, 16

Jensen, Michael, 16, 37, 162

Jerz, Dennis, 99

Johns, Adrian, 58

Johns Hopkins University Press, 175–176

Mellon Foundation: digital humanities publishing projects, funding for, 166; preservation projects sponsored by, 148, 149, 150; toolsets for university publishers, development of, 186

Merck, 198n5

Merton, Robert K., 29, 199n21

metadata, 128, 137–144, 208n18

"metadata train wreck," 139

metalanguages, 132

metatextuality, 89

Middlebury College, 16–17, 198n2

Miller, Linda, 26

Mini vMac, 123–124

Mirzoeff, Nick, 9

Mitchell, Catherine, 182

MLA Handbook, 209n26

MLA International Bibliography, 183

MLIS (Masters of Library and Information Sciences) programs, 126–127

Modern Language Association (MLA): Committee on Scholarly Editions, 134; inclusion of URLs in citations deprecated, 142, 209n26; "Keywords for a Digital Profession" workshop, 1; Task Force on Evaluating Scholarship for Tenure and Promotion, 7–8, 199n22

modern literary system, 59, 77

Monro, Alexander, 198n9

Montfort, Nick, 124, 128, 130

Mosaic browser, 131

Moulthrop, Stuart, 85–86, 87–88

MP3.com, 41, 44

"multimodal," meaning of, 85

multimodal scholarship, 83–84, 90, 152

Muto, Albert, 175

MySpace, 41, 44

National Academies Press (NAP), 162, 163

National Endowment for the Arts (NEA), 2, 197n1

National Endowment for the Humanities (NEH), 9, 134–135, 166

National Institutes of Health (NIH), 165, 166

National Science Foundation (NSF), 165, 166

Nature (journal), 25–26, 27, 195

Nelson, Ted, 96, 98

network technologies: authorship, 52, 60; emergent nature of, 195

networked scholarly publishing: authority, 73; collaboration, unavoidability of, 75–76; originality, 77; reputation economy, 35–37; "trust metrics," 36–37. *See also* electronic publishing

New Everyday, The (Mirzoeff), 9

New York University Center for Religion and Media, 112

New York University Digital Library Technology Services, 9

New York University Press, 163, 168, 186

"Newspapers and Thinking the Unthinkable" (Shirky), 1

Newton, Isaac, 50

NINES (Networked Infrastructure for Nineteenth-century Electronic Scholarship), 101–102, *103*, 119, 170

Nowviskie, Bethany, 73, 102

Nunberg, Geoffrey, 92, 139

obsolescence: of digital media, 6; of first scholarly monographs, 4, 5; in humanities, 13–14; of hypertext fiction, 6; as a political project, 2; of scholarly monographs, 7, 10. *See also* preservation of digital data

O'Donnell, James, 53

Office of Digital Humanities (ODH), 166

Office of Digital Scholarly Publishing, Pennsylvania State University, 168

Omeka, 102–103

Ong, Walter, 106

"online" literary reading, 197n1

ontologies, 140

open-access publishing models, 145, 160–161, 162

Open Archives Initiative Protocol for Metadata Harvesting (OAI-PMH), 139

Open Humanities Press, 170

Open Journal Systems (OJS), 160, 169–170

Open Monograph Press (OMP), 160

open-source software, 82–83, 133. *See also* CommentPress

OpenURL, 144

originality: authorship, 76–79; book publishing, 57; individuality, 76; networked scholarly publishing, 77; scholarship, 12

Orkut, 44

Owens, Howard, 202n8

Oxford University Press, 158, 175

Pachoda, Philip, 167

PageRank, 139, 200n29

Parry, David, 173, 200n23

Patchwork Girl (Jackson), 64

"pay what you will" downloading, 81–82

PDF (Portable Document Format), 93–94

Pearson plc, 158

"peer," meaning of, 32

peer review, 15–49, 189–193; academic life, centrality in, 10–11, 16; advancement of the community, 50; authority, creation of, 32; blind review, 29–30; blog-based review, 33–35, 116; in book publishing, 21–22; "Climategate," 198n5; core notion behind, 31–32; credentialing, 30–32, 47–49; definition, 20; discussion and feedback function, 26, 30, 42; electronic publishing, 16, 18; *Electronic Transactions on Artificial Intelligence (ETAI),* dual-stage process used by, 26–27; epistemological practices, 18–19; faculty performance evaluations, 30, 48–50; filtering function ("publish-then-filter" rather than "filter-then-publish"), 38–43, 80; future of, 23–27; gatekeeping function, 32, 38, 48, 193; history, 20–23; humanities, adoption by, 198n7; in journal publishing, 21, 22; knowledge, communal production of, 42–43; knowledge, disciplining of, 21–22; labor requirements, 11, 32, 43; open peer review, absence of reviewer's comments, 191, 192; open peer review, *Nature* experiment, 25–26, 27, 195; open peer review, participation rates, 192; open peer review, resistance to, 19–20; open peer review, site statistics about, 189–191; open peer review, space for dissensus, 42–43; open peer review, traditional reviews compared

to, 115–116, 190–193; open peer review on MediaCommons, 9; outcomes across disciplines, 199n21; outsourcing to junior scholars, 30, 199n22; peer-to-peer review, 43, 44–45, 46, 50, 80; power and prestige, potential loss of, 19–20; from pre-publication to post-publication, movement from, 11; publishable, determining whether manuscripts are, 38, 198n4; purposes, 26–27; quality control function, 22–23, 26–28, 30–31, 193; rejection rate, 199n21; reputation economy, 32–38; reviewers, anonymity of, 27–30; reviewers, biases of, 28–29; reviewers, comments by, 28; reviewers, review of, 37–38, 45; reviewers, selection of, 23, 29; reviews, quality of, 40; state censorship, role in, 21; traditional reviews, binary result of, 193; traditional reviews, consensus model of community, 42–43; traditional reviews, defenses of, 18–20; traditional reviews, open reviews compared to, 115–116, 190–193; traditional reviews, quality control and, 27–28; "trust metrics," 36–37; Wikipedia, ongoing in, 17; "wisdom of the crowds," 47

"Peer Review Practices of Psychological Journals" (Peters and Ceci), 28–29

peer-reviewed digital objects, 101–102

Pennsylvania State University Office of Digital Scholarly Publishing, 168

Peters, Douglas, 28–29

Philica, 38–41, 43–44

Philosophical Transactions (journal), 20–21

"Places of Books in the Age of Electronic Reproduction" (Nunberg), 92

plagiarism, 77

Planned Obsolescence (blog), 6–7, 191

Pliny (software for scholarship), 104

Porcello, Tom, 86

Portico, 149–150, 210n36

Poster, Mark: author's rights, 59; on digital writing, 50; movement of writing to networked computers, 57; print culture, principles of, 57; separation of authors from texts, 65, 74; writing with computers, 201n4 poststructuralism, 60

"Poughkeepsie Principles," 133–134

preservation of digital data, 121–154; accessibility, Document Type Definitions (DTDs) in ensuring, 131–132; accessibility, findability and, 137, 142–144; accessibility, handle systems for ensuring, 142–144; accessibility, human-legible information in ensuring, 131; accessibility, retrievability and, 141; accessibility and interpretability, importance of, 124; accessibility of digital objects, need for, 128, 144–152; accessibility of licensed materials, 146–148, 207n5; "acid-free bits" campaign, 6; backups, 145, 209n30; in CLOCKSS (Controlled LOCKSS), 149, 154, 210n35; community-oriented systems and practices, 128, 136–137; costs of, 152–154; "crowdsourced" information, 140–141; decisions about, need for early, 125; Digital Item Declaration Language, 136; durability of data written to hard disk, 121–122; of e-books, 150–152; emulation, emulators in, 123–124, 125–126, 206n3; "free riders" problem, 153; individual/proprietary solutions, 126; institutional repositories, 145–146; by libraries, 126 –127; "link rot" problem, 142–144; in LOCKSS (Lots Of Copies Keeps Stuff Safe), 148–150, 210n36; Media Art Notation System (MANS), 136; metadata for texts, changes over time in, 208n18; metadata for texts, extensible and customizable, 140–141; metadata for texts, machine-generated, 139; metadata for texts, need for rich, 128, 137–144; metadata for texts, user-created, 138, 140–141; mobility of digital resources, 142–144; of multimodal scholarship, 152; ontologies, 140; open-source software, 133; in Portico, 149–150, 210n36; preservation of books compared to, 209n33; selection decisions, 127–128; separation of structure from design, 130–132; as serving the public good, 153–154; social systems for, importance of, 126, 128–129; source file preservation *vs.* harvesting

presentation files (rendition archiving), 149–150, 210n36; standard, HTML as a, 130–132, 205n9; standard, XML as a, 132, 135, 136; standards, de facto *vs.* community, 207n12; standards, markup, need for, 129–137; standards, open, 132–133; standards, proprietary/closed, 132; technical solutions, 125–126; TEI (Text Encoding Initiative), 133–137; theory of, 125; "tragedy of the commons" problem, 153; URLs, 142–143, 209n26, 209n27; "vendor neutral" interoperability, 130; X-Lit Initiative, 136 –137

Price, Leah, 104–105

Pride and Prejudice and Zombies (Grahame-Smith), 5

print culture: authority of, 58, 69; authorship, 57–58; completeness, textual, 76; modern literary system, 59, 77; principles of, 57

print-on-demand publishing, 162

print publishing: assumptions about, 67; backwards compatibility with, 84; economics of scarcity, 37

Printing Press as an Agent of Change, The (Eisenstein), 58

Professors as Writers (Boice), 52

Project Gutenberg, 101

property ownership: authorship, 58–59, 77, 83; book publishing, 57; closed texts, 77

Public Knowledge Project (PKP), 160

Public Library of Science, 161

public sphere, 105, 205n15

Publishers International Linking Association, 143–144

publishing: "author-pays" model of, 161–162; gap between publishing "haves" and "have nots," 195; in a networked environment, 55–56, 74; open-access models of, 145, 160–161, 162; print-on-demand publishing, 162; textbook publishing, 202n11; zombie publishing, 4–5, 196n6. *See also* book publishing; electronic publishing; journal publishing; networked scholarly publishing; print publishing; scholarly publishing

Radiohead, 81–82

Radway, Janice, 17

Rascoff, Matthew: cost recovery model for university presses, 210n1; experimentation by university libraries, 169; Ithaka Report ("University Publishing in a Digital Age") (with Brown and Griffiths), 115, 155, 172, 178–179, 181, 182

readers: activation of, 62–63; expectations of being allowed to write, 107

reading: adult literary reading, 197n1; coffee-house model of public reading and debate, 106, 108; "online" literary reading, 197n1; privatization of, 105; reading hypertext, 63; of scholarly monographs, 192–193; social aspects, 104–106, 109

Reading at Risk (National Endowment for the Arts), 2

Reading on the Rise (National Endowment for the Arts), 197n1

Readings, Bill: dissensus, 42–43, 173; function of scholarly publishing, 187; mission of universities, 172–174; obligation to listen, 36, 43; scholarly productivity, 67–68, 74; "University of Thought" *vs.* "University of Excellence," 42–43

rear-view mirrorism, 94, 205n9

Recording Industry Association of America, 16

recursive publics, 82–83

remixing: authorship, 79–80, 83; database-driven scholarship, 100; scholarship, 12–13

Rennie, Drummond, 22, 29–30

reputation economy, 32–38

reputation systems, 45

"'Research': How Peer Review Counts and Doesn't" (Davidson), 15

Rheingold, Howard, 107

Rice University Press, 195

Rinehart, Richard, 136

Roma, 134

Romantic Circles, 170

Rosetta (an emulator), 123

Royal Society of Edinburgh, 21

Royal Society of London, 20–21

Ruecker, Stan, 92

Rutgers University Press, 163

Salo, Dorothea, 205n9, 211n10

Santo, Avi, 15

Schneider, Karen, 149–150

scholarly monographs, 3–5; aggregating and indexing texts published by, 183; average lifetime sales in the humanities, 189; first monographs, 4, 5, 7; intellectual successors to, 84–85; obsolescence, 7, 10; overproducing and underpricing of, 157; production and distribution, 7; reading of, 192–193; replacement for, 5; requirements for, 4; royalties from, 181, 212n15; sales to libraries, 3; as undead, 4–5; viability as a mode of communication, 4

scholarly publishing, 5–14; as *all* tail, 41; business models, 13; coauthorship and collaboration in, 73; consortial publishing centers, 182; contemporary culture, being part of, 17–18; content *vs.* tools in future of, 185; copyright property ownership, 13; "crisis in," 3; development of scholarly thought, importance to, 7; economic basis, 212n15; editorial practices, 13; electronic distribution, move to, 5–6; facilitation of scholarly communication, 13; function of, 187; grant-based funding, 165; MediaCommons, 110; MLA task force recommendations for improving, 7–8; motivation for, 82; new systems and practices, advocates of, 9–10; optimism about, author's, 194–195; ossification of, potential for, 196; purposes, 110; remixing, 79–80; resistance to non-textual forms of, 86; reviewer's comments, 199n16; royalties, 181, 212n15; structures of texts, 13; technologies for ensuring viability of, 14; toolsets for, 84; trade publishers, abandoning it to, 149; university-subvention model of funding, 161–162; value added by scholarly publishing process, 185; on the web, value of, 10. *See also* electronic publishing; MediaCommons; networked scholarly publishing; university presses

traditions, Cass Sunstein on, 1
transdiscursivity, 62
Trettien, Whitney, 102
"trust metrics," 36–37
Twitter, 208n18
typing, 54, 87, 170

UCPubS (UC Publishing Services), 182
University in Ruins, The (Readings), 67
university libraries: academics' resistance
to changes in, 127; collaboration with
university presses, 167–169, 171, 210n10;
deaccessioning print copies of journals, 127; effect of 2000 recession on, 3;
experimentation by, 169; "library of the
21st century," 126; moving print copies
offsite, 127; possession of files constitut-
ing scholarly record, 147–148; preservation function, 126–127
University of Bergen, 134
University of California, 178, 182
University of California Press: Anthro-
Source, 183–184; E-Books Collection,
168; history of, 175, 176–178; as institutional publishing system, 182
"University of Excellence," 42
University of Michigan Press, 167
University of Pennsylvania Press, 163
University of Southern California, 211n8;
Institute for Multimedia Literacy, 164–165
"University of Thought," 42
University of Virginia, 134
university presses, 155–187; advancement of
specific academic fields, 182–183; aggrega-
tion and indexing of texts published by,
183; "author-pays" model of publishing,
161–162; collaboration with academic
authors, 169–170, 171; collaboration with
information technology centers, 169;
collaboration with university libraries,
167–169, 171, 210n10; collaborations, cross-
institutional, 186; consortial publishing
centers, 182; corpus model of publishing, 163; developmental editing, 171, 180;
distribution channels, 182–183; effect of
dot-com crash on, 3; expenses incurred

in, 163–164; financial basis, 155–166, 178,
184–187, 210n1; function of, 157–158, 172,
180; history of, 175–178; institutional
repositories, involvement in, 182; institutional subsidies, 3–4, 157; largest market,
159; library cutbacks, 3; open-access
publishing models, adoption of, 160–161;
press-less institutions, 181–182; prestige
imprinted by, 211n10; pricing, 157–158, 159;
print-on-demand publishing, 162; profit-
ability, 158; selectivity in publishing, 159;
services rather than products, charging
for, 162–163, 181–182; serving needs of host
institutions, focusing on, 175, 176, 178–184,
186–187; shuttering of, 210n1; toolsets
for, development of, 186; trade publishing model, movement toward, 178, 179;
university's infrastructure, as part of, 187;
university's mission, relationship to, 155,
157–185, 160–161, 166, 171–175, 176, 178
"University Publishing in a Digital Age"
(Ithaka Report) (Brown, Griffiths and
Rascoff), 115, 155, 172, 178–179, 181, 182
URLs, 142–143, 209n26, 209n27

Vaidhyanathan, Siva, 16
Valve, The (blog), 7–8, 107–108
Variable Media Network, 136–137, 208n17
Vectors (journal), 90, 164–165, 166
versioning: authorship, 69, 71–72; blogs, 67;
textbook publishing, 202n11
Vioxx, 198n5
Virtual Community, The (Rheingold), 107
viXra, 199n13
Voyager Company, 94

Wales, Jimmy, 200n25
Walt Whitman Archive, The (digital
archive), 101
Wardrip-Fruin, Noah: blog-based review,
116; critic *and* creator of interactive
works, 86; *Expressive Processing,* 33, 116,
188, 191; *Grand Text Auto (GTxA)* blog,
33–35; HTML validators, 130; preservation of digital data, 124, 128; temporal
demands on bloggers, 118–119

About the Author

KATHLEEN FITZPATRICK is Director of Scholarly Communication of the Modern Language Association and Professor of Media Studies (on leave) at Pomona College. She is the founding editor of the digital scholarly network MediaCommons. She is the author of *The Anxiety of Obsolescence: The American Novel in the Age of Television* (2006). She has published essays in journals including the *Journal of Electronic Publishing, Contemporary Literature*, and *Cinema Journal* and has blogged at *Planned Obsolescence* since 2002.